Deep Learnin the Basics

Python and Deep Learning: Theory and Implementation

Koki Saitoh

Deep Learning from the Basics

Author: Koki Saitoh

Managing Editor: Ashish James

Acquisitions Editor: Bridget Neale

Production Editor: Salma Patel

Editorial Board: Megan Carlisle, Mahesh Dhyani, Heather Gopsill, Manasa Kumar, Alex Mazonowicz, Monesh Mirpuri, Bridget Neale, Abhishek Rane, Brendan Rodrigues, Ankita Thakur, Nitesh Thakur, and Jonathan Wray

First Published: March 2021

Production Reference: 1040321

ISBN: 978-1-80020-613-7

Published by Packt Publishing Ltd.

Livery Place, 35 Livery Street

Birmingham B3 2PB, UK

Table of Contents

ᛅ

Chapter 7: Convolutional Neural Networks 221

Preface

About

This section briefly introduces the author and the material covered in this book.

About the Book

Deep learning is rapidly becoming the most preferred way of solving data problems. This is thanks, in part, to its huge variety of mathematical algorithms and their ability to find patterns that are otherwise invisible to us.

Deep Learning from the Basics begins with a fast-paced introduction to deep learning with Python, its definition, characteristics, and applications. You'll learn how to use the Python interpreter for the script files. You'll also learn how to utilize NumPy and Matplotlib in your deep learning applications. As you progress through the book, you'll discover backpropagation—an efficient way to calculate the gradients of weight parameters—and study multilayer perceptrons and their limitations before finally implementing a three-layer neural network and calculating multidimensional arrays.

By the end of the book, you'll have the knowledge to apply the relevant technologies in deep learning.

About the Authors

Koki Saitoh was born in Nagasaki, Japan in 1984. He graduated from the engineering department of the Tokyo Institute of Technology and completed a master's course at the Graduate School of Interdisciplinary Information Studies at the University of Tokyo. Currently, he conducts research and development in computer vision and machine learning. He has authored *Deep Learning from the Basics series* (Vol.1-3), which are published by O'Reilly, Japan.

Learning Objectives

- Use Python with minimum external libraries to implement deep learning programs
- Study the various deep learning and neural network theories
- Learn how to set initial values of weights
- Implement techniques such as batch normalization, dropout, and Adam
- Explore applications like automatic driving, image generation, and reinforcement learning

Audience

Deep Learning from the Basics is designed for data scientists, data analysts, and developers who want to use deep learning techniques to develop efficient solutions. This book is ideal for those who want a deeper understanding as well as an overview of the technologies. Some working knowledge of Python is a must. Knowledge of NumPy and pandas will be beneficial but not essential.

Approach

This book takes a practical approach to deep learning. Exploring the concepts through guided practice, you will write code and implement mathematical algorithms from a programmer's point of view.

Introduction

As technology advances, what was once termed science fiction begins to look increasingly plausible—even, at times, realistic. Artificial intelligence has beaten shogi, chess, and even igo champions. Smartphones can understand human speech, and video calls can provide real-time machine interpretation. "No-crash cars" with built-in cameras protect human lives, and automatic vehicles are getting closer to practical use. When we look around, we find that artificial intelligence flawlessly performs what we once thought exclusively human tasks—even, at times, surpassing us. The development of artificial intelligence is changing our world, making it anew.

"Deep learning" technology plays an important role in such remarkable developments. Researchers around the world praise deep learning as an innovative technology, even calling it a once-in-decade breakthrough. The term is now as familiar to the general public as it is to researchers and engineers.

This book focuses on deep learning, which has been receiving a lot of attention. The purpose is for readers to understand deep learning technologies as comprehensively as possible.

Approaching the essence of deep learning through a process of implementing deep learning programs, this book attempts to exhaustively detail required technologies and functional, practical examples with which readers can experiment.

Deep learning is already used all around the world—in smartphones, in self-driving cars, and in servers that empower Web services. Deep learning is operating today in places where many people do not notice it. In the future, deep learning will more clearly step out into the light. This book will help you understand and be fascinated by its associated technologies.

Concept of this book

This book is about deep learning and covers the knowledge required to understand it step by step from the basics, including what it is, what it entails, and how it works as simply as possible to give readers a deeper understanding of the relevant technologies.

Then what should we do to better understand deep learning? Well, one of the best ways is by making something—for example, performing practical tasks to create a program that runs from scratch that promotes critical thinking while reading a source code. Now, "from scratch" in this context means using as little external already-made items (such as libraries and tools) as possible. The goal of this book is to use as little as possible of these "black boxes", whose contents are unknown, meaning that you begin with minimal basic knowledge, upon which you will build, analyze, and implement to understand and make state-of-the-art deep learning programs. If you were to compare this book to a car manual, it is not a manual that shows how to drive a car but rather one that focuses on understanding the principle of a car. It directs you to open the hood of the car, remove and examine each individual piece for its form, function, and placement before putting it back together and building your model to its exact dimensions and operations. The goal of this book is to make you feel that you can make a car and be familiar with the technologies around it through the process of making it.

In this book, we will use a programming language called Python to carry out deep learning. Python is a very popular programming language that is easy for beginners to use. It is especially suitable for making prototypes. You can try your ideas immediately and conduct various experiments while checking the results. This book describes the theoretical aspects of deep learning while implementing Python programs and conducting experiments.

What you cannot understand only with a mathematical expression or theoretical description, you can often discern by reading and running a source code, getting a feel for the flow of technologies. This book puts emphasis on "engineering"–understanding deep learning through making something by writing codes. You will see many mathematical expressions and also many source codes from a programmer's point of view.

For whom is this book written?

This book provides activities for implementation so that you can better understand deep learning. The following lists the lesson objectives for this course:

- Use Python and the minimum possible external libraries to implement deep learning programs from scratch.

- Describe how to use Python for Python beginners.

- Provide Python source codes that you can run and a learning environment where you can experiment.

- Implement a system that recognizes images with high precision, starting from simple machine learning problems

- Clearly explain deep learning and neural network theories.

- Explain technologies that look complicated, such as backpropagation and convolution, so that you can understand them on an implementation level.

- Describe useful and practical techniques for deep learning, such as how to determine learning coefficients and the initial values of weights.

- Describe and implement trends such as Batch Normalization, Dropout, and Adam.

- Determine the reasons why deep learning is excellent, why a deeper layer improves recognition precision, and why a hidden layer is important.

- Introduce applications of deep learning, such as automatic driving, image generation, and reinforcement learning.

For whom is this book not written?

It is also important to show for whom this book is not written. The following lists what we will not do in this book.

This book...

- does not describe or introduce the latest research about deep learning in detail.
- does not describe how to use deep learning frameworks, such as Caffe, TensorFlow, and PyTorch.
- does not provide a detailed theoretical descriptions about deep learning, particularly neural networks.
- does not provide detailed description about tuning for improving recognition precision in deep learning.
- does not deal with GPU implementation to accelerate deep learning.
- focuses on image recognition. It does not cover natural language processing or speech recognition.

Thus, this book does not cover the latest research or theoretical details. However, when you are nearing the end of this book, you can then proceed with the latest research papers and theoretical books about neural networks.

This book focuses on image recognition. You can mainly learn the technologies required for image recognition using deep learning. It does not cover natural language processing or speech recognition.

How to read this book

When we learn something new, we often fail to understand it or may soon forget it by only listening to explanations. As an ancient Chinese philosopher said, You forget what you heard. You learn what you saw. You can understand what you did. Practice is the most important when you learn something new. This book often provides practical examples (source codes that you can run) after explaining a concept.

This book provides Python code that you can run on your computer for practical implementation to reinforce and apply theory, as well as experimentation through trial and error.

This book will advance on the pair of wheels of "theoretical explanation" and "implementation by Python." It is recommended that you have an environment for programming. You can use a Windows, Mac, or Linux computer with this book. *Chapter 1 Introduction to Python* describes how to install and use Python. You can download the programs used in this book from the following GitHub repository.

https://github.com/koki0702/deep-learning-from-the-basics

This ends the introduction and should have given you an overview of what you will be doing in this book and, hopefully, the desire to continue reading further.

In these next chapters, you will conduct various experiments during the process. Sometimes we are at a loss and stop to think why something has happened. Such time-consuming activities give us important knowledge in understanding technology deeply. The knowledge obtained after such a long time is surely useful also in using existing libraries, reading cutting-edge papers, and making an original system. Above all, making something is fun. Now, we are ready. Let's start on our journey of deep learning!

Acknowledgments

First, I would like to thank the researchers and engineers who have conducted research of technologies about deep learning: machine learning and computer science. It is thanks to them that I can write this book. I also thank those who have published useful information in books and on the Web. Above all, I learned a lot from the spirit of generously providing useful technologies and information in the open class CS231n (*Convolutional Neural Networks for Visual Recognition* (http://cs231n.github.io/) at Stanford University.

The following people have contributed to my writing. Tetsuro Kato, Shinya Kita, Yuka Tobinaga, Kota Nakano, Masatatu Nakamura, Akihiro Hayashi, and Ryo Yamamoto at teamLab, Inc., Kenshi Muto and Moe Masuko at Top Studio Co., Kenji Nomura at Flickfit, and Hidetaka Tanno, JSPS oversea research fellow in The University of Texas at Austin. These people read the manuscript of this book and provided much advice. I would like to thank them here. I say clearly that the author is responsible for any defects and errors in this book.

Finally, I thank Naoki Miyagawa at O'Reilly Japan for his continuous support for about one year and half from the conception to completion of this book. Thank you.

September 1, 2016
Koki Saitoh

1

Introduction to Python

More than 20 years have passed since the Python programming language was released. During that period, it has evolved and increased its user base. Python is currently the most popular programming language in the world.

In this book, we will use this powerful language to implement a deep learning system. This chapter explains Python briefly and describes how to use it. If you are familiar with Python, NumPy, and Matplotlib, you can skip this chapter.

What is Python?

Python is a simple programming language that is easy to read and learn. It is open-source software that you can use as you like for free. You can write a program that uses English-like grammar without the time-consuming compilation. This makes Python easy to use and, therefore a great choice for beginner programmers. In fact, many computer science courses in universities and professional schools choose Python as the first language they teach.

Python enables you to write both readable and high-performance (fast) code. If massive data processing and high-speed responses are required, Python will meet your needs. This is why Python is a favorite both with beginners and professionals. Cutting-edge IT companies such as Google, Microsoft, and Facebook frequently use Python.

Python is often used in scientific fields, particularly in machine learning and data science. Because of its high performance and excellent libraries for numerical calculations and statistical processing (NumPy and SciPy, for example), Python occupies a solid position in the realm of data science. It is often used as the backbone of deep learning frameworks such as Caffe, TensorFlow, and PyTorch, which provide Python interfaces. Therefore, learning Python is also useful when you wish to use a framework for deep learning.

Python is an optimal programming language, particularly in data science, as it offers various user-friendly and efficient features for beginners and professionals alike. For these reasons, it is the natural choice for achieving the goal of this book: *Deep Learning from the Basics*.

Installing Python

The following section describes some precautions you will need to take when installing Python in your environment (PC).

Python Versions

Python has two major versions: version 2 and version 3. Currently, both are in active use. So, when you install Python, you must carefully choose which version to install. These two versions are not completely compatible (to be accurate, no **backward compatibility** is available). Some programs written in Python 3 cannot be run in Python 2. This book uses Python 3. If you have only Python 2 installed, installing Python 3 is recommended.

External Libraries That We Use

The goal of this book is to implement *Deep Learning from the Basics*. So, our policy is that we will use external libraries as little as possible, but we will use the following two libraries by way of exception: NumPy and Matplotlib. We will use these two libraries to implement deep learning efficiently.

NumPy is a library for numerical calculations. It provides many convenient methods for handling advanced mathematical algorithms and arrays (matrices). To implement deep learning in this book, we will use these convenient methods for efficient implementation.

Matplotlib is a library for drawing graphs. You can use Matplotlib to visualize experimental results and visually check the data while executing deep learning. This book uses these libraries to implement deep learning.

This book uses the following programming language and libraries:

- Python 3
- NumPy
- Matplotlib

Now, we will describe how to install Python for those who need to install it. If you have already met these requirements, you can skip this section.

Anaconda Distribution

Although numerous methods are available for installing Python, this book recommends that you use a distribution called **Anaconda**. Distributions contain the required libraries so that the user can install them collectively. The Anaconda distribution focuses on data analysis. It also contains libraries useful for data analysis, such as NumPy and Matplotlib, as described earlier.

As we mentioned previously, this book uses Python 3. Therefore, you will need to install the Anaconda distribution for Python 3. Use the following link to download the distribution suitable for your OS and install it:

https://docs.anaconda.com/anaconda/install/

Python Interpreter

After installing Python, start by checking the version. Open a Terminal (Command Prompt for Windows) and enter the `python --version` command. This command outputs the version of Python you have installed:

```
$ python --version
Python 3.4.1 :: Anaconda 2.1.0 (x86_64)
```

If Python 3.4.1 (the number will be different, depending on your installed version) is displayed, as shown in the preceding code, then Python 3 has been installed successfully. Now, enter `python` and start the Python interpreter:

```
$ python
Python 3.4.1 |Anaconda 2.1.0 (x86_64)| (default, Sep 10 2014, 17:24:09)
[GCC 4.2.1 (Apple Inc. build 5577)] on darwin
Type "help", "copyright", "credits" or "license" for more information.
>>>
```

The Python interpreter is also referred to as **interactive mode**, through which you can interact with Python to write programs. An interaction means that, for example, the Python interpreter answers 3 when you ask, "What is 1+2?". Enter the following:

```
>>> 1 + 2
3
```

Hence, the Python interpreter enables you to write programs interactively. In this book, we will use an interactive mode to work with simple examples of Python programming.

Mathematical Operations

You can conduct mathematical operations, such as addition and multiplication, as follows:

```
>>> 1 - 2
-1
>>> 4 * 5
20
>>> 7 / 5
1.4
>>> 3 ** 2
9
```

Here, * means multiplication, / means division, and ** means exponentiation. (3 ** 2 is the second power of 3.) In Python 2, when you divide two integers, an integer is returned. For example, the result of 7/5 is 1. Meanwhile, in Python 3, when you divide two integers, a floating-point number is returned.

Data Types

Programming has data types. A data type indicates the character of the data, such as an integer, a floating-point number, or a string. Python provides the `type()` function to check the data's type:

```
>>> type(10)
<class 'int'>
>>> type(2.718)
<class 'float'>
>>> type("hello")
<class 'str'>
```

The preceding results indicate that 10 is `int` (integer type), 2.718 is `float` (floating-point type), and `hello` is `str` (string type). The words `type` and `class` are sometimes used in the same way. The resulting output, `<class 'int'>`, can be interpreted as 10 is an `int` `class` (type).

Variables

You can define **variables** by using alphabetical letters such as x and y. You can also use variables to calculate or assign another value to a variable:

```
>>> x = 10 # Initialize
>>> print(x)
10
>>> x = 100 # Assign
>>> print(x)
100
>>> y = 3.14
>>> x * y
314.0
>>> type(x * y)
<class 'float'>
```

Python is a dynamically typed programming language. **Dynamic** means that the type of a variable is determined automatically, depending on the situation. In the preceding example, the user does not explicitly specify that the type of x is int (integer). Python determines that the type of x is int because it is initialized to an integer, 10. The preceding example also shows that multiplying an integer by a decimal returns a decimal (automatic type conversion). The # symbol comments out subsequent characters, which are ignored by Python.

Lists

You can use a list (array) to assign multiple numbers to a variable:

```
>>> a = [1, 2, 3, 4, 5] # Create a list
>>> print(a) # Print the content of the list
[1, 2, 3, 4, 5]
>>> len(a) # Get the length of the list
5
>>> a[0] # Access the first element
1
>>> a[4]
5
>>> a[4] = 99 # Assign a value
>>> print(a)
[1, 2, 3, 4, 99]
```

To access an element, you can write `a[0]`, for example. The number in this `[ ]` is called an index, which starts from 0 (the index 0 indicates the first element). A convenient notation called `slicing` is provided for Python lists. You can use slicing to access both a single element and a sublist of the list:

```
>>> print(a)
[1, 2, 3, 4, 99]
>>> a[0:2] # Obtain from the zero index to the second index (the second
one is not included!)
[1, 2]
>>> a[1:] # Obtain from the first index to the last
[2, 3, 4, 99]
>>> a[:3] # Obtain from the zero index to the third index (the third one
is not included!)
[1, 2, 3]
>>> a[:-1] # Obtain from the first element to the second-last element
[1, 2, 3, 4]
>>> a[:-2] # Obtain from the first element to the third-last element
[1, 2, 3]
```

You can slice a list by writing `a[0:2]`. In this example, `a[0:2]` obtains the elements from the zeroth index to the one before the second index. So, it will show the elements for the zeroth index and the first index only in this case. An index number of `-1` indicates the last element, while `-2` indicates the second-last element.

Dictionaries

In a list, values are stored with index numbers (0, 1, 2, ...) that start from 0. A dictionary stores data as key/value pairs. Words associated with their meanings are stored in a dictionary, just as in a language dictionary:

```
>>> me = {'height':180} # Create a dictionary
>>> me['height'] # Access an element
180
>>> me['weight'] = 70 # Add a new element
>>> print(me)
{'height': 180, 'weight': 70}
```

Boolean

Python has a bool type. Its value is **True** or **False**. The operators for the bool type are **and**, **or**, and **not** (a type determines which operators can be used, such as +, -, *, and / for numbers):

```
>>> hungry = True # Hungry?
>>> sleepy = False # Sleepy?
>>> type(hungry)
<class 'bool'>
>>> not hungry
False
>>> hungry and sleepy
False
>>> hungry or sleepy
True
```

if Statements

You can use **if/else** to switch a process, depending on a condition:

```
>>> hungry = True
>>> if hungry:
...    print("I'm hungry")
...
I'm hungry
>>> hungry = False
>>> if hungry:
...     print("I'm hungry") # Indent with spaces
... else:
...     print("I'm not hungry")
...     print("I'm sleepy")
...
I'm not hungry
I'm sleepy
```

In Python, spaces have an important meaning. In this **if** statement example, the next statement after **if hungry** starts with four spaces. This is an indent that indicates the code that is executed when the condition (**if hungry**) is met. Although you can use tab characters for an indent, Python recommends using spaces.

In Python, use spaces to represent an indent. Four spaces are usually used for each indent level.

for Statements

Use a `for` statement for a loop:

```
>>> for i in [1, 2, 3]:
...     print(i)
...
1
2
3
```

This example outputs the elements of a list, `[1, 2, 3]`. When you use a `for ... in ...:` statement, you can access each element in a dataset, such as a list, in turn.

Functions

You can define a group of processes as a **function**:

```
>>> def hello():
...     print("Hello World!")
...
>>> hello()
Hello World!
```

A function can take an argument:

```
>>> def hello(object):
...     print("Hello " + object + "!")
...
>>> hello("cat")
Hello cat!
```

Use + to combine strings.

To close the Python interpreter, enter *Ctrl+D* (press the *D* key while holding down the *Ctrl* key) for Linux and macOS X. Enter *Ctrl+Z* and press the *Enter* key for Windows.

Python Script Files

The examples shown so far have used a Python interpreter that provides a mode in which you can interact with Python and which is useful for simple experiments. However, it is a little inconvenient if you want to do large processing because you have to enter a program every time. In such a case, you can save a Python program as a file and execute it (at one time). This next section provides examples of Python script files.

Saving in a File

Open your text editor and create a `hungry.py` file. The `hungry.py` file has only one line in it, as shown here:

```
print("I'm hungry!")
```

Then, open a Terminal (Command Prompt for Windows) and move to the location where the `hungry.py` file was created. Execute the `python` command with the argument of the filename, `hungry.py`. Here,

it is assumed that `hungry.py` is located in the `~/deep-learning-from-zero/ch01` directory (in the source code provided by this book, `hungry.py` is located under the `ch01` directory):

```
$ cd ~/deep-learning-from-zero/ch01 # Move to the directory
$ python hungry.py
I'm hungry!
```

Thus, you can use the `python hungry.py` command to run the Python program.

Classes

So far, you have learned about data types such as `int` and `str` (you can use the `type()` function to check the object type). These data types are called **built-in** data types since they are built into Python. Here, you will define a new class to create your data type. You can also define your original method (function for a class) and attributes.

In Python, you can use the `class` keyword to define a class. You must use the following format:

```
class name:
    def __init__ (self, argument, …): # Constructor
        ...
    def method name 1 (self, argument, …): # Method 1
        ...
    def method name 2 (self, argument, …): # Method 2
        ...
```

The `__init__` method is a special method for initialization. This method for initialization is also referred to as a **constructor** and is called only once when the instance of a class is created. In Python, you need to write `self` explicitly as the first argument of a method to represent yourself (your instance). (This practice may seem strange to those who are familiar with other languages.)

Create a class as a simple example as shown below, and save the following program as **man.py**:

```python
class Man:
    def __init__(self, name):
        self.name = name
        print("Initialized!")

    def hello(self):
        print("Hello " + self.name + "!")

    def goodbye(self):
        print("Good-bye " + self.name + "!")

m = Man("David")
m.hello()
m.goodbye()
```

Execute **man.py** from the Terminal:

```
$ python man.py
Initialized!
Hello David!
Good-bye David!
```

Here, you defined a new class, **Man**. In the preceding example, an instance (object), m, was created from the **Man** class.

The constructor (initialization method) of the **Man** class takes **name** as an argument and uses it to initialize the instance variable, **self.name**. An **instance** variable is a variable that is stored in each instance. In Python, you can create and access an instance variable by appending an attribute name to **self**.

NumPy

When implementing deep learning, arrays and matrices are often calculated. The array class of NumPy **(numpy.array)** provides many convenient methods that are used to implement deep learning. This section provides a brief description of NumPy, which we will use later.

Importing NumPy

NumPy is an external library. The word **external** here means that NumPy is not included in standard Python. So, you must load (import) the NumPy library first:

```
>>> import numpy as np
```

In Python, an import statement is used to import a library. Here, `import numpy as np` means that `numpy` is loaded as `np`. Thus, you can now reference a method for NumPy as `np`.

Creating a NumPy Array

You can use the `np.array()` method to create a NumPy array. `np.array()` takes a Python list as an argument to create an array for NumPy—that is, `numpy.ndarray`:

```
>>> x = np.array([1.0, 2.0, 3.0])
>>> print(x)
[ 1. 2. 3.]
>>> type(x)
<class 'numpy.ndarray'>
```

Mathematical Operations in NumPy

The following are a few sample mathematical operations involving NumPy arrays:

```
>>> x = np.array([1.0, 2.0, 3.0])
>>> y = np.array([2.0, 4.0, 6.0])
>>> x + y # Add arrays
array([ 3., 6., 9.])
>>> x - y
array([ -1., -2., -3.])
>>> x * y # element-wise product
array([ 2.,8., 18.])
>>> x / y
array([ 0.5, 0.5, 0.5])
```

Take note that the numbers of elements of arrays **x** and **y** are the same (both are one-dimensional arrays with three elements). When the numbers of elements of **x** and **y** are the same, mathematical operations are conducted for each element. If the numbers of elements are different, an error occurs. So, it is important that they are the same. "For each element" is also called **element-wise**, and the "product of each element" is called an **element-wise product**.

In addition to element-wise calculations, mathematical operations of a NumPy array and a single number (scalar value) are also available. In that case, calculations are performed between each element of the NumPy array and the scalar value. This feature is called **broadcasting** (more details on this will be provided later):

```
>>> x = np.array([1.0, 2.0, 3.0])
>>> x / 2.0
array([ 0.5, 1. , 1.5])
```

N-Dimensional NumPy Arrays

In NumPy, you can create multi-dimensional arrays as well as one-dimensional arrays (linear arrays). For example, you can create a two-dimensional array (matrix) as follows:

```
>>> A = np.array([[1, 2], [3, 4]])
>>> print(A)
[[1 2]
 [3 4]]
>>> A.shape
(2, 2)
>>> A.dtype
dtype('int64')
```

Here, a 2x2 matrix, **A**, was created. You can use **shape** to check the shape of the matrix, **A**, and use **dtype** to check the type of its elements. Here are the mathematical operations of matrices:

```
>>> B = np.array([[3, 0],[0, 6]])
>>> A + B
array([[ 4, 2],
 [ 3, 10]])
>>> A * B
array([[ 3, 0],
 [ 0, 24]])
```

As in arrays, matrices are calculated element by element if they have the same shape. Mathematical operations between a matrix and a scalar (single number) are also available. This is also conducted by broadcasting:

```
>>> print(A)
[[1 2]
 [3 4]]
>>> A * 10
array([[ 10, 20],
 [ 30, 40]])
```

A NumPy array (**np.array**) can be an N-dimensional array. You can create arrays of any number of dimensions, such as one-, two-, three-, ... dimensional arrays. In mathematics, a one-dimensional array is called a **vector**, and a two-dimensional array is called a **matrix**. Generalizing a vector and a matrix is called a **tensor**. In this book, we will call a two-dimensional array a matrix, and an array of three or more dimensions a tensor or a multi-dimensional array.

Broadcasting

In NumPy, you can also do mathematical operations between arrays with different shapes. In the preceding example, the 2x2 matrix, **A**, was multiplied by a scalar value of **s**. *Figure 1.1* shows what is done during this operation: a scalar value of 10 is expanded to 2x2 elements for the operation. This smart feature is called **broadcasting**:

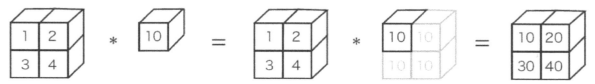

Figure 1.1: Sample broadcasting – a scalar value of 10 is treated as a 2x2 matrix

Here is a calculation for another broadcasting sample:

```
>>> A = np.array([[1, 2], [3, 4]])
>>> B = np.array([10, 20])
>>> A * B
array([[ 10, 40],
 [ 30, 80]])
```

Here (as shown in *Figure 1.2*), the one-dimensional array **B** is transformed so that it has the same shape as the two-dimensional array **A**, and they are calculated element by element.

Thus, NumPy can use broadcasting to do operations between arrays with different shapes:

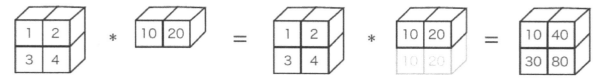

Figure 1.2: Sample broadcasting

Accessing Elements

The index of an element starts from 0 (as usual). You can access each element as follows:

```
>>> X = np.array([[51, 55], [14, 19], [0, 4]])
>>> print(X)
[[51 55]
[14 19]
[ 0 4]]
>>> X[0]  # 0th row
```

```
array([51, 55])
>>> X[0][1] # Element at (0,1)
55
```

Use a `for` statement to access each element:

```
>>> for row in X:
...     print(row)
...
[51 55]
[14 19]
[0 4]
```

In addition to the index operations described so far, NumPy can also use arrays to access each element:

```
>>> X = X.flatten( ) # Convert X into a one-dimensional array
>>> print(X)
[51 55 14 19 0 4]
>>> X[np.array([0, 2, 4])] # Obtain the elements of the 0th, 2nd, and 4th
indices
array([51, 14, 0])
```

Use this notation to obtain only the elements that meet certain conditions. For example, the following statement extracts values that are larger than 15 from `x`:

```
>>> X > 15
array([ True, True, False, True, False, False], dtype=bool)
>>> X[X>15]
array([51, 55, 19])
```

An inequality sign used with a NumPy array (`x > 15`, in the preceding example) returns a Boolean array. Here, the Boolean array is used to extract each element in the array, extracting elements that are `True`.

> **Note**
>
> It is said that dynamic languages, such as Python, are slower in terms of processing than static languages (compiler languages), such as C and C++. In fact, you should write programs in C/C++ to handle heavy processing. When performance is required in Python, the content of a process is implemented in C/C++. In that case, Python serves as a mediator for calling programs written in C/C++. In NumPy, the main processes are implemented by C and C++. So, you can use convenient Python syntax without reducing performance.

Matplotlib

In deep learning experiments, drawing graphs and visualizing data is important. With Matplotlib, you can draw visualize easily by drawing graphs and charts. This section describes how to draw graphs and display images.

Drawing a Simple Graph

You can use Matplotlib's `pyplot` module to draw graphs. Here is an example of drawing a sine function:

```
import numpy as np
import matplotlib.pyplot as plt

# Create data
x = np.arange(0, 6, 0.1) # Generate from 0 to 6 in increments of 0.1
y = np.sin(x)
# Draw a graph
plt.plot(x, y)
plt.show()
```

Here, NumPy's `arange` method is used to generate the data of [0, 0.1, 0.2, ..., 5.8, 5.9] and name it `x`. NumPy's sine function, `np.sin()`, is applied to each element of `x`, and the data rows of `x` and `y` are provided to the `plt.plot` method to draw a graph. Finally, a graph is displayed by `plt.show()`. When the preceding code is executed, the image shown in *Figure* 1.3 is displayed:

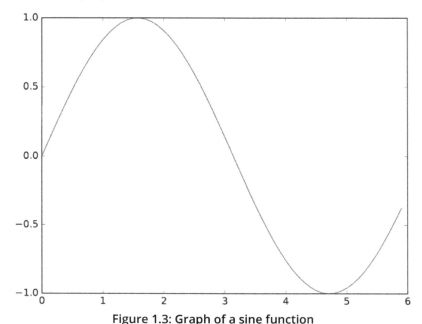

Figure 1.3: Graph of a sine function

Features of pyplot

Here, we will draw a cosine function (`cos`) in addition to the sine function (`sin`) we looked at previously. We will use some other features of `pyplot` to show the title, the label name of the x-axis, and so on:

```python
import numpy as np
import matplotlib.pyplot as plt

# Create data
x = np.arange(0, 6, 0.1) # Generate from 0 to 6 in increments of 0.1
y1 = np.sin(x)
y2 = np.cos(x)

# Draw a graph
plt.plot(x, y1, label="sin")
plt.plot(x, y2, linestyle = "--", label="cos") # Draw with a dashed line
plt.xlabel("x") # Label of the x axis
plt.ylabel("y") # Label of the y axis
plt.title('sin & cos') # Title
plt.legend()
plt.show()
```

Figure 1.4 shows the resulting graph. You can see that the title of the graph and the label names of the axes are displayed:

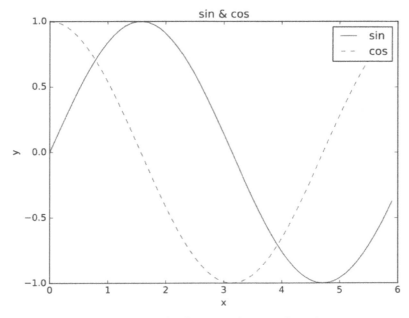

Figure 1.4: Graph of sine and cosine functions

Displaying Images

The `imshow()` method for displaying images is also provided in `pyplot`. You can use `imread()` in the `matplotlib.image` module to load images, as in the following example:

```python
import matplotlib.pyplot as plt
from matplotlib.image import imread

img = imread('lena.png') # Load an image (specify an appropriate path!)
plt.imshow(img)

plt.show()
```

When you execute this code, the image shown in *Figure* 1.5 is displayed:

Figure 1.5: Displaying an image

Here, it is assumed that the image, `lena.png`, is located in the current directory. You need to change the name and path of the file as required, depending on your environment. In the source code provided with this book, `lena.png` is located under the `dataset` directory as a sample image. For example, to execute the preceding code from the `ch01` directory in the Python interpreter, change the path of the image from `lena.png` to `../dataset/lena.png` for proper operation.

Summary

This chapter has given you some of the Python programming basics required to implement deep learning and neural networks. In the next chapter, we will enter the world of deep learning and look at some actual Python code.

This chapter provided only a brief overview of Python. If you want to learn more, the following materials may be helpful. For Python, *Bill Lubanovic: Introducing Python, Second Edition, O'Reilly Media, 2019* is recommended. This is a practical primer that elaborately explains Python programming from its basics to its applications. For NumPy, *Wes McKinney: Python for Data Analysis, O'Reilly Media, 2012* is easy to understand and well organized. In addition to these books, the *Scipy Lecture Notes* (https://scipy-lectures.org) website describes NumPy and Matplotlib in scientific and technological calculations in depth. Refer to them if you are interested.

This chapter covered the following points:

- Python is a programming language that is simple and easy to learn.
- Python is an open-source piece of software that you can use as you like.
- This book uses Python 3 to implement deep learning.
- NumPy and Matplotlib are used as external libraries.
- Python provides two execution modes: interpreter and script files.
- In Python, you can implement and import functions and classes as modules.
- NumPy provides many convenient methods for handling multi-dimensional arrays.

2

Perceptrons

This chapter describes an algorithm called a *perceptron*. Invented by the US researcher Frank Rosenblatt in 1957, it is from this traditional algorithm that neural networks (i.e., deep learning) originated and is thus a necessary first step to the more advanced study of both. This chapter will describe a perceptron and use one to solve easy problems. Throughout this process, you will familiarize yourself with the mechanics of perceptrons.

What Is a Perceptron?

A perceptron receives multiple signals as inputs and outputs one signal. The "signal" here "flows" like an electric current or a river. In the same way that an electric current flows through a conductor and pushes electrons forward, the signal in a perceptron makes flow and transfers information. Unlike an electric current, the signal in a perceptron is binary: "Flow (1) or Do not flow (0)." In this book, 0 indicates "do not flow a signal" and 1 indicates "flow a signal."

(In the interest of precision, note that the perceptron described in this chapter is more accurately called an "artificial neuron" or a "simple perceptron." Here, we will call it a "perceptron" because the basic processes are often the same.)

Figure 2.1 shows an example of a perceptron that receives two signals as input:

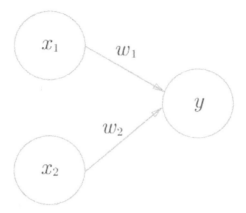

Figure 2.1: Perceptron with two inputs

x_1 and x_2 are input signals, y is an output signal, and w_1 and w_2 are weights (w is the initial letter of "weight"). The circle in the preceding diagram is called a "neuron" or a "node." When input signals are sent to a neuron, each of them is multiplied by its own weight (w_1x_1 and w_2x_2). The neuron sums the signals that it receives and outputs 1 when the sum exceeds a certain limit value. This is sometimes called "firing a neuron." Here, the limit value is called a **threshold** and is represented by the θ symbol.

This is all about the operating principle of a perceptron. Equation (2.1) shows what we described here:

$$y = \begin{cases} 0 & (w_1x_1 + w_2x_2 \leq \theta) \\ 1 & (w_1x_1 + w_2x_2 > \theta) \end{cases} \qquad (2.1)$$

A perceptron has a specific weight for each of multiple inputs, while the weight controls the importance of each signal. The larger the weight, the more important the signal for the weight.

> **Note**
>
> A weight is equivalent to electrical "resistance." Resistance is a parameter that measures the difficulty of passing an electric current. The smaller the resistance, the larger the current. Meanwhile, when the weight of a perceptron is larger, the signal that flows becomes larger. Both resistance and weight work in the same way in that they both control the difficulty (or ease) of passing a signal.

Simple Logic Circuits

AND Gate

The following are some easy problems that use a perceptron. We will look at logic circuits here. Let's think about an AND gate first. An AND gate consists of two inputs and one output. The table of input and output signals in *Figure 2.2* is called a "truth table." As shown in *Figure 2.2*, the AND gate outputs 1 when two inputs are 1. Otherwise, it outputs 0:

x_1	x_2	y
0	0	0
1	0	0
0	1	0
1	1	1

Figure 2.2: Truth table of an AND gate

Now, we will use a perceptron to express this AND gate. We will determine the values of w_1, w_2, and θ so that they satisfy the truth table of *Figure 2.2*. What values can we set to create a perceptron that satisfies the conditions of *Figure 2.2*?

Actually, there is an infinite number of combinations of the parameters that satisfy *Figure 2.2*. For example, when $(w_1, w_2, \theta) = (0.5, 0.5, 0.7)$, the perceptron works as shown in *Figure 2.2*. (0.5, 0.5, 0.8) and (1.0, 1.0, 1.0) also satisfy the conditions of the AND gate. If these parameters are set, the sum of weighted signals exceeds the given threshold, θ, when both x_1 and x_2 are 1.

NAND and OR gates

Now, let's look at a NAND gate. NAND means Not AND, and the output of the NAND gate is the opposite of the AND gate. As shown in the truth table provided in *Figure* 2.3, it outputs 0 when both x_1 and x_2 are 1. Otherwise, it outputs 1. What combinations of parameters are available for a NAND gate?

x_1	x_2	y
0	0	1
1	0	1
0	1	1
1	1	0

Figure 2.3: Truth table of a NAND gate

A combination of $(w_1, w_2, \theta) = (-0.5, -0.5, -0.7)$ can represent a NAND gate, and there is an infinite number of other combinations. In fact, you can build a NAND gate by inverting all the signs of the parameter values that build an AND gate.

Now, let's look at an OR gate, as shown in *Figure* 2.4. This is a logic circuit that outputs 1 if at least one of the input signals is 1. What parameters do you think we can set for the OR gate?

x_1	x_2	y
0	0	0
1	0	1
0	1	1
1	1	1

Figure 2.4: Truth table of an OR gate

> **Note**
>
> We are the ones that determine the perceptron parameters here—not a computer. While looking at the "training data," also known as a truth table, we considered (found) the parameter values manually. In machine learning problems, we have a computer determines the parameter values automatically. **Training** is the task that determines the appropriate parameters, and we consider the structure (model) of the perceptron and give training data to the computer.

As described previously, we can use a perceptron to build AND, NAND, and OR logic circuits. What is important here is that the structure of a perceptron is the same for all of the AND, NAND, and OR gates. The differences between the three gates lie in the parameter values (weights and thresholds). Just like a versatile actor plays a wide variety of characters, the perceptron of the same structure changes into AND, NAND, and OR when the parameter values are adjusted appropriately.

Implementing Perceptrons

Easy Implementation

Let's implement the preceding logic circuits with Python. Here, we will define the AND function, which takes **x1** and **x2** as arguments:

```python
def AND(x1, x2):
    w1, w2, theta = 0.5, 0.5, 0.7
    tmp = x1*w1 + x2*w2
    if tmp <= theta:
        return 0
    elif tmp > theta:
        return 1
```

The **w1**, **w2**, and **theta** parameters are initialized within the function. When the sum of the weighted inputs exceeds the threshold, it returns 1; otherwise, it returns 0. Let's check that the outputs are the same as the ones shown in *Figure 2.2*:

```python
AND(0, 0) # 0 (output)
AND(1, 0) # 0 (output)
AND(0, 1) # 0 (output)
AND(1, 1) # 1 (output)
```

The outputs are as we expected. With that, you have built an AND gate. Although you can use a similar procedure to build a NAND or OR gate, we will change the implementation a little.

Introducing Weights and Bias

Although the preceding implementation of an AND gate is simple and easy to understand, we will change it to a different implementation for the subsequent sections, switching θ in equation (2.1) to -b and representing the behavior of the perceptron in equation (2.2):

$$y = \begin{cases} 0 & (b + w_1 x_1 + w_2 x_2 \leq 0) \\ 1 & (b + w_1 x_1 + w_2 x_2 > 0) \end{cases} \tag{2.2}$$

Although the notation of the symbols has changed, equations (2.1) and (2.2) represent exactly the same thing. Here, b is called a bias and w_1 and w_2 are called **weights**. As equation (2.2) shows, the perceptron sums the input signal values multiplied by the weights and the bias. It outputs 1 if the sum exceeds 0, and outputs 0 otherwise. Now, let's use NumPy to implement equation (2.2). We will use the Python interpreter to check the results one by one:

```
>>> import numpy as np
>>> x = np.array([0, 1]) # Input
>>> w = np.array([0.5, 0.5]) # Weight
>>> b = -0.7      # Bias
>>> w*x
array([ 0. ,  0.5])
>>> np.sum(w*x)
0.5
>>> np.sum(w*x) + b
-0.19999999999999996 # About -0.2 (Operation error with floatingpoint
numbers)
```

As shown in this example, when NumPy arrays are multiplied, each of their elements is multiplied if the two arrays have the same number of elements. Therefore, when calculating `w*x`, each element is multiplied, ([0, 1] * [0.5, 0.5] => [0, 0.5]). In `np.sum(w*x)`, each element is summed. When the bias is added to this weighted sum, the calculation of equation (2.2) is complete.

Implementation with Weights and Bias

You can use weights and bias to implement an AND gate, as follows:

```
def AND(x1, x2):
    x = np.array([x1, x2])
    w = np.array([0.5, 0.5])
    b = -0.7
    tmp = np.sum(w*x) + b
    if tmp <= 0:
        return 0
    else:
        return 1
```

Here, $-\theta$ is called the bias, b. Note that the bias works differently from the weights, w_1 and w_2. Specifically, w_1 and w_2 work as parameters that control the importance of input signals, while the bias works as the parameter that adjusts the ease of firing–that is, how likely it is that the output signal is 1. For example, if b is -0.1, the neuron fires when the weighted sum of the input signals exceeds 0.1. On the other hand, if b is -20.0, the neuron fires only when the weighted sum of input signals exceeds 20.0. Thus, the value of the bias determines how easily the neuron fires. Although w_1 and w_2 are called "weights" and b is called "bias," all the parameters (that is, b, w_1, and w_2) are sometimes called "weights," depending on the context.

> **Note**
>
> The word "bias" also means "padding." It indicates that the output is increased if nothing is input (if the input is 0). Actually, if inputs x_1 and x_2 are 0, the output is just the value of the bias when $b + w_1x_1 + w_2x_2$ is calculated in equation (2.2).

Now, let's implement the NAND and OR gates:

```
def NAND(x1, x2):
    x = np.array([x1, x2])
    w = np.array([-0.5, -0.5]) # Only the weights and bias are different
from AND!
    b = 0.7
    tmp = np.sum(w*x) + b
    if tmp <= 0:
        return 0
    else:
        return 1

def OR(x1, x2):
    x = np.array([x1, x2])
    w = np.array([0.5, 0.5]) # Only the weights and bias are different from
AND!
    b = -0.2
    tmp = np.sum(w*x) + b
    if tmp <= 0:
        return 0
    else:
        return 1
```

As described in the previous section, the AND, NAND, and OR gates are the same in terms of structure for the perceptron and differ only in terms of the values of the weight parameters. When implementing the NAND and OR gates, only the values of the weights and bias are different from the AND gate.

Limitations of Perceptrons

As described so far, we can use a perceptron to implement AND, NAND, and OR logic gates. In this next section, you will consider an XOR gate.

XOR Gate

An XOR gate is a gate circuit that is also called an *exclusive* OR. As shown in *Figure* 2.5, the output is 1 when either x_1 or x_2 is 1 ("exclusive" means "limited to only one person"). What should be the value of the weights to realize the XOR gate by using a perceptron?

x_1	x_2	y
0	0	0
1	0	1
0	1	1
1	1	0

Figure 2.5: Truth table of an XOR gate

In fact, we cannot build this XOR gate by using the perceptron that we have learned about so far. Why can we not build XOR even though we can build AND and OR gates?

First, let's examine the behavior of an OR gate visually. An OR gate satisfies the truth table in *Figure* 2.5 when the weight parameters are (b, w_1, w_2) = (-0.5, 1.0, 1.0), for example. In this case, the perceptron is represented by equation (2.3):

$$y = \begin{cases} 0 & (-0.5 + x_1 + x_2 \le 0) \\ 1 & (-0.5 + x_1 + x_2 > 0) \end{cases} \qquad (2.3)$$

The perceptron represented by equation (2.3) generates two areas that are divided by the straight line $-0.5 + x_1 + x_2 = 0$. One of the areas divided by the straight line outputs 1, while the other outputs 0. *Figure 2.6* shows this graphically:

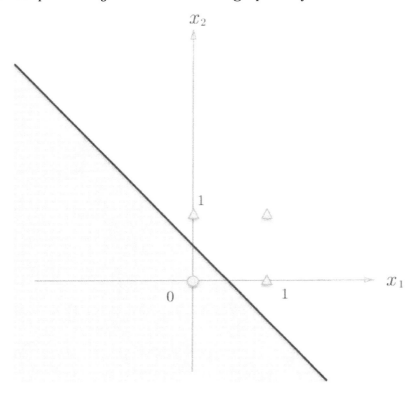

Figure 2.6: Visualizing a perceptron – the perceptron outputs 0 in the gray area, which satisfies the characteristics of an OR gate

An OR gate outputs 0 when $(x_1, x_2) = (0, 0)$ and outputs 1 when $(x_1, x_2) = (0, 1)$, $(1, 0)$, and $(1, 1)$. Here, a circle indicates 0, and a triangle indicates 1. To create an OR gate, we must divide between circles and triangles with a straight line. The straight line can actually divide four points correctly.

So, how about the case of an XOR gate? Can we create areas that divide between circles and triangles with a straight line, as in the case of an OR gate?

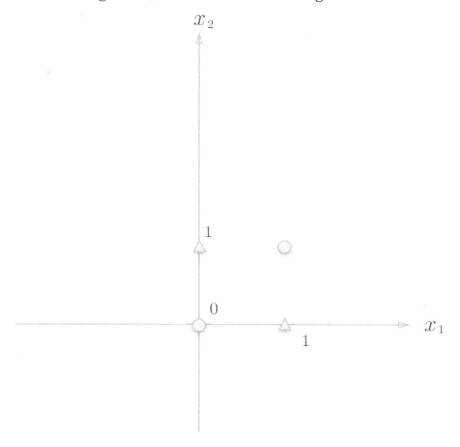

Figure 2.7: Circles and triangles indicate the outputs of an XOR gate.

However hard you may be trying to solve this, you cannot divide between circles and triangles with a straight line. One straight line cannot divide them.

Linear and Nonlinear

You cannot divide between circles and triangles with a straight line. However, you can divide them if you can remove the restriction of a "straight line." For example, you can create the areas that divide between circles and triangles, as shown in *Figure 2.8.*

The limit of a perceptron is that it can only represent the areas divided by a straight line. It cannot represent a curve, as shown in *Figure 2.8*. The areas divided by a curve in *Figure 2.8* are called *nonlinear* areas, while those divided by a straight line are called *linear* areas. The words *linear* and *nonlinear* are often used in machine learning. You can visualize them with *Figures 2.6* and *2.8*:

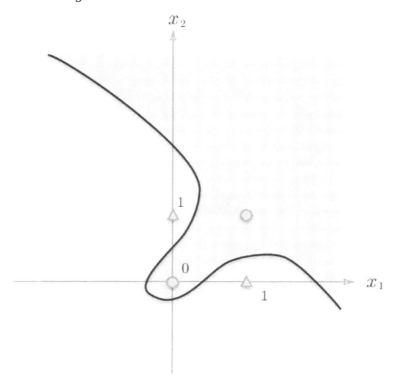

Figure 2.8: A curve can divide between circles and triangles

Multilayer Perceptrons

Unfortunately, we cannot use a perceptron to represent an XOR gate. However, this is not terrible news. Actually, the merit of a perceptron lies in the fact that multiple layers of perceptrons can be stacked (the outline of this section is that multiple layers can represent XOR). We will look at the stacking layers later. Here, we can consider the problem of the XOR gate from another viewpoint.

Combining the Existing Gates

There are some methods we can follow to make an XOR gate. One of them is to combine the AND, NAND, and OR gates that we have created so far and wire them. Here, the AND, NAND, and OR gates are shown with symbols in *Figure* 2.9. The circle at the tip of the NAND gate in *Figure* 2.9 indicates that an output has been reversed.

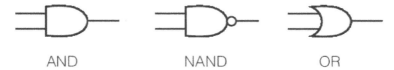

AND   NAND   OR

Figure 2.9: Symbols of the AND, NAND, and OR gates

Now, let's think about how we can wire AND, NAND, and OR to create an XOR gate. Note that you can assign AND, NAND, or OR to each of the ? symbols in *Figure* 2.10 to complete an XOR gate:

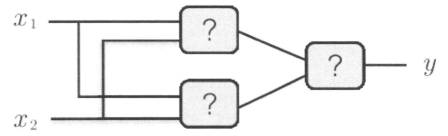

Figure 2.10: Replace the "?" symbols with an AND, NAND, or OR gate to complete an XOR gate!

To be specific, the limitation of a perceptron described in the previous section is that a single layer of a perceptron cannot represent an XOR gate or divide nonlinear areas. Here, we will see that an XOR gate can be built by combining perceptrons (i.e., stacking layers).

The wiring in *Figure 2.11* can build an XOR gate. Here, x_1 and x_2 indicate input signals, while y indicates an output signal. x_1 and x_2 are the inputs to the NAND and OR gates, and the outputs of the NAND and OR gates are the inputs to the AND gate:

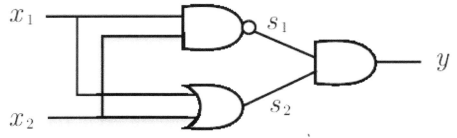

Figure 2.11: A combination of the AND, NAND, and OR gates constructs an XOR gate

Let's check that the wiring in *Figure 2.11* can really form an XOR gate. Assuming that the output of the NAND is s_1 and that of the OR is s_2, we will complete the truth table. *Figure 2.12* shows the results. When we look at x_1, x_2, and y, we can see that they represent the outputs of the XOR:

x_1	x_2	s_1	s_2	y
0	0	1	0	0
1	0	1	1	1
0	1	1	1	1
1	1	0	1	0

Figure 2.12: Truth table of an XOR gate

Implementing an XOR Gate

Now, we will use Python to implement the XOR gate represented by the wiring in *Figure 2.11*. By using the AND, NAND, and OR functions that we defined previously, we can implement this as follows:

```
def XOR(x1, x2):
    s1 = NAND(x1, x2)
    s2 = OR(x1, x2)
    y = AND(s1, s2)
    return y
```

The XOR function outputs the results as expected:

```
XOR(0, 0) # 0 (output)
XOR(1, 0) # 1 (output)
XOR(0, 1) # 1 (output)
XOR(1, 1) # 0 (output)
```

Now, we can build an XOR gate. After doing this, we will represent the XOR that we have just implemented with perceptrons (by showing neurons explicitly). *Figure 2.13* shows this representation.

An XOR is a multilayer network, as shown in *Figure 2.13*. Here, we will call the leftmost column `Layer 0`, the next `Layer 1`, and the rightmost `Layer 2`.

The perceptron in *Figure 2.13* differs in shape from the AND and OR perceptrons we have looked at so far (*Figure 2.1*). The AND and OR perceptrons are single-layer, while the XOR perceptron is two-layer. A perceptron with multiple layers is sometimes called a **multilayered perceptron**:

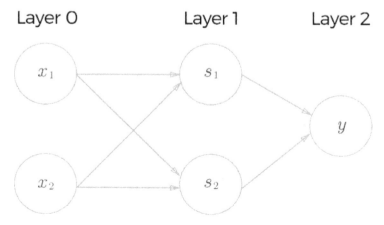

Figure 2.13: Representation of an XOR by perceptrons

> **Note**
>
> Although the perceptron in *Figure 2.13* consists of three layers, we will call it a "two-layer perceptron" because only the two layers (between layers 0 and 1 and between layers 1 and 2) have weight. Some literature calls the perceptron in *Figure 2.13* a "three-layer perceptron" because it consists of three layers.

A two-layer perceptron, as shown in *Figure* 2.13, sends and receives signals between the neurons in layers 0 and 1 and then between layers 1 and 2. The following describes this behavior in more detail:

1. Two neurons in layer 0 receive input signals and send signals to the neurons in layer 1.

2. The neurons in layer 1 send signals to the neuron in layer 2, which outputs y.

The behavior of this two-layer perceptron can be compared to an assembly through a pipeline. The worker on the first level (or first layer) works on the "component" that arrives and passes it to the worker on the second level (the second layer) when the task is finished. The worker in the second layer works on the "component" that was received from the worker in the first layer to complete and ship (output) it.

Thus, the perceptrons in an XOR gate "pass components" between workers. This two-layer structure enables perceptrons to build an XOR gate. This can be interpreted as "what cannot be achieved with a single-layer perceptron can be achieved by adding one layer." Perceptrons can provide a more flexible representation by stacking layers (deepening layers).

From NAND to a Computer

Multilayer perceptrons can create more complicated circuits than those we have examined so far. For example, an adder circuit that add numbers can be created with perceptrons. An encoder that converts a binary number into a decimal number and a circuit that outputs 1 when certain conditions are met (circuit for parity checks) can be represented with perceptrons. As a matter of fact, we can even use perceptrons to represent a computer.

A computer is a machine that processes information. When it receives input, a computer processes it in a certain way and outputs the result. Processing in a certain way means that both a computer and a perceptron have inputs and outputs and calculate them based on fixed rules.

Although it seems that a computer conducts very complicated processes inside it, in fact (surprisingly), a combination of NAND gates can reproduce what a computer does. The surprising fact that NAND gates are all we need to create a computer means that perceptrons can also represent a computer because a NAND gate can itself be made with perceptrons. Simply put, if we can create a computer by combining NAND gates, we can also represent one by combining only perceptrons (a combination of perceptrons can be represented as one multilayer perceptron).

> **Note**
>
> You may find it hard to believe that a combination of NAND gates can create a computer. If you are interested in this topic, *The Elements of Computing Systems: Building a Modern Computer from First Principles* (The MIT Press) is recommended. This book aims to understand computers deeply. Under the motto "From NANDs to Tetris," it uses NANDs to create a computer that runs Tetris. If you read this book, you will realize that computers can be created from simple elements—that is, NANDs.

Thus, multilayer perceptrons can achieve as complicated a representation as creating a computer. So, what perceptron structure can represent a computer? How many layers are needed to create a computer?

The answer is that, theoretically, a computer can be created with two-layer perceptrons. It has been proven that any function can be represented with two-layer perceptrons (to be accurate, when an activation function is a nonlinear sigmoid function – refer to the next chapter for details). However, it will be a very laborious job to create a computer by specifying the appropriate weights in a structure of two-layer perceptrons. Actually, to start from low-level components such as NANDs to create a computer, creating the required components (modules) step by step is natural—starting from AND and OR gates and proceeding to half adders and full adders, **arithmetic and logic units** (**ALUs**), and a CPU. Therefore, creating a structure of many layers is a natural way when representing a computer with perceptrons.

Although we will not create a computer in this book, please keep in mind that multilayer perceptrons enable nonlinear representations and that they can, in principle, represent what a computer does.

Summary

In this chapter, we covered perceptrons. The perceptron is a very simple algorithm, so you should be able to understand how it works quickly. The perceptron is the basis of a neural network, which we will learn about in the next chapter. These points may be summed up in the following list:

- A perceptron is an algorithm with inputs and outputs. When it receives a certain input, it outputs a fixed value.

- A perceptron has "weight" and "bias" parameters.

- You can use perceptrons to represent logic circuits such as AND and OR gates.

- An XOR gate cannot be represented with a single-layer perceptron.

- A two-layer perceptron can be used to represent an XOR gate.

- A single-layer perceptron can only represent linear areas, while a multilayer perceptron can represent nonlinear areas.

- Multilayer perceptrons can represent a computer (theoretically).

3

Neural Networks

We learned about perceptrons in the previous chapter, and there is both good news and bad news. The good news is that perceptrons are likely to represent complicated functions. For example, the perceptron can (theoretically) represent complicated processes performed by a computer, as described in the previous chapter. The bad news is that weights must be defined manually first before the appropriate weights are determined in order to meet the expected inputs and outputs. In the previous chapter, we used the truth tables with AND and OR gates to determine the appropriate weights manually.

Neural networks exist to solve the bad news. More specifically, one important property of a neural network is that it can learn appropriate weight parameters from data automatically. This chapter provides an overview of neural networks and focuses on what distinguishes them. The next chapter will describe how it learns weight parameters from data.

From Perceptrons to Neural Networks

A neural network is similar to the perceptron described in the previous chapter in many ways. How a neural network works, as well as how it differs from a perceptron, will be described in this section.

Neural Network Example

Figure 3.1 shows a neural network example. Here, the left column is called an **input layer**, the right column is called an **output layer**, and the center column is called the **middle layer**. The middle layer is also known as a hidden layer. "Hidden" means that the neurons in the hidden layer are invisible (unlike those in the input and output layers). In this book, we'll call the layers layer 0, layer 1, and layer 2 from the input layer to the output layer (layer numbers start from layer 0 because doing so is convenient when the layers are implemented in Python later). In *Figure* 3.1, layer 0 is the input layer, layer 1 is the middle layer, and layer 2 is the output layer:

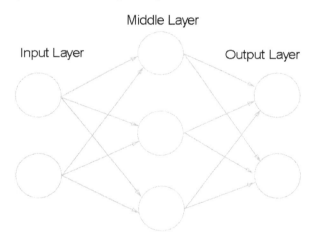

Figure 3.1: Neural network example

> **Note**
>
> Although the network in *Figure 3.1* consists of three layers, we call it a "two-layer network" because it has two layers with weights. Some books call it a "three-layer network" based on the number of layers that constitute the network, but in this book, the network name is based on the number of layers that have weights (that is, the total number of input, hidden, and output layers, minus 1).

The neural network in *Figure 3.1* is similar to the perceptron in the previous chapter in terms of its shape. In fact, in terms of how neurons are connected, it is no different from the perceptron we saw in the previous chapter. So, how are signals transmitted in a neural network?

Reviewing the Perceptron

To answer this question, we first need to review the perceptron. Consider a network that has the following structure:

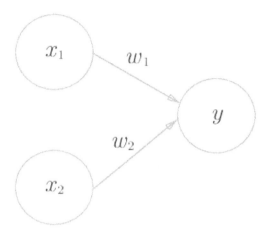

Figure 3.2: Reviewing the perceptron

Figure 3.2 shows a perceptron that receives two input signals (x_1 and x_2) and outputs y. As described earlier, the perceptron in *Figure 3.2* is represented by equation (3.1):

$$y = \begin{cases} 0 & (b + w_1 x_1 + w_2 x_2 \leq 0) \\ 1 & (b + w_1 x_1 + w_2 x_2 > 0) \end{cases} \tag{3.1}$$

Here, b is a parameter called "bias" and controls how easily the neuron fires. Meanwhile, w_1 and w_2 are the parameters that indicate the "weights" of individual signals to control their importance.

You may have noticed that the network in *Figure* 3.2 has no bias, b. We can indicate the bias shown in *Figure* 3.3, if we want to. A signal of weight b and input 1 has been added in *Figure* 3.3. This perceptron receives three signals (x_1, x_2, and 1) as the inputs to the neuron, and multiplies the signals by each weight before transmitting them to the next neuron. The next neuron sums the weighted signals and then outputs 1 if the sum exceeds 0. It outputs 0 if it doesn't. The neuron in the following diagram is shown in solid gray to distinguish it from other neurons. This is because the input signal of the bias is always 1:

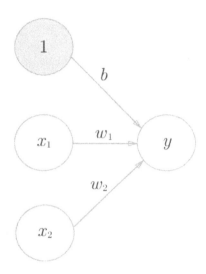

Figure 3.3: Showing the bias explicitly

Now, we want to simplify equation (3.1). To do that, we use a single function to express the condition, where 1 is the output if the sum exceeds 0, and 0 is the output if it does not. Here, we will introduce a new function, $h(x)$, and rewrite equation (3.1) to equations (3.2) and (3.3) shown here:

$$y = h(b + w_1 x_1 + w_2 x_2) \tag{3.2}$$

$$h(x) = \begin{cases} 0 & (x \le 0) \\ 1 & (x > 0) \end{cases} \tag{3.3}$$

Equation (3.2) indicates that the $h(x)$ function converts the sum of input signals into the output, y. The $h(x)$ function represented by equation (3.3) returns 1 if the input exceeds 0 and returns 0 if it does not. Therefore, equations (3.2) and (3.3) operate in the same way as equation (3.1).

Introducing an Activation Function

The $h(x)$ function that appears here is generally called an **activation function**. It converts the sum of input signals into an output signal. As the name "activation" indicates, the activation function determines how the sum of the input signals activates (that is, how it fires).

Now, we can rewrite equation (3.2) again. Equation (3.2) performs two processes: the weighted input signals are summed, and the sum is converted by the activation function. Therefore, you can divide equation (3.2) into the following two equations:

$$a = b + w_1x_1 + w_2x_2 \tag{3.4}$$

$$y = h(a) \tag{3.5}$$

In equation (3.4), the sum of the weighted input signals and biases becomes a. In equation (3.5), a is converted by $h()$, and y is output.

So far, a neuron has been shown as one circle. *Figure 3.4* shows equations (3.4) and (3.5) explicitly:

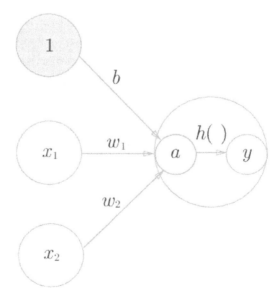

Figure 3.4: Showing the process performed by the activation function explicitly

Figure 3.4 explicitly shows the process that is performed by the activation function in the circle of the neuron. We can clearly see that the sum of the weighted signals becomes node a and that it is converted into node y by the activation function, $h()$. In this book, the terms "neuron" and "node" are used interchangeably. Here, circles a and y are called "nodes," which are used in the same sense as "neurons" that were used earlier.

We will continue to show a neuron as one circle, as shown on the left of *Figure* 3.5. In this book, we will also show the activation process (to the right of *Figure* 3.5), if the behavior of the neural network can be clarified:

Figure 3.5: The left-hand image is an ordinary image that shows a neuron, while the right-hand image explicitly shows the process of activation in a neuron (a is the sum of input signals, h() is the activation function, and y is the output)

Now, let's focus on the activation function, which serves as the bridge from a perceptron to a neural network.

> **Note**
>
> In this book, the algorithm indicated by the word "perceptron" is not strictly defined. Generally, a "simple perceptron" is a single-layer network where a step function that changes the output values at a threshold is used as the activation function. A "multilayer perceptron" usually means a neural network that contains multiple layers and uses a smooth activation function, such as a sigmoid function.

Activation Function

The activation function represented by equation (3.3) changes output values at a threshold and is called a "step function" or a "staircase function." Therefore, we can say, "a perceptron uses a step function as the activation function." In other words, a perceptron chooses a "step function" as the activation function from many candidate functions. When a perceptron uses a step function as the activation function, what happens if a function other than a step function is used as the activation function? Well, by changing the activation function from a step function to another function, we can move to the world of a neural network. The next section will introduce an activation function for a neural network.

Sigmoid Function

One of the activation functions often used in neural networks is the **sigmoid function**, represented by equation (3.6):

$$h(x) = \frac{1}{1 + \exp(-x)} \qquad (3.6)$$

exp(-x) in equation (3.6) indicates e^{-x}. The real number, e, is Napier's number, 2.7182... The sigmoid function represented by equation (3.6) seems complicated, but it is only a "function." A function is a converter that returns output when input is provided. For example, when a value such as 1.0 and 2.0 is provided to the sigmoid function, values such as $h(1.0) = 0.731...$ and $h(2.0) = 0.880...$ are returned.

In a neural network, a sigmoid function is often used as the activation function to convert signals, and the converted signals are transmitted to the next neuron. In fact, the main difference between the perceptron described in the previous chapter and the neural network described here is the activation function. Other aspects, such as the structure where neurons are connected in multiple layers and how signals are transmitted, are basically the same as they are for perceptrons. Now, let's look more closely at a sigmoid function (used as the activation function) by comparing it with a step function.

Implementing a Step Function

Here, we will use Python to show the graph of a step function. As represented by equation (3.3), the step function outputs 1 when the input exceeds 0 and outputs 0 if it does not. The following shows a simple implementation of the step function:

```
def step_function(x):
    if x > 0:
        return 1
    else:
        return 0
```

This implementation is simple and easy to understand, but it only takes a real number (a floating-point number) as argument **x**. Therefore, `step_function(3.0)` is allowed. However, the function cannot take a NumPy array as the argument. Thus, `step_function(np.array([1.0, 2.0]))` is not allowed. Here, we want to change to the future implementation so that it can take a NumPy array. For that purpose, we can write an implementation like the following:

```
def step_function(x):
    y = x > 0
    return y.astype(np.int)
```

Although the preceding function contains only two lines, it may be a little difficult to understand because it uses a useful "trick" from NumPy. Here, the following example from the Python interpreter is used to describe what kind of trick is used. In this example, the NumPy **x** array is provided. For the NumPy array, a comparison operator is conducted:

```
>>> import numpy as np
>>> x = np.array([-1.0, 1.0, 2.0])
>>> x
array([-1., 1., 2.])
>>> y = x > 0
>>> y
array([False, True, True], dtype=bool)
```

When a *greater than* comparison is conducted for a NumPy array, each element in the array is compared to generate a Boolean array. Here, each element in the **x** array is converted into **True** when it exceeds 0 or into **False** when it does not. Then, the new array, **y**, is generated.

The **y** array is Boolean, and the desired step function must return 0 or 1 of the **int** type. Therefore, we convert the type of elements of array **y** from Boolean into **int**:

```
>>> y = y.astype(np.int)
>>> y
array([0, 1, 1])
```

As shown here, the **astype()** method is used to convert the type of the NumPy array. The **astype()** method takes the desired type (**np.int**, in this example) as the argument. In Python, **True** is converted into 1, and **False** is converted into 0 by converting the Boolean type into the int type. The preceding code explains NumPy's "trick" that's used when implementing the step function.

Step Function Graph

Now, let's draw the graph of the step function we defined previously. To do that, we need to use the Matplotlib library:

```python
import numpy as np
import matplotlib.pylab as plt

def step_function(x):
    return np.array(x > 0, dtype=np.int)

x = np.arange(-5.0, 5.0, 0.1)
y = step_function(x)
plt.plot(x, y)
plt.ylim(-0.1, 1.1) # Specify the range of the y-axis
plt.show()
```

np.arange(-5.0, 5.0, 0.1) generates a NumPy array containing values from **-5.0** to **5.0** in **0.1** steps, **([-5.0, -4.9, ..., 4.9])**. **step_function()** takes a NumPy array as the argument. It executes the step function for each element in the array and returns an array as the result. When these **x** and **y** arrays are plotted, the graph shown in *Figure 3.6* is displayed:

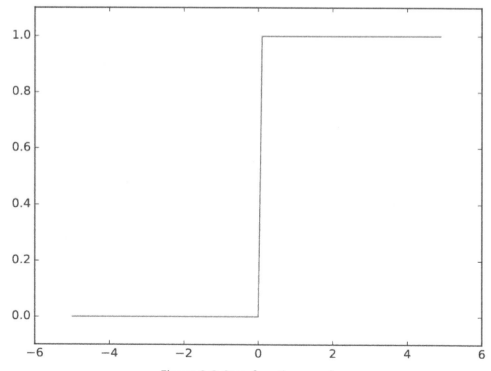

Figure 3.6: Step function graph

As shown in *Figure* 3.6, the output of the step function changes from 0 to 1 (or 1 to 0) at the threshold of 0. A step function is sometimes called a "staircase function" because the output represents the steps of stairs, as shown in *Figure* 3.6.

Implementing a Sigmoid Function

Now, let's implement a sigmoid function. We can write the sigmoid function of equation (3.6) in Python as follows:

```
def sigmoid(x):
    return 1 / (1 + np.exp(-x))
```

Here, `np.exp(-x)` corresponds to `exp(-x)` in the equation. This implementation is not very difficult. The correct results are returned even when a NumPy array is provided as the **x** argument. When this sigmoid function receives a NumPy array, it calculates correctly, as shown here:

```
>>> x = np.array([-1.0, 1.0, 2.0])
>>> sigmoid(x)
array([0.26894142,  0.73105858,  0.88079708])
```

The implementation of the sigmoid function supports a NumPy array due to NumPy's broadcasting (refer to the *Broadcasting* section in *Chapter 1*, *Introduction to Python* for details). When an operation is performed on a scalar and a NumPy array, thanks to the broadcast, the operation is performed between the scalar and each element of the NumPy array.

```
>>> t = np.array([1.0, 2.0, 3.0])
>>> 1.0 + t
array([2., 3., 4.])
>>> 1.0 / t
array([1.  ,  0.5 ,   0.33333333])
```

In the preceding example, arithmetic operations (such as + and /) are performed between the scalar value (1.0 here) and the NumPy array. As a result, the scalar value and each element of the NumPy array is used in the operations, and the results are output as a NumPy array. In this implementation of the sigmoid function, because `np.exp(-x)` generates a NumPy array, `1 / (1 + np.exp(-x))` also uses each element of the NumPy array for the operation.

Now, let's draw the graph of the sigmoid function. The code for drawing is almost the same as the code for the step function. The only difference is that the function that outputs y is changed to the sigmoid function:

```
x = np.arange(-5.0, 5.0, 0.1)
y = sigmoid(x)
plt.plot(x, y)
plt.ylim(-0.1, 1.1) # Specify the range of the y-axis
plt.show()
```

The preceding code creates the graph shown in *Figure* 3.7 when it is executed:

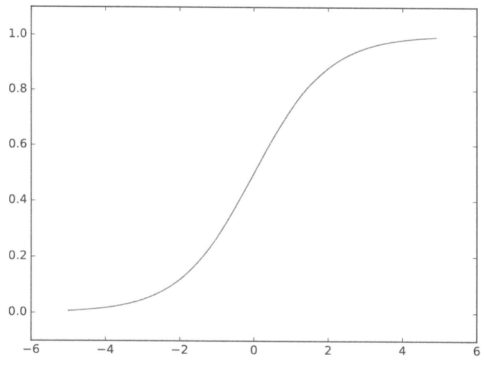

Figure 3.7: Graph of the sigmoid function

Comparing the Sigmoid Function and the Step Function

Let's compare the sigmoid function and the step function. *Figure* 3.8 shows the sigmoid function and the step function. In what ways are the two functions different? In what ways are they alike? We can consider *Figure* 3.8 and think about this for a moment.

When you look at *Figure 3.8*, you may notice the difference in smoothness. The sigmoid function is a smooth curve, where the output changes continuously based on the input. On the other hand, the output of the step function changes suddenly at 0. This smoothness of the sigmoid function has an important meaning when training neural networks:

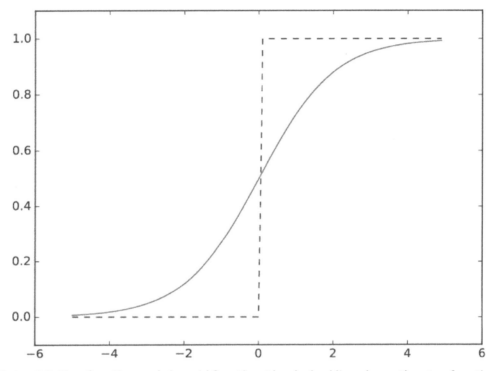

Figure 3.8: Step function and sigmoid function (the dashed line shows the step function)

In connection with the smoothness mentioned previously, they are different in that the step function returns only 0 or 1, while the sigmoid function returns real numbers such as 0.731... and 0.880... That is, binary signals of 0 and 1 flow among neurons in a perceptron, while signals of continuous real numbers flow in a neural network.

When we use "water" to describe the behaviors of these two functions, the step function can be compared to a "shishi-odoshi" (a bamboo tube that clacks against a stone after water flows out of a tube), and the sigmoid function can be compared to a "waterwheel." The step function conducts two actions: it drains or stores water (0 or 1), while the sigmoid function controls the flow of water like a "waterwheel" based on the amount of water that reaches it.

Now, consider the ways in which the step and sigmoid functions are similar. They are different in "smoothness," but you may notice that they are similar in shape when you view *Figure 3.8* from a broader perspective. Actually, both of them output a value near/ of 0 when the input is small, and, as the input becomes larger, the output approaches/ reaches 1. The step and sigmoid functions output a large value when the input signal contains important information and output a small value when it don't. They are also similar in that they output a value between 0 and 1, no matter how small or large the value of the input signal is.

Nonlinear Function

The step and sigmoid functions are similar in another way. One important similarity is that they are both **nonlinear functions**. The sigmoid function is represented by a curve, while the step function is represented by straight lines that look like stairs. They are both classified as nonlinear functions.

> **Note**
>
> The terms "nonlinear function" and "linear function" often appear when an activation function is used. A function is a "converter" that returns a value when a value is provided. A function that outputs the input values multiplied by a constant is called a linear function (represented by the equation $h(x) = cx$, where c is a constant). Therefore, the graph of a linear function is a straight line. Meanwhile, as its name suggests, the graph of a nonlinear function is not a simple straight line.

In a neural network, a nonlinear function must be used as the activation function. In other words, a linear function may not be used as the activation function. Why may a linear function not be used? The reason is that increasing the number of layers in a neural network becomes useless if a linear function is used.

The problem with a linear function is caused by the fact that a "network without a hidden layer" that does the same task always exists, no matter how many layers are added. To understand this specifically (and somewhat intuitively), let's consider a simple example. Here, a linear function, $h(x) = cx$, is used as the activation function and the calculation of $y(x) = h(h(h(x)))$ is performed as in a three-layer network. It contains multiplications of $y(x) = c \times c \times c \times x$, and the same operation can be represented by one multiplication of $y(x) = ax$ (where $a = c^3$). Thus, it can be represented by a network without a hidden layer. As this example shows, using a linear function offsets the advantage of multiple layers. Therefore, to take advantage of multiple layers, a nonlinear function must be used as the activation function.

ReLU Function

Thus far, we have learned about step and sigmoid functions as activation functions. While a sigmoid function has been used for a long time in the history of neural networks, a function called **Rectified Linear Unit (ReLU)** is mainly used these days.

If the input exceeds 0, the ReLU function outputs the input as it is. If the input is equal to or smaller than 0, it outputs 0 (see *Figure* 3.9):

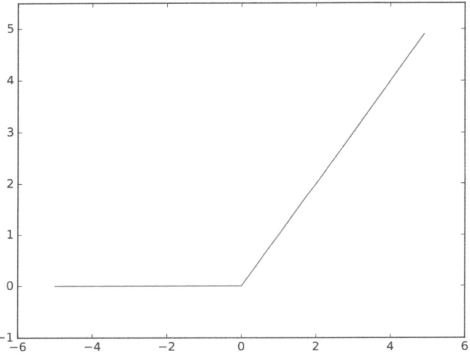

Figure 3.9: ReLU function

Equation (3.7) represents the ReLU function:

$$h(x) = \begin{cases} x & (x > 0) \\ 0 & (x \leq 0) \end{cases} \qquad (3.7)$$

As the graph and the equation shows, the ReLU function is very simple. Therefore, we can also implement it easily, as shown here:

```
def relu(x):
    return np.maximum(0, x)
```

Here, NumPy's maximum function is used. It outputs the larger of the input values.

While a sigmoid function will be used as the activation function later in this chapter, the ReLU function is mainly used in the latter half of this book.

Calculating Multidimensional Arrays

If you learn how to calculate multidimensional arrays using NumPy, you will be able to implement a neural network efficiently. First, we will look at how to use NumPy to calculate multidimensional arrays. Then, we will implement a neural network.

Multidimensional Arrays

Simply put, a multidimensional array is "a set of numbers" arranged in a line, in a rectangle, in three dimensions, or (more generally) in N dimensions, called a multidimensional array. Let's use NumPy to create a multidimensional array. First, we will create a one-dimensional array, as described so far:

```
>>> import numpy as np
>>> A = np.array([1, 2, 3, 4])
>>> print(A)
[1 2 3 4]
>>> np.ndim(A)
1
>>> A.shape
(4,)
>>> A.shape[0]
4
```

As shown here, you can use the `np.ndim()` function to obtain the number of dimensions of an array. You can also use the instance variable, `shape`, to obtain the shape of the array. The preceding example shows that `A` is a one-dimensional array consisting of four elements. Please note that the result of `A.shape` is a tuple. This is because the result is returned in the same format both for a one-dimensional array and for a multidimensional array. For example, a (4,3) tuple is returned for a two-dimensional array, and a (4,3,2) tuple is returned for a three-dimensional one. Therefore, a tuple is also returned for a one-dimensional array. Now, let's create a two-dimensional array:

```
>>> B = np.array([[1,2], [3,4], [5,6]])
>>> print(B)
[[1 2]
 [3 4]
 [5 6]]
>>> np.ndim(B)
2
>>> B.shape
(3, 2)
```

Here, a 3x2 array, B, is created. A 3x2 array means that it has three elements in the first dimension and two elements in the next dimension. The first dimension is dimension 0, and the next dimension is dimension 1 (an index starts from 0 in Python). A two-dimensional array is called a matrix. As shown in *Figure 3.10*, a horizontal sequence in an array is called a **row**, while a vertical sequence is called a **column**:

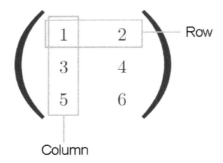

Figure 3.10: A horizontal sequence is called a "row," and a vertical one is called a "column"

Matrix Multiplication

Now, consider the product of matrices (two-dimensional arrays). For 2x2 matrices, matrix multiplication is calculated as shown in *Figure 3.11* (defined as the calculation in this procedure):

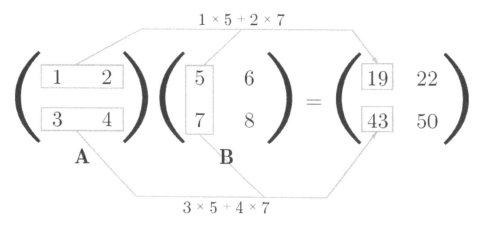

Figure 3.11: Calculating matrix multiplication

As this example indicates, matrix multiplication is calculated by multiplying the elements between the (horizontal) rows of the left matrix and the (vertical) columns of the right matrix and adding the results. The calculation result is stored as the elements of a new multidimensional array. For example, the result between A's first row and B's first column becomes the first element in the first row, while the result between A's second row and B's first column becomes the first element in the second row. In this book, a matrix in an equation is shown in bold. For example, a matrix is shown as A to differentiate it from a scalar value (for example, a or b) with one element. This calculation is implemented in Python as follows:

```
>>> A = np.array([[1,2], [3,4]])
>>> A.shape
(2, 2)
>>> B = np.array([[5,6], [7,8]])
>>> B.shape
(2, 2)
>>> np.dot(A, B)
array([[19, 22],
       [43, 50]])
```

A and B are 2x2 matrices. NumPy's `np.dot()` function is used to calculate the product of matrices A and B (the "dot" here indicates a dot product). `np.dot` (dot product) calculates the inner product of vectors for one-dimensional arrays and matrix multiplication for two-dimensional arrays. You should note that `np.dot(A, B)` and `np.dot(B, A)` can return different values. Unlike regular operations (+, *, and so on), the product of matrices becomes different when the order of operands (A and B) is different.

The preceding example shows the product of 2x2 matrices. You can also calculate the product of matrices in different shapes. For example, the product of 2x3 and 3x2 matrices can be implemented in Python as follows:

```
>>> A = np.array([[1,2,3], [4,5,6]])
>>> A.shape
(2, 3)
>>> B = np.array([[1,2], [3,4], [5,6]])
>>> B.shape
(3, 2)
>>> np.dot(A, B)
array([[22, 28],
       [49, 64]])
```

The preceding code shows how the product of the 2x3 matrix A and the 3x2 matrix B can be implemented. Here, you must be careful about the "shapes of matrices." Specifically, the number of elements (number of columns) in dimension 1 of matrix A must be the same as the number of elements (number of rows) in dimension 0 of matrix B. Actually, in the preceding example, matrix A is 2x3, and matrix B is 3x2. The number of elements in dimension 1 of matrix A (3) is the same as the number of elements in dimension 0 of matrix B (3). If they are different, the product of the matrices cannot be calculated. So then, if you try to calculate the product of the 2x3 matrix A and the 2x2 matrix C in Python, the following error occurs:

```
>>> C = np.array([[1,2], [3,4]])
>>> C.shape
(2, 2)
>>> A.shape
(2, 3)
>>> np.dot(A, C)
```

Traceback (most recent call last):

```
    File "<stdin>", line 1, in <module>
ValueError: shapes (2,3) and (2,2) not aligned: 3 (dim 1) != 2 (dim 0)
```

This error says that dimension 1 of matrix A and dimension 0 of matrix C are different in terms of the numbers of their elements (the index of a dimension starts from zero). In other words, to calculate the product of a multidimensional array, the number of elements in the corresponding dimensions of two matrices must be the same. Because this is an important point, let's check it again in *Figure 3.12*:

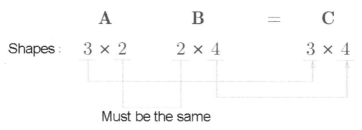

Figure 3.12: The number of elements in corresponding dimensions must be the same for matrix multiplication

Figure 3.12 shows an example of the product of the 3x2 matrix A and the 2x4 matrix B, resulting in the 3x4 matrix C. As we can see, the number of elements in the corresponding dimensions of matrices A and B must be the same. The resulting matrix, C, consists of as many rows as matrix A and as many columns as matrix B. This is also important.

Even when A is a two-dimensional matrix and B is a one-dimensional array, the same principle (that the number of elements in the corresponding dimensions must be the same) applies, as shown in *Figure 3.13*:

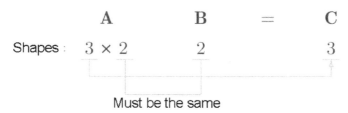

Figure 3.13: The number of elements in the corresponding dimensions must be the same, even when A is a two-dimensional matrix and B is a one-dimensional array

The sample in *Figure 3.13* can be implemented in Python as follows:

```
>>> A = np.array([[1,2], [3, 4], [5,6]])
>>> A.shape
(3, 2)
>>> B = np.array([7,8])
>>> B.shape
(2,)
>>> np.dot(A,  B)
array([23, 53, 83])
```

Matrix Multiplication in a Neural Network

Now, let's use NumPy matrices to implement a neural network, as shown in *Figure 3.14*. Let's assume that the neural network only has weights. Bias and an activation function have been omitted.

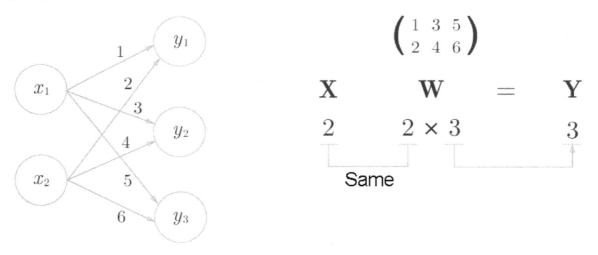

Figure 3.14: Using matrix multiplication to calculate a neural network

In this implementation, we must be careful about the shapes of **x**, **w**, and **y**. It is very important that the number of elements in the corresponding dimensions of **x** and **w** are the same:

```
>>> X = np.array([1, 2])
>>> X.shape
(2,)
>>> W = np.array([[1, 3, 5], [2, 4, 6]])
>>> print(W)
[[1 3 5]
 [2 4 6]]
>>> W.shape
(2, 3)
>>> Y = np.dot(X, W)
>>> print(Y)
[ 5  11  17]
```

As shown here, you can use `np.dot` (dot product of multidimensional matrices) to calculate the result, **y**, at one time. This means that, even if the number of elements of **y** is 100 or 1,000, you can calculate it all at once. Without `np.dot`, you must take out each element of **y** (and use a `for` statement) for calculation, which is very tiresome. Therefore, we can say that the technique of using matrix multiplication to calculate the product of multidimensional matrices is very important.

Implementing a Three-Layer Neural Network

Now, let's implement a "practical" neural network. Here, we will implement the process from its input to its output (a process in the forward direction) in the three-layer neural network shown in *Figure 3.15*. We will use NumPy's multidimensional arrays (as described in the previous section) for implementation. By making good use of NumPy arrays, you can write some short code for a forward process in the neural network.

Examining the Symbols

Here, we will use symbols such as $w_{12}^{(1)}$ and $a_1^{(1)}$ to explain the processes performed in the neural network. They may seem a little complicated. You can skim through this section because the symbols are only used here:

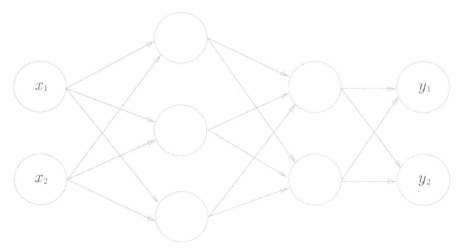

Figure 3.15: A three-layer neural network consisting of two neurons in the input layer (layer 0), three neurons in the first hidden layer (layer 1), two neurons in the second hidden layer (layer 2), and two neurons in the output layer (layer 3)

> **Note**
>
> What is important in this section is that calculating a neural network can be conducted collectively as a matrix calculation. Calculating each layer in a neural network can be conducted collectively using matrix multiplication (this can be considered from a larger viewpoint). So, there is no problem in understanding subsequent explanations, even if you forget the detailed rules relating to these symbols.

Let's begin by defining the symbols. Look at *Figure 3.16*. This diagram illustrates the weight from the input layer x_2 to the neuron $a_1^{(1)}$ in the next layer.

As shown in *Figure 3.16*, "(1)" is placed at the upper right of a weight or a hidden layer neuron. This number indicates the weight or neuron of layer 1. A weight has two numbers at the lower right, which are the index numbers of the next and previous layer neurons. For example, $w_{12}^{(1)}$ indicates that it is the weight from the second neuron (x_2) in the previous layer to the first neuron ($a_1^{(1)}$) in the next layer. The index numbers at the lower right of weight must be in the order of "the number for the next layer and the number for the previous layer":

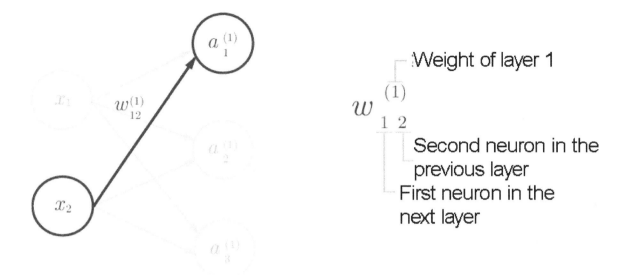

Figure 3.16: Weight symbols

Implementing Signal Transmission in Each Layer

Now, let's look at transmitting signals from the input layer to "the first neuron in layer 1." *Figure* 3.17 shows this graphically:

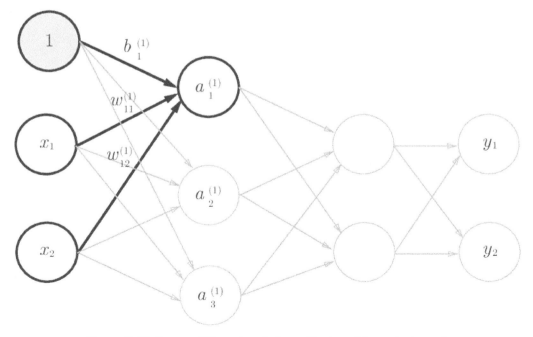

Figure 3.17: Transmitting signals from the input layer to layer 1

As shown in *Figure 3.17*, ① is added as a neuron for a bias. Note that there is only one index at the lower right of the bias. This is because only one bias neuron (① neuron) exists in the previous layer. Now, let's express $a_1^{(1)}$ as an equation to review what we have learned so far. $a_1^{(1)}$ is the sum of the weighted signals and the bias and is calculated as follows:

$$a_1^{(1)} = w_{11}^{(1)} x_1 + w_{12}^{(1)} x_2 + b_1^{(1)} \tag{3.8}$$

By using matrix multiplication, you can express "the weighted sum" of layer 1 collectively as follows:

$$\mathbf{A}^{(1)} = \mathbf{X}\mathbf{W}^{(1)} + \mathbf{B}^{(1)} \tag{3.9}$$

Here, $A^{(1)}$, X, $B^{(1)}$, and $W^{(1)}$ are as follows:

$$\mathbf{A}^{(1)} = \begin{pmatrix} a_1^{(1)} & a_2^{(1)} & a_3^{(1)} \end{pmatrix}, \ \mathbf{X} = \begin{pmatrix} x_1 & x_2 \end{pmatrix}, \ \mathbf{B}^{(1)} = \begin{pmatrix} b_1^{(1)} & b_2^{(1)} & b_3^{(1)} \end{pmatrix}$$

$$\mathbf{W}^{(1)} = \begin{pmatrix} w_{11}^{(1)} & w_{21}^{(1)} & w_{31}^{(1)} \\ w_{12}^{(1)} & w_{22}^{(1)} & w_{32}^{(1)} \end{pmatrix}$$

Now, let's use NumPy's multidimensional arrays to implement equation (3.9). Arbitrary values are set for input signals, weights, and biases here:

```
X = np.array([1.0, 0.5])
W1 = np.array([[0.1, 0.3, 0.5], [0.2, 0.4, 0.6]])
B1 = np.array([0.1, 0.2, 0.3])

print(W1.shape) # (2, 3)
print(X.shape)  # (2,)
print(B1.shape) # (3,)

A1 = np.dot(X, W1) + B1
```

This calculation is the same as the one in the previous section. W1 is a 2x3 array and X is a one-dimensional array with two elements. Also, in this case, the number of elements in the corresponding dimensions of W1 and X are the same.

Now, consider the processes performed by the activation function in layer 1. *Figure 3.18* shows these processes graphically.

As shown in *Figure 3.18*, the weighted sums in a hidden layer (the total of the weighted signals and the biases) are shown as a's, and the signals converted with the activation function are shown as z's. Here, the activation function is shown as $h()$ using a sigmoid function:

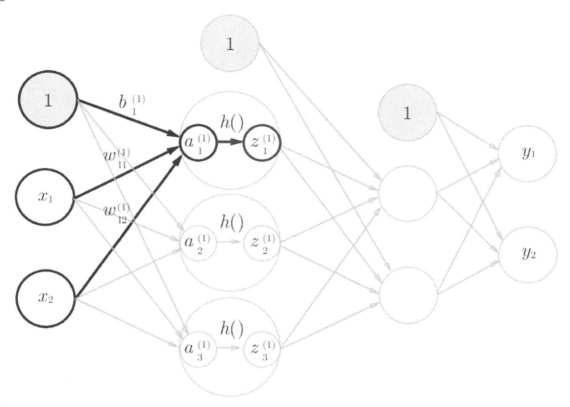

Figure 3.18: Transmitting signals from the input layer to layer 1

This process is implemented in Python as follows:

```
Z1 = sigmoid(A1)
print(A1) # [0.3, 0.7, 1.1]
print(Z1) # [0.57444252, 0.66818777, 0.75026011]
```

This **sigmoid()** function is the one we defined previously. It takes a NumPy array and returns a NumPy array with the same number of elements.

Let's now move on to the implementation from layer 1 to layer 2 (*Figure* 3.19):

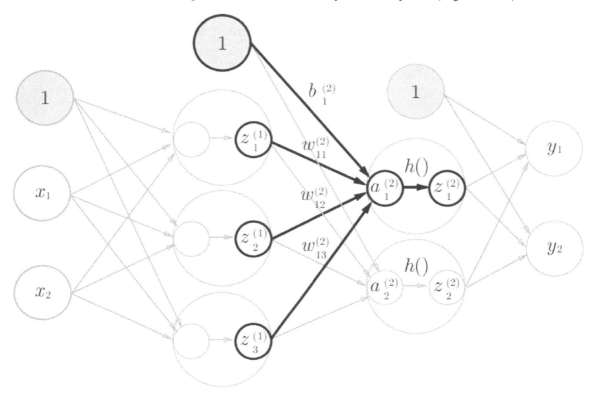

Figure 3.19: Transmitting signals from layer 1 to layer 2

This implementation is the same as the previous one, except that the output of layer 1 (Z1) is the input of layer 2. As you can see, you can write the transmission of signals from one layer to another easily by using NumPy arrays:

```
W2 = np.array([[0.1, 0.4], [0.2, 0.5], [0.3, 0.6]])
B2 = np.array([0.1, 0.2])

print(Z1.shape) # (3,)
print(W2.shape) # (3, 2)
print(B2.shape) # (2,)
A2 = np.dot(Z1, W2) + B2
Z2 = sigmoid(A2)
```

Finally, let's implement the transmission of signals from layer 2 to the output layer (*Figure* 3.20). You can implement the output layer almost in the same way as the other implementations we've looked at so far. Only the last activation function is different from that of the hidden layers we've seen so far:

```
def identity_function(x):
    return x

W3 = np.array([[0.1, 0.3], [0.2, 0.4]])
B3 = np.array([0.1, 0.2])

A3 = np.dot(Z2, W3) + B3
Y = identity_function(A3) # or Y = A3
```

Here, we will define a function named `identity_function()` and use it as the activation function for the output layer. An identity function outputs the input as it is. Although you do not need to define `identity_function()` in this example, this implementation is used so that it is consistent with the previous ones. In *Figure* 3.20, the activation function of the output layer is shown as σ() to indicate that it is different from the activation function, *h*(), of the hidden layers (σ is called **sigma**):

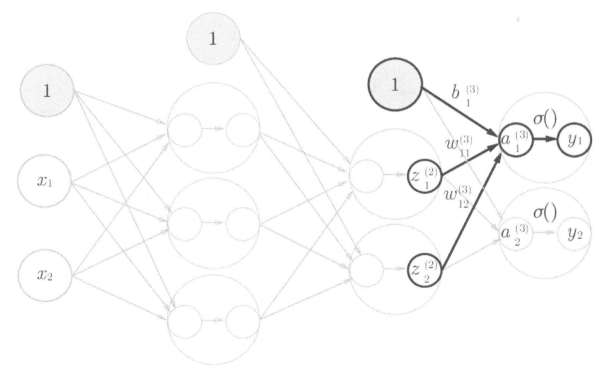

Figure 3.20: Transmitting signals from layer 2 to the output layer

You can select the activation function used in the output layer, depending on what type of problem you wish to solve. Generally, an identity function is used for a regression problem, a sigmoid function for a two-class classification problem, and a softmax function for a multi-class classification problem. The activation function for an output layer will be explained in detail in the next section.

Implementation Summary

This completes our investigation of a three-layer neural network. The following summarizes the implementation we've performed so far. As is customary in the implementation of a neural network, only weights are written in uppercase (for example, W1), while other items (such as a bias and intermediate result) are written in lowercase:

```python
def init_network():
    network = {}
    network['W1'] = np.array([[0.1, 0.3, 0.5], [0.2, 0.4, 0.6]])
    network['b1'] = np.array([0.1, 0.2, 0.3])
    network['W2'] = np.array([[0.1, 0.4], [0.2, 0.5], [0.3, 0.6]])
    network['b2'] = np.array([0.1, 0.2])
    network['W3'] = np.array([[0.1, 0.3], [0.2, 0.4]])
    network['b3'] = np.array([0.1, 0.2])

    return network

def forward(network, x):
    W1, W2, W3 = network['W1'], network['W2'], network['W3']
    b1, b2, b3 = network['b1'], network['b2'], network['b3']

    a1 = np.dot(x, W1) + b1
    z1 = sigmoid(a1)
    a2 = np.dot(z1, W2) + b2
    z2 = sigmoid(a2)
    a3 = np.dot(z2, W3) + b3
    y = identity_function(a3)
```

```
    return y
```

```
network = init_network()
x =  np.array([1.0,  0.5])
y = forward(network, x)
print(y) # [ 0.31682708 0.69627909]
```

Here, the `init_network()` and `forward()` functions are defined. The `init_network()` function initializes the weights and biases and stores them in a dictionary type variable, `network` which stores the parameters required for individual layers, weights, and biases. The `forward()` function collectively implements the process of converting an input signal into an output signal.

The word "forward" here indicates the transmission process from an input to an output. Later, we will look at the process in the backward direction (from output to input) when we train a neural network.

This completes the implementation of a three-layer neural network in the forward direction. By using NumPy's multidimensional arrays, we were able to implement a neural network efficiently.

Designing the Output Layer

You can use a neural network both for a classification problem and for a regression problem. However, you must change the activation function of the output layer, depending on which of the problems you use a neural network for. Usually, an identity function is used for a regression problem, and a softmax function is used for a classification problem.

> **Note**
>
> Machine learning problems can be broadly divided into "classification problems" and "regression problems." A classification problem is a problem of identifying which class the data belongs to—for example, classifying the person in an image as a man or a woman—while a regression problem is a problem of predicting a (continuous) number from certain input data—for example, predicting the weight of the person in an image.

Identity Function and Softmax Function

An identity function outputs the input as it is. The function that outputs what is entered without doing anything is an identity function. Therefore, when an identity function is used for the output layer, an input signal is returned as-is. Using the diagram of the neural network we've used so far, you can represent the process by an identity function as shown in *Figure 3.21*. The process of conversion by the identity function can be represented with one arrow, in the same way in the same way as the activation function we have seen so far:

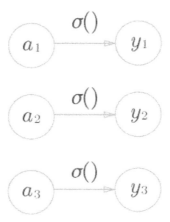

Figure 3.21: Identity function

The softmax function, which is used for a classification problem, is expressed by the following equation:

$$y_k = \frac{\exp(a_k)}{\sum_{i=1}^{n} \exp(a_i)} \tag{3.10}$$

`exp(x)` is an exponential function that indicates e^x (e is Napier's constant, 2.7182...). Assuming the total number of output layers is n, the equation provides the k-th output, y_k. As shown in equation (3.10), the numerator of the softmax function is the exponential function of the input signal, a_k, and the denominator is the sum of the exponential functions of all the input signals.

Figure 3.22 shows the softmax function graphically. As you can see, the output of the softmax function is connected from all the input signals with arrows. As the denominator of equation (3.10) indicates, each neuron of the output is affected by all the input signals:

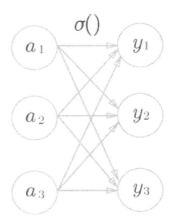

Figure 3.22: Softmax function

Now, let's implement the softmax function,using the Python interpreter to check the results, one by one:

```
>>> a = np.array([0.3, 2.9, 4.0])
>>>
>>> exp_a = np.exp(a)  # Exponential function
>>> print(exp_a)
[ 1.34985881 18.17414537 54.59815003]
>>>
>>> sum_exp_a = np.sum(exp_a)  # Sum of exponential functions
>>> print(sum_exp_a)
74.1221542102
>>>
>>> y = exp_a / sum_exp_a
>>> print(y)
[ 0.01821127 0.24519181 0.73659691]
```

This implementation represents the softmax function of equation (3.10) with Python. Therefore, no special description will be required. When considering the use of the softmax function later, we will define it as a Python function, as follows:

```
def softmax(a):
    exp_a = np.exp(a)
    sum_exp_a = np.sum(exp_a)
    y = exp_a / sum_exp_a

    return y
```

Issues when Implementing the Softmax Function

The preceding implementation of the softmax function represents equation (3.10) correctly, but it is defective for computer calculations. This defect is an overflow problem. Implementing the softmax function involves calculating the exponential functions, and the value of an exponential function can be very large. For example, e^{10} is larger than 20,000, and e^{100} is a large value that has more than 40 digits. The result of e^{1000} returns `inf`, which indicates an infinite value. Dividing these large values returns an "unstable" result.

> **Note**
>
> When a computer handles a "number," it is stored in finite data width, such as four or eight bytes. This means that a number has a number of significant figures. The range of a number that can be represented is limited. Therefore, there is a problem in that a very large value cannot be expressed. This is called an overflow, so we must be careful when we use a computer for calculation.

Improved implementation of the softmax function is obtained from the following equation:

$$
y_k = \frac{\exp(a_k)}{\sum\limits_{i=1}^{n} \exp(a_i)} = \frac{C \exp(a_k)}{C \sum\limits_{i=1}^{n} \exp(a_i)}
$$

$$
= \frac{\exp(a_k + \log C)}{\sum\limits_{i=1}^{n} \exp(a_i + \log C)} \qquad (3.11)
$$

$$
= \frac{\exp(a_k + C')}{\sum\limits_{i=1}^{n} \exp(a_i + C')}
$$

First, equation (3.11) is transformed by multiplying both the numerator and the denominator by an arbitrary constant, C (the same calculations are performed because both the numerator and the denominator are multiplied by the same constant). Then, C is moved into the exponential function (exp) as log C. Finally, log C is replaced with another symbol, C'.

Equation (3.11) says that adding or subtracting a certain constant does not change the result when the exponential functions in the softmax function are calculated. Although you can use any number as C' here, the largest value from the input signals is usually used to prevent an overflow. Consider the following example:

```
>>> a = np.array([1010, 1000, 990])
>>> np.exp(a) / np.sum(np.exp(a)) # Calculating the softmax function
array([ nan,   nan,   nan]) # Not calculated correctly
>>>
>>> c = np.max(a) # 1010
>>> a - c
array([  0, -10, -20])
>>>
>>> np.exp(a - c) / np.sum(np.exp(a - c))
array([   9.99954600e-01,    4.53978686e-05,    2.06106005e-09])
```

As this example indicates, when the largest value of the input signals (c, here) is subtracted, you can calculate the function properly. Otherwise, nan (not a number: unstable) values are returned. Based on this description, we can implement the softmax function as follows:

```
def softmax(a):
    c = np.max(a)
    exp_a = np.exp(a - c) # Prevent an overflow
    sum_exp_a = np.sum(exp_a)
    y = exp_a / sum_exp_a

    return y
```

Characteristics of the Softmax Function

You can use the **softmax()** function to calculate the output of the neural network, as follows:

```
>>> a = np.array([0.3, 2.9, 4.0])
>>> y = softmax(a)
>>> print(y)
```

```
[ 0.01821127 0.24519181 0.73659691]
>>> np.sum(y)
1.0
```

The softmax function outputs a real number between 0 and 1.0. The total of the outputs of the softmax function is 1. The fact that the total is 1 is an important characteristic of the softmax function as it means we can interpret the output of the softmax function as "probability."

For instance, in the preceding example, we could interpret the probability of y[0] as 0.018 (1.8%), the probability of y[1] as 0.245 (24.5%), and the probability of y[2] as 0.737 (73.7%). From these probabilities, we can say, "because the second element is the most probable, the answer is the second class." We can even answer probabilistically: "the answer is the second class with a probability of 74%, the first class with a probability of 25%, and the zeroth class with a probability of 1%." Thus, you can use the softmax function to handle a problem probabilistically (statistically).

We should note that applying the softmax function does not change the order of the elements. This is because an exponential function, ($y = exp(x)$), increases monotonically. Actually, in the preceding example, the order of the elements in a is the same as those of the elements in y. The largest value in a is the second element, and the largest value in y is also the second element.

Generally, class classification by a neural network recognizes only the class that corresponds to the neuron with the largest output. Using the softmax function does not change the position of the neuron of the largest output. Therefore, you can omit the softmax function for the output layer from neural network classification. In reality, the softmax function for the output layer is usually omitted because the exponential function requires some computation.

> **Note**
>
> The procedure for solving a machine learning problem consists of two phases: "training" and "predicting." First, you train a model in the training phase and then use the trained model to predict (classify) unknown data in the inference phase. As described earlier, the softmax function for the output layer is usually omitted in the inference phase. The reason we use the softmax function for the output layer will be relevant when the neural network trains (for more details, refer to the next chapter).

Number of Neurons in the Output Layer

You must determine the number of neurons in the output layer as appropriate, depending on the problem to solve. For classification problems, the number of classes to classify is usually used as the number of neurons in the output layer. For example, to predict a number from 0 to 9 from an input image (10-class classification), 10 neurons are placed in the output layer, as shown in *Figure* 3.23:

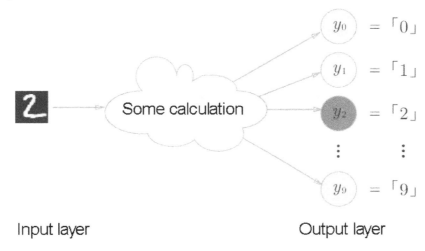

Figure 3.23: The neuron in the output layer corresponds to each number

As shown in *Figure* 3.23, the neurons in the output layer correspond to the numbers 0, 1, ..., 9 from the top. Here, the various shades of gray represent the values of the neurons in the output layer. In this example, the color of y_2 is the darkest because the y_2 neuron outputs the largest value. It shows that this neural network predicts that the input belongs to the class that corresponds to y_2; that is, "2."

Handwritten Digit Recognition

Now that we have covered the mechanisms of a neural network, let's consider a practical problem. We will classify some handwritten digit images. Assuming that training has already been completed, we will use trained parameters to implement "inference" in the neural network. This inference is also called forward propagation in a neural network.

> **Note**
>
> In the same way as the procedure for solving a machine learning problem (which consists of two phases, "training" and "inference"), to solve a problem using a neural network, we will use training data to train the weight parameters and then use the trained parameters while predicting to classify the input data.

MNIST Dataset

Here, we will use a set of images of handwritten digits called MNIST. MNIST is one of the most famous datasets in the field of machine learning and is used in various ways, from simple experiments to research. When you read research papers on image recognition or machine learning, you will often notice that the MNIST dataset is used as experimental data.

The MNIST dataset consists of images of numbers from 0 to 9 (*Figure 3. 24*). It contains 60,000 training images and 10,000 test images, and they are used for training and inference. When we use the MNIST dataset, we usually use training images for training and measure how correctly the trained model can classify the test images:

Figure 3.24: Examples from the MNIST image dataset

MNIST's image data is a 28x28 gray image (one channel), and each pixel has a value from 0 to 255. Each image data is labeled, such as "7", "2", and "1."

This book provides a convenient Python script, `mnist.py`, which is located in the `dataset` directory. It supports downloading the MNIST dataset and converting image data into NumPy arrays. To use the `mnist.py` script, the current directory must be the `ch01`, `ch02`, `ch03`, ..., or `ch08` directory. By using the `load_mnist()` function in `mnist.py`, you can load the MNIST data easily, as follows:

```python
import sys, os
sys.path.append(os.pardir) # Configure to import the files in the parent
directory
from dataset.mnist import load_mnist


# Waits for a few minutes for the first call ...
(x_train, t_train), (x_test, t_test) = \
    load_mnist(flatten=True, normalize=False)


# Output the shape of each data
print(x_train.shape) # (60000, 784)
print(t_train.shape) # (60000,)
print(x_test.shape) # (10000, 784)
print(t_test.shape) # (10000,)
```

First, configure the details for importing the files in the parent directory. Then, import the `load_mnist` function from `dataset/mnist.py`. Finally, use the imported `load_mnist` function to load the MNIST dataset. When you call `load_mnist` for the first time, an internet connection is required to download the MNIST data. A subsequent call completes immediately because it only loads the locally saved files (pickle files).

> **Note**
>
> The files for loading the MNIST images exist in the dataset directory of the source code provided in this book. It is assumed that this MNIST dataset is used only from the `ch01`, `ch02`, `ch03`, ..., or `ch08` directory. Therefore, to use the dataset, the `sys.path.append(os.pardir)` statement is required. This is because the files in the parent directory (dataset directory) must be imported.

The `load_mnist` function returns the loaded MNIST data in the format of `(training image, training label)`, `(test image, test label)`. It can take three arguments: `load_mnist(normalize=True, flatten=True, one_hot_label=False)`. The first argument, `normalize`, specifies whether to normalize the input image between 0.0 and 1.0. If `False` is set, the pixel of the input image remains between 0 and 255. The second argument, `flatten`, specifies whether to flatten the input image (convert it into a one-dimensional array). If `False` is set, the input image is stored as an array with three dimensions ($1 \times 28 \times 28$). If `True` is set, it is stored as a one-dimensional array with 784 elements. The third argument, `one_hot_label`, specifies whether to store the label using one-hot encoding. In a one-hot encoded array, only the element for the correct label is 1 and the other elements are 0, such as in [0,0,1,0,0,0,0,0,0,0]. When `one_hot_label` is `False`, only the correct label, such as 7 or 2, is stored. If `one_hot_label` is `True`, the labels are stored as a one-hot encoded array.

> **Note**
>
> Python has a convenient feature called pickle, which saves objects as files while a program is being executed. By loading the saved pickle file, you can immediately restore the object that was used during the execution of the program. The `load_mnist()` function, which loads the MNIST dataset, also uses pickle (for the second or subsequent loading phases). By using pickle's feature, you can prepare the MNIST data quickly.

Now, let's display MNIST images to check the data. We will use the **Python Image Library (PIL)** module to display the images. When you execute the following code, the first training image will be displayed, as shown in *Figure* 3.25 (the source code is located at `ch03/mnist_show.py`):

```python
import sys, os
sys.path.append(os.pardir)
import numpy as np
from dataset.mnist import load_mnist
from PIL import Image

def img_show(img):
    pil_img = Image.fromarray(np.uint8(img))
    pil_img.show()

(x_train, t_train), (x_test, t_test) = /
    load_mnist(flatten=True, normalize=False)
    img = x_train[0]
    label = t_train[0]
    print(label) # 5

    print(img.shape)    # (784,)
    img = img.reshape(28, 28) # Reshape the image based on the original
size
    print(img.shape)    # (28, 28)
    img_show(img)
```

This results in the following output:

Figure 3.25: Displaying an MNIST image

Please note that when `flatten=True`, the loaded image is stored as a NumPy array in a line (one-dimensionally). Therefore, to display the image, you must reshape it into its original 28x28 size. You can use the `reshape()` method to reshape a NumPy array by specifying the desired shape with an argument. You must also convert the image data stored as a NumPy array into the data object for PIL. You can use `Image.fromarray()` for this conversion.

Inference for Neural Network

Now, let's implement a neural network that predicts over this MNIST dataset. The network consists of an input layer containing 784 neurons and an output layer containing 10 neurons. The number 784 for the input layer comes from the image size (28 x 28 = 784), while the number 10 for the output layer comes from 10-class classification (10 classes of numbers 0 to 9). There are two hidden layers: the first one has 50 neurons, and the second one has 100 neurons. You can change the numbers 50 and 100 as you like. First, let's define the three functions, `get_data()`, `init_network()`, and `predict()` (the following source code is located at `ch03/neuralnet_mnist.py`):

```python
def get_data():
    (x_train, t_train), (x_test, t_test) = /
        load_mnist(normalize=True, flatten=True, one_hot_label=False)
    return x_test, t_test

def init_network():
    with open("sample_weight.pkl", 'rb') as f:
        network = pickle.load(f)

    return network

def predict(network, x):
    W1, W2, W3 = network['W1'], network['W2'], network['W3']
    b1, b2, b3 = network['b1'], network['b2'], network['b3']

    a1 = np.dot(x, W1) + b1
    z1 = sigmoid(a1)
    a2 = np.dot(z1, W2) + b2
    z2 = sigmoid(a2)
    a3 = np.dot(z2, W3) + b3
    y = softmax(a3)

    return y
```

The `init_network()` function loads the trained weight parameters that are stored in the pickle file `sample_weight.pkl`. This file contains weight and bias parameters as a dictionary type variable. The remaining two functions are almost the same as in the implementations described so far, so these don't need to be described. Now, we will use these three functions to predict using a neural network. We want to evaluate the recognition precision—that is, how correctly it can classify:

```
x, t = get_data()
network = init_network()

accuracy_cnt = 0
for i in range(len(x)):
    y = predict(network, x[i])
    p = np.argmax(y) # Obtain the index of the most probable element

    if p == t[i]:
        accuracy_cnt += 1

print("Accuracy:" + str(float(accuracy_cnt) / len(x)))
```

Here, we will obtain the MNIST dataset and build a network, then use a `for` statement to get each image data stored in `x` and use the `predict()` function to classify it. The `predict()` function returns a NumPy array containing the probability of each label. For example, an array such as [0.1, 0.3, 0.2, ..., 0.04] is returned, which indicates that the probability of "0" is 0.1, that of "1" is 0.3, and so on. The index with the largest value in this probability list, which indicates the most probable element, is obtained as the prediction result. You can use `np.argmax(x)` to obtain the index of the largest element in an array. It returns the index of the largest element in the array specified by the `x` argument. Finally, the answers predicted by the neural network and the correct labels are compared, and the rate of correct predictions is displayed as the recognition precision (accuracy).

When the preceding code is executed, `Accuracy:0.9352` is displayed. This shows that 93.52% of the classifications were correct. We will not discuss the recognition accuracy here as our goal is to run a trained neural network, but later in this book, we will improve the structure and training method of the neural network to gain higher recognition accuracy. In fact, the accuracy will exceed 99%.

In this example, the argument of the `load_mnist` function, `normalize`, is set to `True`. When `normalize` is `True`, the function divides the value of each pixel in the image by 255 so that the data values are between 0.0 and 1.0. Converting data so that it fits in a certain range is called **normalization**, while converting the input data for a neural network in a defined way is called **pre-processing**. Here, the input image data was normalized as pre-processing.

> **Note**
>
> In practical usage, pre-processing is often used in a neural network (deep learning). The validity of pre-processing, as in improved discrimination and faster learning, has been proven through experiments. In the preceding example, simple normalization was conducted by dividing the value of each pixel by 255 using pre-processing. Actually, pre-processing is often conducted while considering the distribution of the whole data. Normalization is conducted by using the average and standard deviation of the whole data so that all of the data is distributed around 0 or fits in a certain range. In addition, **whitening** is also conducted so that all the data is distributed more evenly.

Batch Processing

This process is all about implementing a neural network using the MNIST dataset. Here, we will re-examine the preceding implementation while paying attention to the "shapes" of the input data and weight parameters.

Let's use the Python interpreter to output the shape of the weights for each layer in the preceding neural network:

```
>>> x, _ = get_data( )
>>> network = init_network( )
>>> W1, W2, W3 = network['W1'], network['W2'], network['W3']
>>>
>>> x.shape
(10000, 784)
>>> x[0].shape
(784,)
>>> W1.shape
(784, 50)
>>> W2.shape
(50, 100)
>>> W3.shape
(100, 10)
```

Let's check that the number of elements in the corresponding dimensions of the multidimensional arrays are the same as they are in the preceding result (biases are omitted). *Figure* 3.26 shows this graphically. Here, the number of elements in the corresponding dimensions of the multidimensional arrays are the same. Verify that a one-dimensional array with 10 elements, y, is returned as the final result:

X
W1
W2
W3
→
Y
Shapes : 784
784 × 50
50 × 100
100 × 10
10
Same
Same
Same

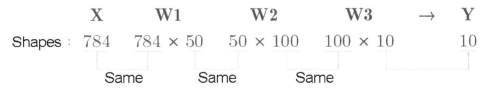

Figure 3.26: Transition of the shapes of arrays

Figure 3.26 shows the flow where a one-dimensional array with 784 elements (originally a two-dimensional 28x28 array) is provided, and a one-dimensional array with 10 elements is returned. This is the process when a single image is input.

Now, let's think about the process when multiple images are entered at once. For example, let's assume that you want to use the `predict()` function to process 100 images at one time. To do that, you can change the shape of `x` to `100×784` so that you can enter 100 images collectively as input data. *Figure* 3.27 shows this graphically:

X
W1
W2
W3
→
Y
Shapes : 100 × 784
784 × 50
50 × 100
100 × 10
100 × 10

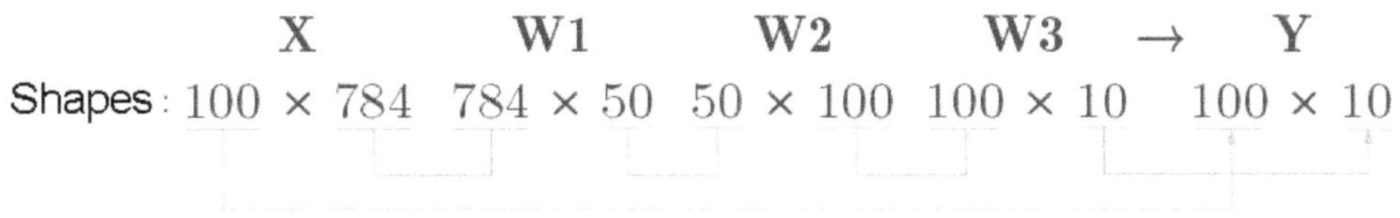

Figure 3.27: Transition of the shapes of arrays in batch processing

As shown in *Figure* 3.27, the shape of the input data is 100x784, and that of the output data is 100x10. This indicates that the results for the input data of 100 images are returned in one go. For example, `x[0]` and `y[0]` store the image and predict the result of the 0th image, `x[1]`, and `y[1]` store the image and predicting the result of the first image, and so on.

An organized set of input data, as described here, is called a **batch**. A batch is a stack of images, such as a wad of bills.

> **Note**
>
> Batch processing has a big advantage in computer calculation. It can greatly reduce the processing time of each image since many of the libraries that handle numerical calculations are highly optimized so that large arrays can be calculated efficiently. When data transfer causes a bottleneck in neural network calculation, batch processing can reduce the load on the bus band (i.e.: the ratio of operations to data loading can be increased). Although batch processing requires a large array to be calculated, calculating a large array in one go is faster than calculating by dividing small arrays little by little.

Now, let's use batch processing for our implementation. Here, the differences from the previous code are shown in bold:

```
x, t = get_data( )
network = init_network( )

batch_size = 100 # Number of batches
accuracy_cnt = 0

for i in range(0, len(x), batch_size):
    x_batch = x[i:i+batch_size]
    y_batch = predict(network, x_batch)
    p = np.argmax(y_batch, axis=1)
    accuracy_cnt += np.sum(p == t[i:i+batch_size])

print("Accuracy:" + str(float(accuracy_cnt) / len(x)))
```

Now, we will describe each section shown in bold. First, let's look at the `range()` function. You can use the `range()` function, such as `range(start, end)`, to generate a list of integers from `start` to `end-1`. By specifying three integers, as in `range(start, end, step)`, you can generate a list of integers where values are incremented by the value specified with the `step`, as in the following example:

```
>>> list( range(0, 10) )
[0, 1, 2, 3, 4, 5, 6, 7, 8, 9]
>>> list( range(0, 10, 3) )
[0, 3, 6, 9]
```

Based on the list returned by the `range()` function, `x[i:i+batch_size]` is used to extract a batch from the input data. `x[i:i+batch_n]` obtains from the `i`-th to `i+batch_n`-th data in the input data. In this example, 100 items of data are obtained from the beginning, such as x[0:100], x[100:200], ...

Then, `argmax()` obtains the index of the largest value. Please note that an argument, `axis=1`, is specified here. It indicates that, in a 100x10 array, the index of the largest value is found among the elements in dimension 1 (the axis is almost the same as the dimension), as shown below:

```
>>> x = np.array([[0.1, 0.8, 0.1], [0.3, 0.1, 0.6],
... [0.2, 0.5, 0.3], [0.8, 0.1, 0.1]])
>>> y = np.argmax(x, axis=1)
>>> print(y)
[1 2 1 0]
```

Lastly, the classification results for each batch are compared with the actual answers. To do that, a comparison operator (`==`) is used to compare the NumPy arrays. A Boolean array of `True/False` is returned, and the number of Trues is calculated, as follows:

```
>>> y = np.array([1, 2, 1, 0])
>>> t = np.array([1, 2, 0, 0])
>>> print(y==t)
[True True False True]
>>> np.sum(y==t)
3
```

That's it for implementation using batch processing. Batch processing enables fast and efficient processing. When we learn about neural networks in the next chapter, batches of image data will be used for training. There, we will also build an implementation of batch processing, just like we did in this chapter.

Summary

This chapter described forward propagation in a neural network. The neural network we explained in this chapter is the same as a perceptron in the previous chapter in that the signals of the neurons are transmitted hierarchically. However, a large difference exists in the activation functions that change signals when they are transmitted to the next neurons. As an activation function, a neural network uses a sigmoid function, which changes signals smoothly, and a perceptron uses a step function, which changes signals sharply. This difference is important in neural network training and will be described in the next chapter. This chapter covered the following points:

- A neural network uses a function that changes smoothly, such as a sigmoid function or a ReLU function, as an activation function.

- By using NumPy's multidimensional arrays, you can implement a neural network efficiently.

- Machine learning problems can be broadly divided into classification problems and regression problems.

- When using the activation function for the output layer, an identity function is often used for a regression problem, and a softmax function is used for a classification problem.

- For a classification problem, the number of classes to classify is used as the number of neurons in the output layer.

- A set of input data is called a batch. Predicting per batch accelerates the calculation process.

Neural Network Training

This chapter describes neural network training. When we talk about "training" in this context, we mean obtaining the optimal weight parameters automatically from training data. In this chapter, we will introduce a criterion called a loss function; this enables a neural network to learn. The purpose of training is to discover the weight parameters that lead to the smallest value of the loss function. In this chapter, we will be introduced to the method of using the gradient of a function, called a gradient method, to discover the smallest loss function value.

Learning from Data

The essential characteristic of a neural network is its ability to learn from data. Training from data means that weight parameter values can be automatically determined. If you have to determine all the parameters manually, it is quite hard work. For example, for a sample perceptron, as shown in *Chapter 2, Perceptrons*, we determined the parameter values manually while looking at the truth table. There are as few as three parameters. However, in an actual neural network, the number of parameters can range between thousands and tens of thousands. For deep learning with more layers, the number of parameters may reach hundreds of millions. It is almost impossible to determine them manually. This chapter describes neural network training, or how to determine parameter values from data, and implements a model that learns handwritten digits from the MNIST dataset with Python.

> **Note**
>
> For a linearly separable problem, a perceptron can learn automatically from data. That training, when completed a finite number of times, can solve a linearly separable problem, which is known as "the perceptron convergence theorem." On the other hand, a nonlinear separation problem cannot be solved (automatically).

Data-Driven

Data is critical in machine learning. Machine learning looks for an answer in the data, finds a pattern in the data, and tells a story based on it. It can do nothing without data. Therefore, "data" exists at the center of machine learning. We can say that this data-driven approach is a departure from a "man"-centered approach.

Usually, when we solve a problem—especially when we need to find a pattern—we must consider various things to find an answer. "This problem seems to have this pattern." "No, there may be a cause somewhere else." Based on our experience and intuition, we advance this task through trial and error. Machine learning avoids human intervention as much as possible. It tries to find an answer (pattern) from the collected data. Moreover, a neural network and deep learning have an important characteristic in common in that they can avoid human intervention more than traditional machine learning.

Let's look at a specific problem here. Suppose that we want to implement a program that recognizes the number "5", for example. Let's suppose that our goal is implementing the program that determines whether handwritten images, as shown in *Figure 4.1*, are "5" or not "5". This problem seems relatively simple. What algorithm can we use?

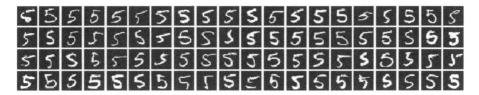

Figure 4.1: Sample handwritten digits – how "5" is written varies from person to person

When you try to design a program that can classify "5" correctly, you will find that it is a more difficult problem than expected. We can easily recognize "5", but it is difficult to clarify the rule for recognizing an image as "5". As shown in *Figure 4.1*, how it is written differs from person to person. This tells us that finding the rule for recognizing "5" will be hard work and that it may take a lot of time.

Now, instead of "working out" the algorithm that recognizes "5" from scratch, we want to use data effectively to solve the problem. One of the methods we can use is to extract features from an image and use machine learning technology to learn the pattern of the features. A feature indicates a converter that is designed to extract essential data (important data) from input data (input image) accurately. The feature of an image is usually described as a vector. Famous features in the field of computer vision include SIFT, SURF, and HOG. You can use these features to convert image data into vectors and use a classifier in machine learning, such as SVM and KNN, to learn the converted vectors.

In this machine learning approach, a "machine" discovers a pattern from the collected data. This can solve a problem more efficiently and reduce the burden on a "person" compared to when we invent an algorithm from scratch. However, we must note that the features that are used when images are converted into vectors are designed by a "man." This is because good results cannot be obtained without using features that are suitable for the problem (or without designing the features). For example, to recognize the face of a dog, a person may need to select the features that are different from those for recognizing "5". After all, even the approach of using features and machine learning may need suitable features to be selected by a "man," depending on the problem.

So far, we have discussed two approaches to machine learning problems. These two approaches are shown in the upper rows in *Figure 4.2*. Meanwhile, the approach to using a neural network (deep learning) is shown in the lower row of *Figure 4.2*. It is represented by a block without human intervention.

As shown in *Figure 4.2*, a neural network learns images "as they are." In the second approach, an example that uses features and machine learning, called human-designed features, are used, while in a neural network, a "machine" learns important features from images:

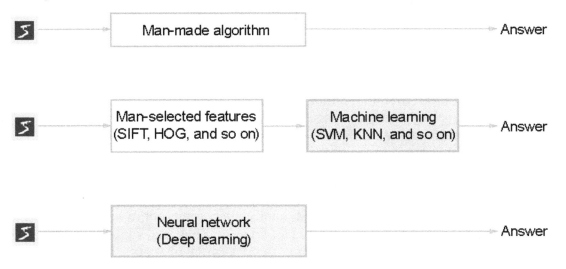

Figure 4.2: A paradigm shift from man-made rules to a "machine" learning from data – a block without human intervention is shown in gray

> **Note**
>
> Deep learning is sometimes called "end-to-end machine learning." "**End-to-end**" means "from one end to the other end," that is, the acquisition of the desired result (output) from raw data (input).

The advantage of a neural network is that it can solve all the problems in the same flow; for example, whether trying to recognize "5", a dog, or a human face, a neural network learns the provided data patiently, trying to discover a pattern in the given problem. A neural network can learn data as it is "end-to-end," regardless of the problem to solve.

Training Data and Test Data

In this chapter, we will cover neural network training, beginning with some best practices when handling data in machine learning.

In machine learning problems, we usually use **training data** and **test data** according to the purpose. First, we use only training data to find optimal parameters. Then, we use test data to evaluate the ability of the trained model. Why should we divide training data and test data? Because we want the generalization capability of the model. We must separate the training data and test data because we want to evaluate this **generalization** correctly.

Generalization means the ability of unknown data (data that is not contained in the training data), and the ultimate goal of machine learning is to obtain this generalization. For example, handwritten digit recognition may be used in a system for reading postal codes on postcards automatically. In that case, handwritten digit recognition must be able to recognize the characters written by "someone." That "someone" is not "a specific character written by a specific person," but "an arbitrary character is written by an arbitrary person." Even if the model can distinguish only your training data well, it may have learned only specific characters of the person's handwriting contained in the data.

Therefore, if you use only one dataset to learn parameters and evaluate them, the correct evaluation will not be provided. This results in a model that can handle a certain dataset well but cannot handle another one. When a model has become too adapted to only one dataset, **overfitting** occurs. Avoiding overfitting is an important challenge in machine learning.

Loss Function

How do you answer when you are asked, "How happy are you now?". We may usually answer vaguely: "I am moderately happy" or "I am not very happy." You may be surprised if someone answers, "My current happiness score is 10.23" because the person can only quantify their happiness with one score. If such a person exists, the person may lead their life only based on their "happiness score."

This "happiness score" is an allegory used to illustrate some similar things which occur in neural network training. In neural network training, one "score" is used to indicate the current status. Based on the score, optimal weight parameters are searched for. As this person looks for an "optimal life" based on the "happiness score," a neural network searches for optimal parameters using "one score" as a guide. The score that's used in neural network training is called a **loss function**. Although any function can be used as the loss function, the sum of squared errors or a cross-entropy error is usually used.

> **Note**
>
> A loss function is an index that indicates the "poorness" of a neural network's ability. It indicates how unfit the current neural network is for labeled data and how it deviates from labeled data. You may feel that it's unnatural for the "poorness of ability" to be the score, but you can interpret the loss function multiplied by a negative value as the score of the opposite of "how poor the ability is" (that is, the score of "how good the ability is"). "To minimize poorness of ability" is the same as "to maximize the goodness of ability." Therefore, the index of the "poorness" of ability is essentially the same as that of the "goodness" of ability.

Sum of Squared Errors

There are a few functions that are used as loss functions. Probably the most famous one is the **sum of squared errors**. It is expressed by the following equation:

$$E = \frac{1}{2} \sum_{k} (y_k - t_k)^2 \qquad (4.1)$$

Here, y_k is the output of the neural network, t_k is labeled data, and k is the number of dimensions of the data. For example, in the section, *Handwritten Digit Recognition*, of *Chapter 3, Neural networks*, y_k, and t_k are data items that consist of 10 elements:

```
>>> y = [0.1, 0.05, 0.6, 0.0, 0.05, 0.1, 0.0, 0.1, 0.0, 0.0]
>>> t = [0, 0, 1, 0, 0, 0, 0, 0, 0, 0]
```

The elements of these arrays correspond to numbers "0," "1," "2," ... in order from the first index. Here, the output of the neural network, y, is the output of a softmax function. The output of the softmax function can be interpreted as a probability. In this example, the probability of "0" is 0.1, that of "1" is 0.05, that of "2" is 0.6, and so on. Meanwhile, t is labeled data. In the labeled data, the correct label is 1 and the other labels are 0. Here, label "2" is 1, which indicates that the correct answer is "2." Setting 1 for the correct label and 0 for other labels is called **one-hot representation**.

As shown in equation (4.1), the sum of squared errors is the sum of the squares of the differences between the outputs of the neural network and the corresponding elements of the correct teacher data. Now, let's implement the sum of squared errors in Python. You can implement it as follows:

```
def sum_squared_error(y,  t):
    return 0.5 * np.sum((y-t)**2)
```

Here, the **y** and **t** arguments are NumPy arrays. Because this simply implements equation (4.1), we won't explain this here. Now, we will use this function to perform a calculation:

```
>>> # Assume that "2" is correct
>>> t = [0, 0, 1, 0, 0, 0, 0, 0, 0, 0]
>>>
>>>  # Example 1: "2" is the most probable (0.6)
>>> y = [0.1, 0.05, 0.6, 0.0, 0.05, 0.1, 0.0, 0.1, 0.0, 0.0]
>>> sum_squared_error(np.array(y), np.array(t))
0.097500000000000031
>>>
>>>  # Example 2: "7" is the most probable (0.6)
>>> y = [0.1, 0.05, 0.1, 0.0, 0.05, 0.1, 0.0, 0.6, 0.0, 0.0]
>>> sum_squared_error(np.array(y), np.array(t))
0.59750000000000003
```

There are two examples here. In the first one, the correct answer is "2", and the output of the neural network is the largest at "2." Meanwhile, in the second one, the correct answer is "2," but the output of the neural network is the largest at "7." As the result of this experiment shows, the loss function of the first example is smaller, which indicates that the difference in the labeled data is smaller. In other words, the sum of squared errors indicates that the output in the first example fits the labeled data better.

Cross-Entropy Error

Other than the sum of squared errors, a **cross-entropy error** is also often used as a loss function. It is expressed by the following equation:

$$E = - \sum_{k} t_k \log y_k$$

(4.2)

Here, log indicates the natural logarithm, that is, the logarithm to the base of e ($\log_e$). y_k is the output of the neural network and t_k is the correct label. In t_k, only the index for the correct label is 1; the other indices are 0 (one-hot representation). Therefore, equation (4.2) only calculates the logarithm of the output that corresponds to the correct label, 1. For example, if "2" is the index of the correct label, and the corresponding output from the neural network is 0.6, a cross-entropy error is `-log 0.6` `= 0.51`. If the output for "2" is 0.1, the error is `-log 0.1` `= 2.30`. A cross-entropy error depends on the output result from the correct label. *Figure* 4.3 shows the graph of this natural logarithm:

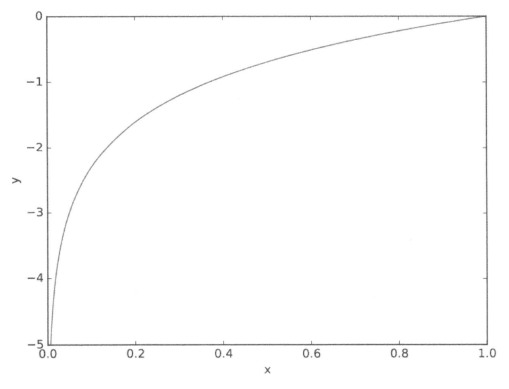

Figure 4.3: Graph of the natural logarithm y = log x

As shown in *Figure* 4.3, y is 0 when x is 1, and the value of y is getting smaller as x approaches 0. Therefore, since the output corresponding to the correct label is larger, equation (4.2) approaches 0. When the output is 1, the cross-entropy error becomes 0. When the output corresponding to the correct label is smaller, the value of equation (4.2) is larger.

Now, let's implement a cross-entropy error:

```
def cross_entropy_error(y, t):
    delta = 1e-7
    return -np.sum(t * np.log(y + delta))
```

Here, the y and t arguments are NumPy arrays. When `np.log` is calculated, a very small value, delta, is added. If `np.log(0)` is calculated, `-inf`, which indicates minus infinity, is returned. At this point, the calculation cannot be advanced further. To avoid this, a very small value is added so that minus infinity does not occur. Now, let's use `cross_entropy_error(y, t)` for ease of calculation:

```
>>> t = [0, 0, 1, 0, 0, 0, 0, 0, 0, 0]
>>> y = [0.1, 0.05, 0.6, 0.0, 0.05, 0.1, 0.0, 0.1, 0.0, 0.0]
>>> cross_entropy_error(np.array(y), np.array(t))
0.51082545709933802
>>>
>>> y = [0.1, 0.05, 0.1, 0.0, 0.05, 0.1, 0.0, 0.6, 0.0, 0.0]
>>> cross_entropy_error(np.array(y), np.array(t))
2.3025840929945458
```

In the first example, the output of the correct label is 0.6 and the cross-entropy error is 0.51. In the next example, the output of the correct label is as small as 0.1 and the cross-entropy error is 2.3. These results are consistent with what we've discussed so far.

Mini-Batch Learning

For a machine learning problem, training data is used for training. To be precise, it means finding the loss function for the training data and finding the parameters that make that value as small as possible. Therefore, all the training data must be used to obtain the loss function. If there are 100 pieces of training data, the sum of their 100 loss functions must be used as the index.

In the example of the loss function we described earlier, the loss function for one piece of data was used. For a cross-entropy error, equation (4.3) can calculate the sum of the loss functions for all training data:

$$E = -\frac{1}{N} \sum_n \sum_k t_{nk} \log y_{nk} \qquad (4.3)$$

Suppose that the number of data elements is N. t_{nk} means the k-th value of the n-th data (y_{nk} is the output of the neural network, and t_{nk} is labeled data). Although this equation seems a little complicated, it is only an extension of equation (4.2), which expresses the loss function for one piece of data for N items of data. In the end, it is divided by N for normalization. Division by N calculates the "average loss function" per data. The average can be used as a consistent index, regardless of the amount of training data. For example, even when the number of training data elements is 1,000 or 10,000, you can calculate the average loss function per data element.

The MNIST dataset contains 60,000 items of training data. Calculating the sum of the loss functions for all this data takes a while. Big data sometimes contains millions or tens of millions of pieces of data. In that case, calculating the loss functions for all the data is not practical. Therefore, some data is extracted to approximate all the data. Also, in neural network training, some training data is selected, and training is conducted for each group of data, which is called a mini-batch (small collection). For example, 100 pieces of data are selected at random from 60,000 items of training data to be used for training. This training method is called **mini-batch training**.

Now, let's write some code that selects the specified amount of data from the training data at random for mini-batch training. Before that, the following is the code for loading the MNIST dataset:

```
import sys, os
sys.path.append(os.pardir)
import numpy as np
from dataset.mnist import load_mnist

(x_train, t_train), (x_test, t_test) = /
    load_mnist(normalize=True, one_hot_label=True)

print(x_train.shape) # (60000, 784)
print(t_train.shape) # (60000, 10)
```

As described in *Chapter 3, Neural Networks*, the `load_mnist` function loads the MNIST dataset. It is located in the **dataset/mnist.py** file provided with this book. This function loads the training and test data. By specifying the `one_hot_label=True` argument, you can use one-hot representation, where the correct label is 1 and the other labels are 0.

When you load the preceding MNIST data, you will find that the number of training data is 60,000 and that the input data contains 784 rows of image data (originally 28x28). Labeled data is data with 10 rows. Therefore, the shapes of **x_train** and **t_train** are (60000, 784) and (60000, 10), respectively.

Now, how can we extract 10 pieces of data at random from the training data? We can write the following code by using NumPy's `np.random.choice()` function:

```
train_size = x_train.shape[0]
batch_size = 10
batch_mask = np.random.choice(train_size, batch_size)
x_batch = x_train[batch_mask]
t_batch = t_train[batch_mask]
```

By using `np.random.choice()`, you can select the desired number of numerals at random from the specified numerals. For example, `np.random.choice(60000, 10)` selects 10 numerals at random from the numerals between 0 and less than 60,000. In the actual code, as shown here, you can obtain the indices as an array for selecting mini-batches:

```
>>> np.random.choice(60000, 10)
array([ 8013, 14666, 58210, 23832, 52091, 10153, 8107, 19410, 27260,
21411])
```

Now, you can specify the randomly selected indices to extract mini-batches. We will use these mini-batches to calculate loss functions.

> **Note**
>
> To measure television viewership, not all households, but selected ones, are targeted. For example, by measuring viewership among 1,000 households randomly selected from Tokyo, you can approximate the viewership throughout Tokyo. The viewership among these 1,000 households is not exactly the same as the whole viewership, but it can be used as an approximate value. Like the viewership described here, the loss function of a mini-batch is measured by using sample data to approximate the whole data. In short, a small group of randomly selected data (mini-batch) is used as the approximation of the whole training data.

Implementing Cross-Entropy Error (Using Batches)

How can we use batch data such as mini-batches to implement a cross-entropy error? By improving the cross-entropy error we implemented earlier, which targets only one piece of data, we can implement it easily. Here, we will support both the input of a single piece of data and the input of data as batches:

```
def cross_entropy_error(y, t):
    if y.ndim == 1:
        t = t.reshape(1, t.size)
```

```
        y = y.reshape(1, y.size)

    batch_size = y.shape[0]
    return -np.sum(t * np.log(y + 1e-7)) / batch_size
```

Here, y is the output of the neural network, and t is labeled data. If y is one-dimensional (that is, to calculate the cross-entropy error for one piece of data), the shape of the data is changed. The average cross-entropy error per data is calculated by normalization based on the amount of data in a batch.

If labeled data is provided as labels (not in one-hot representation format but as labels such as "2" and "7"), we can implement a cross-entropy error as follows:

```
def cross_entropy_error(y, t):
    if y.ndim == 1:
        t = t.reshape(1, t.size)
        y = y.reshape(1, y.size)

    batch_size = y.shape[0]
    return -np.sum(np.log(y[np.arange(batch_size), t] + 1e-7)) / batch_
size
```

Please note that if t of an element is 0 in one-hot representation, its cross-entropy error is also 0, and you can ignore this calculation. In other words, if you can obtain the output of the neural network for a correct label, you can calculate the cross-entropy error. Therefore, for t as the one-hot representation, t * np.log(y) is used, while for t as labels, np.log(y[np.arange(batch_size), t]) is used for the same processing (here, the description of "a very small value, 1e-7" has been omitted for visibility).

For reference, we can cover np.log(y[np.arange(batch_size), t]) briefly. np.arange(batch_size) generates an array from 0 to batch_size-1. When batch_size is 5, np.arange(batch_size) generates a NumPy array, [0, 1, 2, 3, 4]. t contains labels, as in [2, 7, 0, 9, 4] and y[np.arange(batch_size), t] extracts the output of the neural network corresponding to the correct label for each piece of data (in this example, y[np.arange(batch_size), t] generates a NumPy array, [y[0,2], y[1,7], y[2,0], y[3,9], y[4,4]]).

Why Do We Configure a Loss Function?

Some people may wonder why we introduce a loss function. For example, in the case of number recognition, we want parameters to improve recognition accuracy. Isn't it extra work to introduce a loss function? Our goal is to achieve a neural network that maximizes recognition accuracy. So, surely, we should use "recognition accuracy" as a score?

You can find the answer to this question by paying attention to the role of the "derivative" in neural network training. This will be explained in detail in the next section. Neural network training looks for optimal parameters (weights and biases) so that the value of the loss function is the smallest. To look for the position of the smallest loss function, the derivative (gradient, to be precise) of a parameter is calculated, and the parameter value is updated gradually, based on the value of the derivative.

For example, suppose that a virtual neural network exists here. We will pay attention to one weight parameter in the neural network. Here, the derivative of the loss function of the weight parameter indicates how the loss function changes when the value of the weight parameter is changed a little. If the derivative becomes a negative value, you can reduce the loss function by changing the weight parameter in a positive direction. On the other hand, if the derivative is a positive value, you can reduce the loss function by changing the weight parameter in the negative direction. However, when the value of the derivative becomes 0, the value of the loss function does not change, no matter how the weight parameter is moved. Updating the weight parameter is stopped there.

We cannot use recognition accuracy as the score because the derivative becomes 0 at almost all positions, preventing parameters from being updated. Now, let's neatly summarize this.

> **Note**
>
> When training a neural network, we should not use recognition accuracy as the score. The reason is that if you use recognition accuracy as the score, the derivative of the parameters will be zero in most places.

So why does recognition accuracy as the score lead the derivative of the parameter to 0 at almost all positions? Well, to explain this, let's consider another example. Say that a neural network can recognize 32 out of 100 items of training data. This means that the recognition accuracy is 32%. If we use the recognition accuracy as the score, slightly changing the weight parameter will leave it at 32% and cause no change. Slightly adjusting the parameters does not improve recognition accuracy. Even if the recognition accuracy is improved, the change will not be continuous, such as 32.0123...%, but discontinuous, such as 33% and 34%. On the other hand, if the loss function is used as the score, the current value of the loss function is represented as a value, such as 0.92543... Slightly changing the parameter value also changes the loss function continuously, such as 0.93432...

Slightly adjusting the parameter only changes the recognition accuracy a bit, and any change is discontinuous and sudden. This is also true of the "step function" of an activation function. If you use a step function for an activation function, a neural network cannot learn appropriately for the same reason. The reason for this is that the derivative of a step function is 0 almost anywhere (positions other than 0), as shown in *Figure* 4.4. When you use a step function, a slight change to the parameter is erased by the step function, and the value of the loss function shows no changes, even if you use it as the score.

A step function changes only at some moments, like a shishi-odoshi or scarecrow. On the other hand, for the derivative (tangent) of a sigmoid function, the output (value of the vertical axis) changes continuously and the gradient of the curve also changes continuously, as shown in *Figure* 4.4. In short, the derivative of a sigmoid function is not 0 at any position. This is important for "training" in a neural network. Because the gradient is never 0, a neural network can learn correctly:

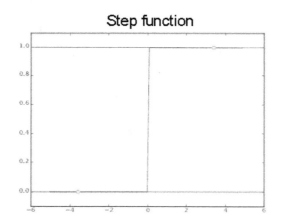 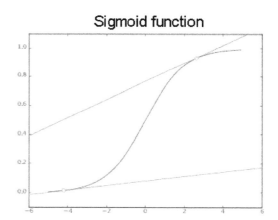

Figure 4.4: Step function and sigmoid function – the gradient of a step function is 0 at almost all positions, while the gradient of a sigmoid function (tangent) is never 0

Numerical Differentiation

The gradient method uses information from the gradient to determine which direction to follow. This section describes what a gradient is and its characteristics, beginning with a "derivative."

Derivative

For example, let's assume that you ran 2 km in 10 minutes from the start of a full marathon. You can calculate the speed as 2 / 10 = 0.2 [km/minute]. You ran at a speed of 0.2 km per minute.

In this example, we calculated how much the "running distance" changed over "time." Strictly speaking, this calculation indicates the "average speed" for 10 minutes because you ran 2 km in 10 minutes. A derivative indicates the amount of change at "a certain moment." Therefore, by minimizing the time of 10 minutes (the distance in the last 1 minute, the distance in the last 1 second, the distance in the last 0.1 seconds, and so on), you can obtain the amount of change at a certain moment (instantaneous speed).

Thus, a derivative indicates the amount of change at a certain moment. This is defined by the following equation:

$$\frac{df(x)}{dx} = \lim_{h \to 0} \frac{f(x+h) - f(x)}{h} \qquad (4.4)$$

Equation (4.4) indicates the derivative of a function. The left-hand side $\frac{df(x)}{dx}$ indicates the derivative of $f(x)$ with respect to x – the degree of changes of f(x) with respect to x. The derivative expressed by equation (4.4) indicates how the value of the function, $f(x)$, changes because of a "slight change" in x. Here, the slight change, h, is brought close to 0 infinitely, which is indicated as $\lim_{h \to 0}$.

Let's write a program to obtain the derivative of a function based on equation (4.4). To implement equation (4.4) directly, you can assign a small value to h for calculation purposes:

```
# Bad implementation sample
def numerical_diff(f,  x):
    h = 10e-50
    return (f(x+h) - f(x)) / h
```

The function is named `numerical_diff(f, x)`, after **numerical differentiation**. It takes two arguments: the function, f, and the argument, x, of the function, f. This implementation seems correct, but two improvements can be made.

The preceding implementation uses a small value of `10e-50` ("0.00...1" containing 50 0s) as h because we want to use the smallest possible value as h (we want to bring h infinitely close to 0 if possible). But the problem of a **rounding error** occurs here. A rounding error occurs in the final calculation result by omitting a numeric value in the small range of a decimal (for example, by omitting eight or more places of decimals). The following example shows a rounding error in Python:

```
>>> np.float32(1e-50)
0.0
```

When you represent 1e-50 in the float32 type (a 32-bit floating-point number), the value becomes 0.0. You cannot express it correctly. Using too small value causes a problem in computer calculation. Now, here is the first improvement. You can use 10^{-4} as the small value, h. It is known that a value of around 10^{-4} brings about good results.

The second improvement is in terms of the difference in the function, f. The preceding implementation calculates the difference in the function f between x + h and x. You should observe that this calculation causes an error in the first place. As shown in *Figure* 4.5, the "true derivative " corresponds to the gradient of the function at the position of x (called a tangent), while the derivative in this implementation corresponds to the gradient between (x + h) and x. Therefore, the true derivative (true tangent) is not strictly identical to the value of this implementation. This difference occurs because you cannot bring h close to 0 infinitely:

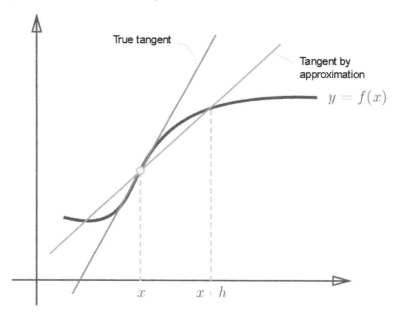

Figure 4.5: True derivative (true tangent) and numerical differentiation (tangent by approximation) are different in value

As shown in *Figure* 4.5, a numerical differential contains an error. To reduce this error, you can calculate the difference of the function, (f), between (x + h) and (x - h). This difference is called a **central difference** because it is calculated around x (on the other hand, the difference between (x + h) and x is called a **forward difference**). Now, let's implement a numerical differentiation (numerical gradient) based on these two improvements:

```
def numerical_diff(f, x):
    h = 1e-4 # 0.0001
    return (f(x+h) - f(x-h)) / (2*h)
```

> **Note**
>
> As the preceding code shows, calculating a derivative by using a very small value difference is called **numerical differentiation**. On the other hand, obtaining a derivative with the expansion is called an "analytical solution" or "analytically obtaining a derivative," for example, by using the word "analytic." You can obtain the derivative of
>
> $y = x^2$ analytically as $\frac{dy}{dx} = 2x$. Therefore, you can calculate the derivative of y as $x = 2$, and this is 4. An analytic derivative is the "true derivative" without errors.

Examples of Numerical Differentiation

Let's differentiate an easy function by using numerical differentiation. The first example is the quadratic function expressed by the following equation:

$$y = 0.01x^2 + 0.1x \qquad\qquad (4.5)$$

Implement equation (4.5) in Python as follows:

```
def function_1(x):
    return 0.01*x**2 + 0.1*x
```

Draw the graph of this function. The following shows the code for drawing a graph and the resulting graph (*Figure 4.6*):

```
import numpy as np
import  matplotlib.pylab  as  plt


x = np.arange(0.0, 20.0, 0.1) # The array x containing 0 to 20 in
increments of 0.1
y = function_1(x)
plt.xlabel("x")
plt.ylabel("f(x)")
plt.plot(x, y)
plt.show()
```

Now calculate the differentials of the function when x=5 and x=10:

```
>>> numerical_diff(function_1, 5)
0.1999999999990898
>>> numerical_diff(function_1, 10)
0.2999999999986347
```

The differential calculated here is the amount of change of $f(x)$ for x, which corresponds to the gradient of the function. By the way, the analytical solution of $f(x) = 0.01x^2 + 0.1x$ is $\frac{\partial f}{\partial x} = 0.02x + 0.1$. The true derivative when x=5 and 10 are 0.2 and 0.3, respectively. They are not strictly identical to the results from numerical differentiation, but the error is very small. Actually, the error is so small that they can be regarded as almost identical values:

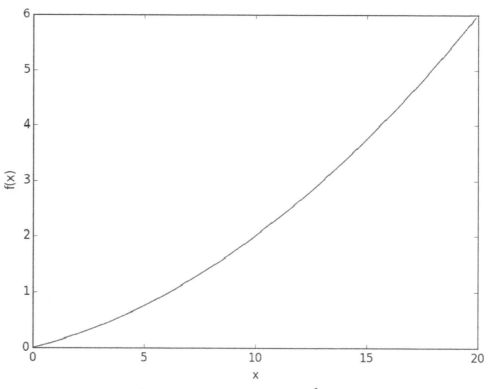

Figure 4.6: Graph of $f(x) = 0.01x^2 + 0.1x$

We will use the preceding results of our numerical differentiation to plot graphs of lines whose gradients are the values of the numerical differentiation. The results are shown in *Figure 4.7*. Here, you can see that the derivatives correspond to the tangents of the function (the source code is located at `ch04/gradient_1d.py`):

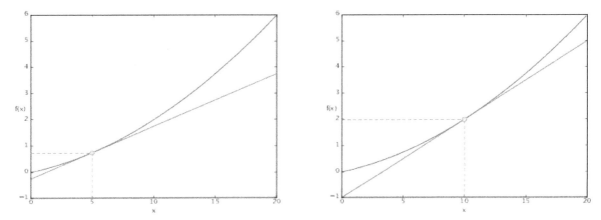

Figure 4.7: Tangents when $x = 5$ and $x = 10$ – using the values from numerical differentiation as the gradients of lines

Partial Derivative

Next, let's look at the function expressed by equation (4.6). This simple equation calculates the square sum of the arguments. Note that it has two variables, unlike the previous example:

$$f(x_0, x_1) = x_0^2 + x_1^2 \qquad (4.6)$$

You can implement it in Python as follows:

```
def function_2(x):
    return x[0]**2 + x[1]**2
    # or return np.sum(x**2)
```

Here, it is assumed that NumPy arrays are passed as arguments. The function simply squares each element of the NumPy arrays and sums it up (`np.sum(x**2)` can implement the same processing). Now, let's draw the graph of this function. This three-dimensional graph appears as follows:

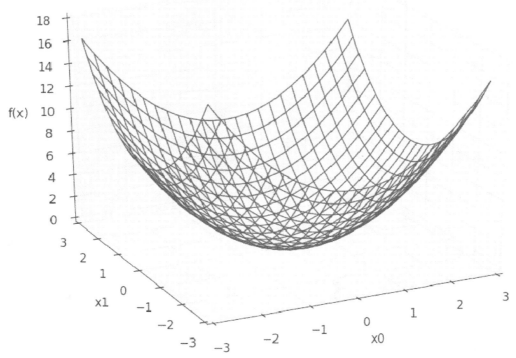

Figure 4.8: Graph of $f(x_0, x_1) = x_0^2 + x_1^2$

Now, we want to calculate the derivative of equation (4.6). Here, please note that equation (4.6) has two variables. Therefore, you must specify for which of the two variables, x_0 and x_1, the differentials are calculated. The derivative of a function that consists of multiple variables is called a **partial derivative**. They are expressed as $\frac{\partial f}{\partial x_0}$, $\frac{\partial f}{\partial x_1}$.

To illustrate this, consider the following two partial derivative problems and their solutions:

Question 1: Calculate the partial derivative, $\frac{\partial f}{\partial x_0}$, for `x0` when `x0 = 3` and `x1 = 4`:

```
>>> def function_tmp1(x0):
...     return x0*x0 + 4.0**2.0
...
>>> numerical_diff(function_tmp1, 3.0)
6.00000000000378
```

Question 2: Calculate the partial derivative, $\frac{\partial f}{\partial x_1}$, for **x1** when **x0 = 3** and **x1 = 4**:

```
>>> def function_tmp2(x1):
...     return 3.0**2.0 + x1*x1
...
>>> numerical_diff(function_tmp2, 4.0)
7.999999999999119
```

To solve these problems, a function with one variable is defined, and the derivative for the function is calculated. For example, in **Question 1**, a new function for **x1=4** is defined, and the function, which has only one variable, **x0**, is passed to the function to calculate a numerical differentiation. Based on the results, the answer to **Question 1** is `6.00000000000378`, and the answer to **Question 2** is `7.999999999999119`. They are mostly the same as the solutions from analytical differentiation.

In this way, the partial derivative calculates the gradient at a certain position, such as the differentiation for one variable. However, for the partial derivative, one of the variables is targeted, and the other variables are fixed at a certain value. In the preceding implementation, a new function was defined to hold the other variables at a specific value. The newly defined function was passed to the previous numerical differential function to calculate the partial derivative.

Gradient

In the previous example, the partial derivatives of x_0 and x_1 were calculated for each variable. Now, we want to calculate the partial derivatives of x_0 and x_1 collectively. For example, let's calculate the partial derivatives of (x_0, x_1) when **x0 = 3** and **x1 = 4** as $\left(\frac{\partial f}{\partial x_0}, \frac{\partial f}{\partial x_1}\right)$ The vector that collectively indicates the partial differentials of all the variables, such as $\left(\frac{\partial f}{\partial x_0}, \frac{\partial f}{\partial x_1}\right)$ is called a **gradient**. You can implement a gradient as follows:

```
def numerical_gradient(f,   x):
    h = 1e-4 # 0.0001
    grad = np.zeros_like(x) # Generate an array with the same shape as x

    for idx in range(x.size):
        tmp_val = x[idx]
        # Calculate f(x+h)
        x[idx] = tmp_val + h
        fxh1 = f(x)

        # Calculate f(x-h)
```

```
        x[idx] = tmp_val - h
        fxh2 = f(x)

        grad[idx] = (fxh1 - fxh2) / (2*h)
        x[idx] = tmp_val # Restore the original value

    return grad
```

Implementing the `numerical_gradient(f, x)` function seems a little complicated, but the processes are almost the same as those in numerical differentiation for one variable. Note that `np.zeros_like(x)` generates an array that has the same shape as `x` and whose elements are all zero.

The `numerical_gradient(f, x)` function takes the `f` (function) and `x` (NumPy array) arguments and obtains numerical differentiations for each element of the NumPy array, `x`. Now, let's use this function to calculate a gradient. Here, we will obtain the gradients at points (3, 4), (0, 2), and (3, 0):

```
>>> numerical_gradient(function_2, np.array([3.0, 4.0]))
array([ 6., 8.])
>>> numerical_gradient(function_2, np.array([0.0, 2.0]))
array([ 0., 4.])
>>> numerical_gradient(function_2, np.array([3.0, 0.0]))
array([ 6., 0.])
```

> **Note**
>
> The actual result is [6.0000000000037801, 7.9999999999991189], but [6., 8.] is returned. This is because a returned NumPy array is formatted to enhance the visibility of the values.

Thus, we can calculate the gradient at each point of (x_0, x_1). The preceding example shows that the gradient for point (3, 4) is (6, 8), that for point (0, 2) is (0, 4), and that for point (3, 0) is (6, 0). What do these gradients mean? To understand this, let's look at the gradients of $f(x_0, x_1) = x_0^2 + x_1^2$. Here, we will make the gradients negative and draw the vectors (the source code is located at `ch04/gradient_2d.py`).

The gradients of $f(x_0, x_1) = x_0^2 + x_1^2$ are shown as the vectors (arrows) that have the direction toward the lowest point, as shown in *Figure 4. 9*. In *Figure 4.9*, the gradients seem to point at "the lowest position (smallest value)" of the function, $f(x_0, x_1)$. Just like a compass, the arrows point to one point. The more distant they are from "the lowest position," the larger the size of the arrow:

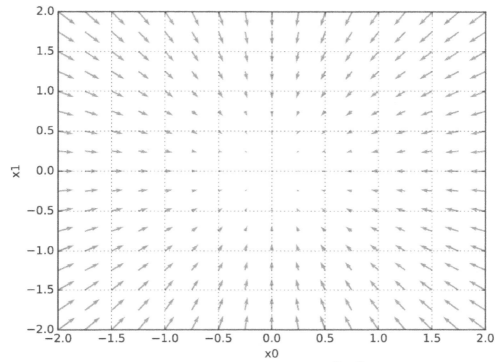

Figure 4.9: Gradients of $f(x_0, x_1) = x_0^2 + x_1^2$

In the example shown in *Figure* 4.9, the gradients point at the lowest position, but this is not always the case. In fact, gradient points in the lower direction at each position. To be more precise, the direction of a gradient is **the direction that reduces the value of the function most at each position**. This is an important point, so please keep this in mind.

Gradient Method

Many machine learning problems look for optimal parameters during training. A neural network also needs to find optimal parameters (weights and biases) during training. The optimal parameter here is the parameter value when the loss function takes the minimum value. However, a loss function can be complicated. The parameter space is vast, and we cannot guess where it takes the minimum value. A gradient method makes good use of gradients to find the minimum value (or the smallest possible value) of the function.

A gradient shows the direction that reduces the value of the function most at each position. Therefore, whether the position that a gradient points in is really the minimum value of the function, in other words, whether the direction is really the one to take, cannot be guaranteed. Actually, in a complicated function, the direction that a gradient points to is not the minimum value in most cases.

Note

The gradient is 0 at the local minimum, the minimum, and at a point called the saddle point of a function. A local minimum is locally the smallest value, which is the minimum value in a limited range. A saddle point is a position of the local maximum in one direction and of the local minimum in another direction. A gradient method looks for the position where a gradient is 0, but where the position is not always the global minimum (it can be the local minimum or a saddle point). When a function has a complicated and distorted shape, learning enters an (almost) flat land and a stagnant period called a "plateau" might occur, leading to stagnation in training.

Even if the direction of a gradient does not always point at the global minimum value, moving in that direction can reduce the value of the function the most. Therefore, to look for the position of the minimum value or to look for the position where the function has the smallest possible value, you should determine the direction of movement based on the information about gradients.

Now, let's look at the gradient method. In the gradient method, you move a fixed distance from the current position in the gradient direction. By doing this, you obtain a gradient at the new position and move in the gradient direction again. Thus, you move in the gradient direction repeatedly. Reducing the value of a function gradually by going in the gradient direction repeatedly is known as the **gradient method**. This method is often used in optimization problems for machine learning. It is typically used when training neural networks.

Note

A gradient method is called by another name if it looks for the minimum or the maximum value. To be precise, the method for the minimum value is called the **gradient descent method**, while the method for the maximum value is called the **gradient ascent method**. However, reversing the sign of a loss function can change this from a problem for the minimum value into a problem for the maximum value. So, the difference between "descent" and "ascent" is not especially important. Generally, a "gradient descent" method is often used in neural networks (deep learning).

Now, let's express a gradient method with an equation. Equation (4.7) shows a gradient method:

$$x_0 = x_0 - \eta \frac{\partial f}{\partial x_0}$$

$$x_1 = x_1 - \eta \frac{\partial f}{\partial x_1} \qquad (4.7)$$

In equation (4.7), η adjusts the amount to be updated. This is called a **learning rate** in neural network. A learning rate determines how much needs to be learned and how much to update the parameters.

Equation (4.7) shows an update equation for one training instance, and the step is repeated. Each step updates the variable values, as shown in equation (4.7), and the step is repeated several times to reduce the value of the function gradually. This example has two variables, but even when the number of variables is increased, a similar equation–a partial differential value for each variable–is used for updating.

You must specify the value of the learning rate, such as 0.01 and 0.001, in advance. Generally, if this value is too large or too small, you cannot reach a "good place." In neural network training, we usually check whether training is successful by changing the value of the learning rate.

Now, let's implement a gradient descent method in Python. This can be done as follows:

```
def gradient_descent(f, init_x, lr=0.01, step_num=100):
    x = init_x

    for i in range(step_num):
        grad = numerical_gradient(f, x)
        x -= lr * grad

    return x
```

The `f` argument is a function to optimize, the `init_x` argument is an initial value, the `lr` argument is a learning rate, and the `step_num` argument is the number of repetitions in a gradient method. The gradient of the function is obtained by `numerical_gradient(f, x)` and the gradient updated by multiplying it by the learning rate, which is repeated the number of times specified by `step_num`.

You can use this function to obtain the local minimum of the function and even the minimum value if you are lucky. Now, let's try solving a problem.

Question: Obtain the minimum value of $f(x_0, x_1) = x_0^2 + x_1^2$ with a gradient method:

```
>>> def function_2(x):
...     return x[0]**2 + x[1]**2
...
>>> init_x = np.array([-3.0, 4.0])
>>> gradient_descent(function_2, init_x=init_x, lr=0.1, step_num=100)
array([ -6.11110793e-10, 8.14814391e-10])
```

Here, specify (-3.0, 4.0) as the initial value and start looking for the minimum value by using a gradient method. The final result is (-6.1e-10, 8.1e-10), which is almost near (0, 0). Actually, the true minimum value is (0, 0). You successfully obtained almost correct results by using a gradient method. *Figure 4.10* shows the process of updating with a gradient method. The origin is the lowest position, and you can see that the result is approaching it gradually. The source code to draw this graph is located at ch04/ `gradient_method.py` (ch04/`gradient_method.py` does not display dashed lines, which show the contour lines in the graph):

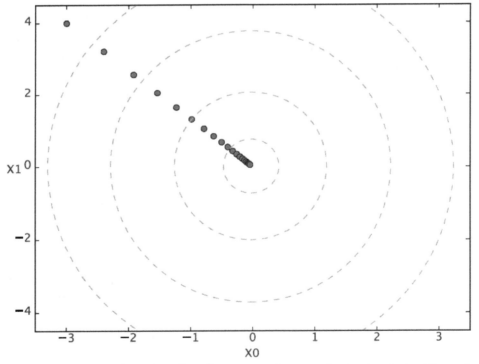

Figure 4.10: Updating $f(x_0, x_1) = x_0^2 + x_1^2$ with a gradient method – the dashed lines show the contour lines of the function

As mentioned earlier, an overly large or small learning rate does not achieve good results. Let's do some experiments regarding both cases here:

```
# When the learning rate is too large: lr=10.0
>>> init_x = np.array([-3.0, 4.0])
>>> gradient_descent(function_2, init_x=init_x, lr=10.0, step_num=100)
array([ -2.58983747e+13, -1.29524862e+12])


# When the learning rate is too small: lr=1e-10
>>> init_x = np.array([-3.0, 4.0])
>>> gradient_descent(function_2, init_x=init_x, lr=1e-10, step_num=100)
array([-2.99999994, 3.99999992])
```

As this experiment shows, the result diverges to a large value if the learning rate is too large. On the other hand, almost no updates occur if the learning rate is too small. Setting an appropriate learning rate is important.

> **Note**
>
> A parameter such as a learning rate is called a **hyperparameter**. It is different from the parameters (weights and biases) of a neural network in terms of its characteristics. Weight parameters in a neural network can be obtained automatically with training data and a training algorithm, while a hyperparameter must be specified manually. Generally, you must change this hyperparameter to various values to find a value that enables good training.

Gradients for a Neural Network

You must also calculate gradients in neural network training. The gradients here are those of a loss function for weight parameters. For example, let's assume that a neural network has the weight W (2x3 array) only, and the loss function is L. In this case, we can express the gradient as $\frac{\partial L}{\partial W}$. The following equation shows this:

$$\mathbf{W} = \begin{pmatrix} w_{11} & w_{12} & w_{13} \\ w_{21} & w_{22} & w_{23} \end{pmatrix}$$

$$\frac{\partial L}{\partial \mathbf{W}} = \begin{pmatrix} \frac{\partial L}{\partial w_{11}} & \frac{\partial L}{\partial w_{12}} & \frac{\partial L}{\partial w_{13}} \\ \frac{\partial L}{\partial w_{21}} & \frac{\partial L}{\partial w_{22}} & \frac{\partial L}{\partial w_{23}} \end{pmatrix}$$

(4.8)

Each element of $\frac{\partial L}{\partial W}$ is the partial derivative for each element. For example, the element at the first row and column, $\frac{\partial L}{\partial w_{11}}$, indicates how a slight change in w_{11} changes the loss function, L. What is important here is that the shape of $\frac{\partial L}{\partial W}$ is the same as that of W. Actually, in equation (4.8), both W and $\frac{\partial L}{\partial W}$ are the same (2x3) in shape.

Now, let's implement a program that calculates a gradient by taking an easy neural network as an example. To do that, we will implement a class named **simpleNet** (the source code is located at **ch04/gradient_simplenet.py**):

```python
import sys, os
sys.path.append(os.pardir)
import numpy as np
from common.functions import softmax, cross_entropy_error
from common.gradient import numerical_gradient


class simpleNet:
    def __init__(self):
        self.W = np.random.randn(2,3) # Initialize with a Gaussian
distribution

    def predict(self, x):
        return np.dot(x, self.W)

    def loss(self, x, t):
        z = self.predict(x)
        y = softmax(z)
        loss = cross_entropy_error(y, t)

        return loss
```

Here, the **softmax** and **cross_entropy_error** methods in **common/functions.py** are being used. The **numerical_gradient** method in **common/gradient.py** is also being used. The **simpleNet** class has only one instance variable, which is the weight parameters with a shape of 2x3. It has two methods: one is **predict(x)** for prediction, and the other is **loss(x, t)** for obtaining the value of the loss function. Here, the **x** argument is the input data and the **t** argument is a correct label. Now, let's try using **simpleNet**:

```python
>>> net = simpleNet()
>>> print(net.W) # Weight parameters
[[ 0.47355232 0.9977393 0.84668094]
 [ 0.85557411 0.03563661 0.69422093]]
>>>
>>> x = np.array([0.6, 0.9])
```

```
>>> p = net.predict(x)
>>> print(p)
[ 1.05414809 0.63071653 1.1328074]
>>> np.argmax(p) # Index for the maximum value
2
>>>
>>> t = np.array([0, 0, 1]) # Correct label
>>> net.loss(x, t)
0.92806853663411326
```

Next, let's obtain the gradients,using `numerical_gradient(f, x)`. The `f(W)` function
defined here takes a dummy argument, `w`. Because the `f(x)` function is executed inside
`numerical_gradient(f, x)`, `f(W)` is defined for consistency:

```
>>> def f(W):
...      return net.loss(x, t)
...
>>> dW = numerical_gradient(f, net.W)
>>> print(dW)
[[ 0.21924763 0.14356247 -0.36281009]
 [ 0.32887144 0.2153437 -0.54421514]]
```

The `f` argument of `numerical_gradient(f, x)` is a function and the `x` argument is the
argument to the function, `f`. Therefore, a new function, `f`, is defined here. It takes `net.W`
as an argument and calculates the loss function. The newly defined function is passed
to `numerical_gradient(f, x)`.

`numerical_gradient(f, net.W)` returns `dW`, which is a two-dimensional 2x3 array.
`dW` shows that $\frac{\partial L}{\partial W_{11}}$ for $\frac{\partial L}{\partial W}$ is around `0.2`, for example. This indicates that when w_{11} is
increased by h, the value of the loss function increases by 0.2h. $\frac{\partial L}{\partial W_{23}}$ is about `-0.5`, which
indicates that when w_{23} is increased by h, the value of the loss function decreases
by 0.5h. Therefore, to reduce the loss function, you should update w_{23} in a positive
direction and w_{11} in a negative direction. You can also see that updating w_{23} contributes
to the reduction more than updating w_{11}.

In the preceding implementation, the new function is written as `def f(x):`… In Python,
you can use a `lambda` notation to write and implement a simple function, as follows:

```
>>> f = lambda w: net.loss(x, t)
>>> dW = numerical_gradient(f, net.W)
```

After obtaining the gradients for a neural network, all you have to do is use a gradient
method to update the weight parameters. In the next section, we will implement all
these training processes for a two-layer neural network.

> **Note**
>
> The `numerical_gradient()` function we used here is slightly different from the previous implementation for handling multi-dimensional arrays such as the weight parameter, **w**. However, these changes are simple and are only for handling multidimensional arrays. For further details, please refer to the source code (`common/gradient.py`).

Implementing a Training Algorithm

So far, we have learned about the basics of neural network training. Important keywords such as "loss function", "mini-batch", "gradient", and "gradient descent method" have appeared in succession. Here, we will look at the procedure of neural network training for review purposes. Let's go over the neural network training procedure.

Presupposition

A neural network has adaptable weights and biases. Adjusting them so that they fit the training data is called "training." Neural network training consists of four steps.

Step 1 (mini-batch)

Select some data at random from the training data. The selected data is called a mini-batch. The purpose here is to reduce the value of the loss function for the mini-batch.

Step 2 (calculating gradients)

To reduce the loss function for the mini-batch, calculate the gradient for each weight parameter. The gradient shows the direction that reduces the value of the loss function the most.

Step 3 (updating parameters)

Update the weight parameters slightly in the gradient direction.

Step 4 (repeating)

Repeat *steps* 1, 2, and 3.

The preceding four steps are used for neural network training. This method uses a gradient descent method to update parameters. Because the data used here is selected at random as a mini-batch, it is referred to as **stochastic gradient descent**. "Stochastic" means "selecting data at random stochastically." Therefore, stochastic gradient descent means "the gradient descent method for randomly selected data." In many deep learning frameworks, stochastic gradient descent is usually implemented as the **SGD** function, which is named after its initials.

Now, let's implement the neural network that actually learns handwritten digits. Here, a two-layer neural network (with one hidden layer) will use the MNIST dataset for training.

A Two-Layer Neural Network as a Class

First, let's implement a two-layer neural network as a class. This class is named `TwoLayerNet` and is implemented as follows (implementing `TwoLayerNet` is based on the Python source code provided by the CS231n (*Convolutional Neural Networks for Visual Recognition* (http://cs231n.github.io/) course at Stanford University). The source code is located at **ch04/two_layer_net.py**:

```python
import sys, os
sys.path.append(os.pardir)
from common.functions import *
from common.gradient import numerical_gradient


class TwoLayerNet:
    def __init__ (self, input_size, hidden_size, output_size,
                        weight_init_std=0.01):
        # Initialize weights
        self.params = {}
        self.params['W1'] = weight_init_std * /
                        np.random.randn(input_size, hidden_size)
        self.params['b1'] = np.zeros(hidden_size)
        self.params['W2'] = weight_init_std * /
                        np.random.randn(hidden_size, output_size)
        self.params['b2'] = np.zeros(output_size)
```

```python
def predict(self, x):
    W1, W2 = self.params['W1'], self.params['W2']
    b1, b2 = self.params['b1'], self.params['b2']

    a1 = np.dot(x, W1) + b1
    z1 = sigmoid(a1)
    a2 =  np.dot(z1, W2) + b2
    y = softmax(a2)

    return y
# x: input data, t: label data
def loss(self, x, t):
    y = self.predict(x)

    return cross_entropy_error(y, t)

def accuracy(self, x, t):
    y = self.predict(x)
    y = np.argmax(y, axis=1)
    t = np.argmax(t, axis=1)

    accuracy = np.sum(y == t) / float(x.shape[0])
    return accuracy

# x: input data, t: teacher data
def numerical_gradient(self, x, t):
    loss_W = lambda  W:  self.loss(x,  t)

    grads = {}
    grads['W1'] = numerical_gradient(loss_W, self.params['W1'])
    grads['b1'] = numerical_gradient(loss_W, self.params['b1'])
    grads['W2'] = numerical_gradient(loss_W, self.params['W2'])
    grads['b2'] = numerical_gradient(loss_W, self.params['b2'])

    return grads
```

The implementation of this class is a little long, but nothing that new appears. It has many things in common with the implementation of forward processing a neural network covered in the previous chapter. First, let's look at the variables and methods that were used in this class. *Table 4.1* shows the important variables, while *Table 4.2* shows all the methods:

Variable	Description
params	Dictionary variable (instance variable) that contains the parameters of the neural network.
	params['W1'] is the weights for layer 1, while params['b1'] is the biases for layer 1.
	params['W2'] is the weights for layer 2, while params['b2'] is the biases for layer 2.
grads	Dictionary variable that contains gradients (return value of the numerical_gradient() method).
	grads['W1'] is the gradients of the weights for layer 1, while grads['b1'] is the gradients of the biases for layer 1.
	grads['W2'] is the gradients of the weights for layer 2, while grads['b2'] is the gradients of the biases for layer 2.

Table 4. 1: Variables used in the TwoLayerNet class

Method	Description
__init__(self, input_size, hidden_size, output_size)	Initialize.
	The arguments are the numbers of neurons in the input layer, in the hidden layer, and the output layer in order from left to right.
predict(self, x)	Conduct recognition (making predictions).
	The x argument is image data.
loss(self, x, t)	Obtain the value of the loss function.
	The x argument is image data, and the t argument is the correct label (the same is true for the arguments of the following three methods).
accuracy(self, x, t)	Obtain recognition accuracy.
numerical_gradient(self, x, t)	Obtain the gradient for the weight parameter.
gradient(self, x, t)	Obtain the gradient for the weight parameter.
	The fast version of the numerical_gradient() method.
	This will be implemented in the next chapter.

Table 4.2: Methods used in the TwoLayerNet class

The TwoLayerNet class has two dictionary variables, params and grads, as instance variables. The params variable contains the weight parameters. For example, the weight parameters for layer 1 are stored in params['W1'] as a NumPy array. You can access the bias for layer 1 using params['b1']. Here is an example:

```
net = TwoLayerNet(input_size=784, hidden_size=100, output_size=10)
net.params['W1'].shape # (784, 100)
net.params['b1'].shape # (100,)
net.params['W2'].shape # (100, 10)
net.params['b2'].shape # (10,)
```

As shown here, the `params` variable contains all the parameters required for this network. The weight parameters contained in the `params` variable are used for predicting (forward processing). You can make a prediction as follows:

```
x = np.random.rand(100, 784) # Dummy input data (for 100 images)
y = net.predict(x)
```

The `grads` variable contains the gradient for each parameter so that it corresponds to the `params` variable. When you calculate gradients by using the `numerical_gradient()` method, gradient information is stored in the `grads` variable, as follows:

```
x = p.random.rand(100, 784) # Dummy input data (for 100 images)
t = np.random.rand(100, 10) # Dummy correct label (for 100 images)

grads = net.numerical_gradient(x, t) # Calculate gradients

grads['W1'].shape # (784, 100)
grads['b1'].shape # (100,)
grads['W2'].shape # (100, 10)
grads['b2'].shape # (10,)
```

Now, let's look at the implementation of the methods in `TwoLayerNet`. The `__init__` (self, input_size, hidden_size, output_size) method is the initialization method of the class (called when `TwoLayerNet` is generated). The arguments are the numbers of neurons in the input layer, in the hidden layer, and the output layer in order from left to right. For handwritten digit recognition, a total of 784 input images that are 28x28 in size are provided and 10 classes are returned. Therefore, we specify the `input_size=784` and `output_size=10` arguments and set an appropriate value for `hidden_size` as the number of hidden layers.

This initialization method also initializes the weight parameters. Determining what values to set as the initial weight parameters is important for successful neural network training. We will discuss the initialization of weight parameters in detail later. Here, the weights are initialized by using the random numbers based on Gaussian distribution, and the biases are initialized by 0. `predict(self, x)`, and `accuracy(self, x, t)` are almost the same as in the implementation of predicting in relation to the neural network, which we looked at in the previous chapter. If you have any questions, please refer to the previous chapter. The `loss(self, x, t)` method calculates the value of the loss function. It obtains a cross-entropy error based on the result of `predict()` and the correct label.

The remaining `numerical_gradient(self, x, t)` method calculates the gradient of each parameter. It uses numerical differentiation to calculate the gradient for the loss function of each parameter. The `gradient(self, x, t)` method will be implemented in the next chapter.

> **Note**
>
> `numerical_gradient(self, x, t)` uses numerical differentiation to calculate the gradients of the parameters. In the next chapter, we will look at how to calculate gradients quickly using backpropagation, which returns almost the same result as using numerical differentiation, but with faster processing. The method for obtaining a gradient through backpropagation will be implemented as `gradient(self, x, t)` in the next chapter. If you want to save time, you can use `gradient(self, x, t)` instead of `numerical_gradient(self, x, t)` because neural network training takes time.

Implementing Mini-Batch Training

Here, we will use mini-batch training to implement neural network training. In mini-batch training, we extract some data randomly from training data (called a mini-batch) and use it to update the parameters using a gradient method. Let's conduct training for the `TwoLayerNet` class by using the MNIST dataset (the source code is located at `ch04/train_neuralnet.py`):

```
import numpy as np
from dataset.mnist import load_mnist
from two_layer_net import TwoLayerNet

(x_train, t_train), (x_test, t_test) = \
    load_mnist(normalize=True, one_hot_label=True)

train_loss_list = []

# Hyper-parameters
iters_num = 10000
train_size = x_train.shape[0]
batch_size = 100
learning_rate = 0.1

network = TwoLayerNet(input_size=784, hidden_size=50, output_size=10)

for i in range(iters_num):
    # Obtain a mini-batch
    batch_mask = np.random.choice(train_size, batch_size)
    x_batch = x_train[batch_mask]
```

```
t_batch = t_train[batch_mask]

# Calculate a gradient
grad = network.numerical_gradient(x_batch, t_batch)
# grad = network.gradient(x_batch, t_batch) # fast version!

# Update the parameters
for key in ('W1', 'b1', 'W2', 'b2'):
    network.params[key] -= learning_rate * grad[key]

# Record learning progress
loss = network.loss(x_batch, t_batch)
train_loss_list.append(loss)
```

Here, the size of a mini-batch is 100. Each time, 100 pieces of data (image data and correct label data) are extracted randomly from 60,000 pieces of training data. Then, gradients are obtained for the mini-batch, and the parameters are updated using **stochastic gradient descent (SGD)**. Here, the number of updates made by a gradient method;that is, the number of iterations is 10,000. At each update, the loss function for the training data is calculated, and the value is added to the array. *Figure 4.11* shows the graph of how the value of this loss function changes.

Figure 4.11 shows that, as the number of training increases, the value of the loss function decreases. It indicates that training is successful. The weight parameters of the neural network are adapting to the data gradually. The neural network is indeed learning. By being exposed to data repeatedly, it is approaching the optimal weight parameters:

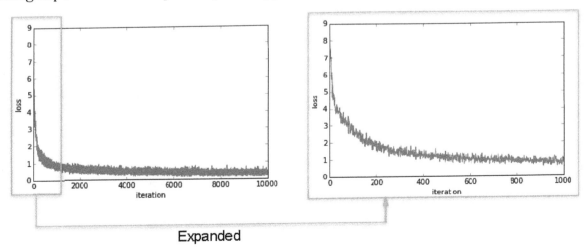

Expanded

Figure 4.11: Transition of the loss function – the image on the left shows the transition up to 10,000 iterations, while the image on the right shows the transition up to 1,000 iterations

Using Test Data for Evaluation

The result of *Figure 4.11* shows that repeatedly training the data reduces the value of the loss function gradually. However, the value of the loss function is the value of "the loss function for the mini-batch of training data." The reduction in the value of the loss function for the training data indicates that the neural network is learning well. However, this result does not prove that it can handle a different dataset as well as this one.

In neural network training, we must check whether data other than training data can be recognized correctly. We must check whether "overfitting" does not occur. Overfitting means that only the number of images contained in the training data can be recognized correctly, and those that are not contained there cannot be recognized, for example.

The goal of neural network training is to obtain generalization capability. To do that, we must use data that is not contained in the training data to evaluate the generalization capability of the neural network. In the next implementation, we will record the recognition accuracy for the test data and the training data periodically during training. We will record the recognition accuracy for the test data and the training data for each epoch.

> **Note**
>
> An epoch is a unit. One epoch indicates the number of iterations when all the training data has been used for training. For example, let's assume that 100 mini-batches are used to learn 10,000 pieces of training data. After a stochastic gradient descent method is repeated 100 times, all the training data has been seen. In this case, 100 `iterations` = 1 `epoch`.

Now, we will change the previous implementation slightly to gain a correct evaluation. Here, the differences from the previous implementation are shown in bold:

```
import numpy as np
from dataset.mnist import load_mnist
from two_layer_net import TwoLayerNet

(x_train, t_train), (x_test, t_test) = \
    load_mnist(normalize=True, one_hot_label=True)

train_loss_list = []
train_acc_list = []
test_acc_list = []
# Number of iterations per epoch
```

```
iter_per_epoch = max(train_size / batch_size, 1)

# Hyper-parameters
iters_num = 10000
batch_size = 100
learning_rate = 0.1
network = TwoLayerNet(input_size=784, hidden_size=50,
output_size=10)

for i in range(iters_num):
    # Obtain a mini-batch
    batch_mask = np.random.choice(train_size, batch_size)
    x_batch = x_train[batch_mask]
    t_batch = t_train[batch_mask]

    # Calculate a gradient
    grad = network.numerical_gradient(x_batch, t_batch)
    # grad = network.gradient(x_batch, t_batch) # Quick version!

    # Update the parameters
    for key in ('W1', 'b1', 'W2', 'b2'):
        network.params[key] -= learning_rate * grad[key]

    loss = network.loss(x_batch, t_batch)
    train_loss_list.append(loss)

    # Calculate recognition accuracy for each epoch
    if i % iter_per_epoch == 0:
        train_acc = network.accuracy(x_train, t_train)
        test_acc = network.accuracy(x_test, t_test)
        train_acc_list.append(train_acc)
        test_acc_list.append(test_acc)
        print("train acc, test acc | " + str(train_acc) + " , " +
str(test_acc))
```

In the preceding example, the recognition accuracy is calculated for all the training and test data and the results are recorded for each epoch. The recognition accuracy is calculated for each epoch because it takes time if it is calculated repeatedly in a `for` statement. Also, we do not need to record recognition accuracy frequently (all we need is the approximate transition of recognition accuracy). Therefore, the transition of recognition accuracy is recorded for each epoch of training data.

Now, let's show the results of the preceding code in a graph:

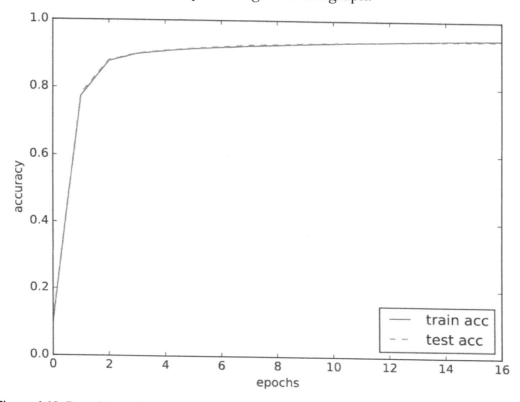

Figure 4.12: Transition of recognition accuracy for training data and test data. The horizontal axis shows the epochs

In *Figure 4.12*, the solid line shows the recognition accuracy of the training data, while the dashed line shows that of the test data. As you can see, as the number of epochs increases (training advances), the recognition accuracies for both the training data and the test data improve. Here, we can see that the two recognition accuracies are almost the same as the two lines mostly overlap. This indicates that overfitting did not occur here.

Summary

This chapter described neural network training. First, we introduced a `score` called a loss function so that a neural network can learn. The goal of neural network training is to discover the weight parameters that lead to the smallest value of the loss function. Then, we learned how to use the gradient of a function, called the gradient method, to discover the smallest loss function value. This chapter covered the following points:

- In machine learning, we use training data and test data.

- Training data is used for training, while test data is used to evaluate the generalization capability of the trained model.

- A loss function is used as a score in neural network training. Weight parameters are updated so that the value of the loss function will decrease.

- To update the weight parameters, their gradients are used to update their values in the gradient direction repeatedly.

- Calculating a derivative based on the difference when very small values are provided is called numerical differentiation.

- You can use numerical differentiation to obtain the gradients for the weight parameters.

- Numerical differentiation takes time to calculate, but its implementation is easy. On the other hand, backpropagation, which will be described in the next chapter, is slightly complicated, but it can calculate gradients quickly.

5

Backpropagation

The previous chapter described neural network training. There, the gradient of a weight parameter in the neural network (i.e., the gradient of the loss function for a weight parameter) was obtained by using numerical differentiation. Numerical differentiation is simple, and its implementation is easy, but it has the disadvantage that calculation takes time. This chapter covers backpropagation, which is a more efficient way to calculate the gradients of weight parameters.

There are two ways to understand backpropagation correctly. One of them uses "equations," while the other uses **computational graphs**. The former is a common way, and many books about machine learning expand on this by focusing on formulas. This is good because it is strict and simple, but it may hide essential details or end in a meaningless list of equations.

Therefore, this chapter will use computational graphs so that you can understand backpropagation "visually." Writing code will deepen your understanding further and convince you of this. The idea of using computational graphs to explain backpropagation is based on Andrej Karpathy's blog (*Hacker's guide to Neural Networks*, (http://karpathy.github.io/neuralnets/)) and the deep learning course (*CS231n: Convolutional Neural Networks for Visual Recognition* (http://cs231n.github.io/)) provided by him and Professor Fei-Fei Li at Stanford University.

Computational Graphs

A computational graph shows the process of calculation. This graph is used as a graph of data structure and is represented by multiple nodes and edges (meaning, straight lines that connect nodes). In this section, we will solve easy problems to familiarize ourselves with computational graphs before advancing step by step into more complex backpropagation.

Using Computational Graphs to Solve Problems

The problems in this section are simple enough that you can solve them with mental arithmetic, but the purpose here is to get familiar with computational graphs. Learning to use computational graphs will be helpful for the complicated calculations we will cover later, so it's important to first master how to use them here.

Question 1: Taro bought 2 apples that were 100 yen apiece. Calculate the amount of money he paid if a 10% consumption tax was applied.

A computational graph shows the process of calculation with nodes and arrows. A node is represented by a circle, and an operation is described in it. The intermediate result of the calculation above an arrow shows the result of each node that flows from left to right. The following diagram shows the computational graph that solves Question 1:

Figure 5.1: Answer to Question 1 using a computational graph

As shown in the preceding diagram, 100 yen for an apple that flows to the "x2" node becomes 200 yen, which is passed to the next node. Then, 200 yen is passed to the "× 1.1" node and becomes 220 yen. The result of this computational graph shows that the answer is 220 yen.

In the preceding diagram, each circle contains "× 2" or "× 1.1" as one operation. You can also place only "x" in a circle to show the operation. In that case, as shown in the following diagram, you can place "2" and "1.1" outside the circles as the "Number of apples" and "Consumption tax" variables.

The solution to this problem can be observed in the figure below:

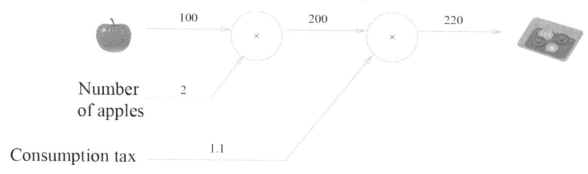

Figure 5.2: Answer to Question 1 using a computational graph: the "Number of apples" and "Consumption tax" variables are placed outside circles

Question 2: Taro bought 2 apples and 3 oranges. An apple was 100 yen, and the orange was 150. A 10% consumption tax was applied. Calculate the amount of money he paid.

As in Question 1, we will use a computational graph to solve Question 2. The following diagram shows the computational graph for this:

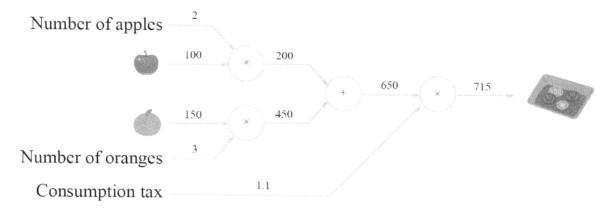

Figure 5.3: Answer to Question 2 using a computational graph

In this question, an addition node, "+", was added to sum the amounts of apples and oranges. After creating a computational graph, we advance the calculation from left to right. The calculation result moves from left to right, just like an electric current flows in a circuit, and the calculation ends when the result reaches the rightmost side. The preceding diagram shows that the answer is 715 yen.

To solve a problem using a computational graph, then, you must perform the following:

1. Create a computational graph.

2. Advance the calculation from left to right on the computational graph.

Step 2 is known as propagating in the forward direction or **forward propagation**. In forward propagation, calculation propagates from start to finish in a computational graph. If forward propagation exists, we can also consider propagation in the backward direction–from right to left. This is called **backward propagation** and is known as backpropagation. It will play an important role when we calculate derivatives later.

Local Calculation

The main characteristic of a computational graph is that it can obtain the final result by propagating "local calculation." The word "local" means "a small range related to the node." A local calculation can return the next result (subsequent result) from information related to the node, no matter what is happening on the whole.

We can break down local calculations using a specific example. For example, let's assume that we bought two apples and many other things at a supermarket. To visualize this, you can create a computational graph like so:

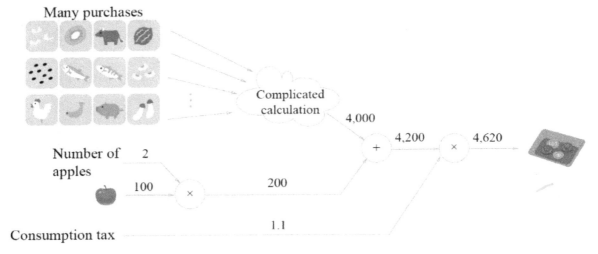

Figure 5.4: Example of buying two apples and many other things

Let's assume that we bought many things and that the total amount was 4,000 yen (after a complicated calculation), as shown in the preceding computational graph. What is important here is that the calculation in each node is a local calculation. To sum the amounts of the apples and the other purchases (4,000 + 200 -> 4,200), you can add the two figures without thinking about how 4,000 was obtained. In other words, what to calculate in each node is only the calculation related to the node–in this example, the addition of the two numbers provided. We do not need to think about the whole graph.

Thus, you can focus on local calculation in a computational graph. However complicated the whole calculation is, what is done at each step is "local calculation" for the target node. By passing the results of simple local calculations, you can obtain the result of the complicated calculations that constitute the whole graph.

> **Note**
>
> For example, the assembly of a car is complicated, but it is usually conducted based on the division of labor on an "assembly line." Each worker (machine) conducts simple work. The outcome of the workflows to the next worker, and finally, a car is built. A computational graph also divides complicated calculations into "simple and local calculations" and passes the calculation result to the next node, just like a car is passed down an assembly line. Like the assembly of a car, complicated calculations can be divided into simple calculations.

Why Do We Use Computational Graphs?

We have solved two problems by using computational graphs and may now consider the advantages. One of them is "local calculation," as described earlier. However complicated the whole calculation is, local calculation enables you to focus on the simple calculations in each node in order to simplify the problem as a whole.

Another advantage is that you can keep all the results of intermediate calculations in a computational graph (for example, 200 yen after 2 apples are calculated and 650 yen before consumption tax is added). However, the largest reason for using computational graphs is that you can calculate "derivatives" efficiently by propagating in the backward direction.

To describe backward propagation in a computational graph, consider Question 1 again. In this problem, you calculated the final amount paid regarding two apples and the consumption tax. Now say that you need to know how the final amount paid will be affected when the price of an apple goes up. This corresponds to obtaining the "derivative of the amount paid with respect to the price of an apple." It corresponds to obtaining $\frac{\partial L}{\partial x}$ when the price of an apple is x and the amount paid is L. The value of this derivative indicates how much the amount paid increases when the price of an apple goes up "slightly."

As we mentioned earlier, you can use backward propagation in a computational graph to obtain a value, such as the "derivative of the amount paid with respect to the price of an apple." First, we will only look at the result. As shown in the following diagram, you can obtain derivatives by using backpropagation in a computational graph:

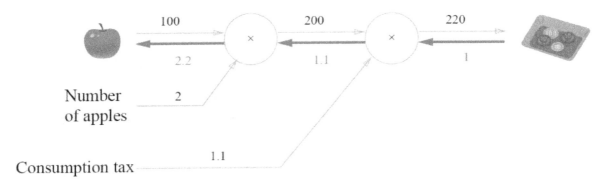

Figure 5.5: Propagating differential values using backward propagation

As shown in the preceding diagram, backward propagation is shown graphically with arrows (thick lines) in the opposite direction to the forward direction. Backward propagation passes "local differentials," and the values are placed below the arrows. In this example, derivative values are passed from right to left, as in 1 -> 1.1 -> 2.2. The result shows that the value of the "derivative of the amount paid with respect to the price of an apple" is 2.2.

This indicates that the final amount paid increases by 2.2 yen when the price of an apple goes up 1 yen. This means that when the price of an apple goes up by a small amount, the final amount increases by 2.2 times that of the small value. Here, only the derivative with respect to the price of an apple was obtained, but you can also obtain the "derivative of the amount paid with respect to consumption tax" and the "derivative of the amount paid with respect to the number of apples" by using similar steps.

During these steps, you can share the intermediate results of the derivatives (the derivatives that are passed halfway) so that you can calculate multiple derivatives efficiently. Thus, the advantage of a computational graph is that forward, and backward propagations enable you to obtain the derivative value of each variable efficiently.

Chain Rule

Forward propagation in a computational graph propagates the calculation result in the forward direction from left to right. These calculations seem natural because they are usually conducted. On the other hand, in backward propagation, a "local derivative" is propagated in the backward direction from right to left. The principle that propagates the "local derivative" is based on the **chain rule**. Let's look at the chain rule and clarify how it corresponds to backward propagation in a computational graph.

Backward Propagation in a Computational Graph

We will now look at an example of backward propagation using a computational graph. Let's assume that a calculation, $y = f(x)$, exists. The following diagram shows the backward propagation of this calculation:

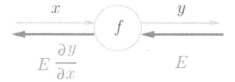

Figure 5.6: Backward propagation in a computational graph – the local derivative is multiplied in the backward direction

As shown in the preceding diagram, backward propagation multiplies the signal E by the local derivative of the node, $\left(\frac{\partial y}{\partial x}\right)$, and propagates it to the next node. The local derivative here means obtaining the derivative of the calculation, $y = f(x)$, in forward propagation and indicates obtaining the derivative, **y**, with respect to x $\left(\frac{\partial y}{\partial x}\right)$; for example, y = f (x) = x², $\left(\frac{\partial y}{\partial x}\right) = 2x$. The local derivative is multiplied by the value propagated from the upper stream (E, in this example) and passed to the previous node.

This is the procedure of backward propagation. It can obtain the target derivative values efficiently. The reason why this is possible can be explained by the principle of the chain rule, defined in the next section.

What Is the Chain Rule?

Before explaining the chain rule, we need to talk about **composite functions**. A composite function is a function that consists of multiple functions. For example, the equation **z = (x + y)²** consists of two equations, as shown in equation (5.1):

$$z = t^2$$
$$t = x + y$$

(5.1)

The chain rule is the characteristic related to the derivative of a composite function and is defined as follows.

When a function is expressed by a composite function, the derivative of the composite function can be expressed by the product of the derivative of each function that constitutes the composite function.

This is called the principle of the chain rule. Although it may seem difficult, it is actually quite simple. In the example given in equation (5.1), $\left(\frac{\partial z}{\partial x}\right)$ (a derivative of z with respect to x) is the product of $\left(\frac{\partial z}{\partial t}\right)$ (a derivative of z with respect to t) and $\left(\frac{\partial t}{\partial x}\right)$ (a derivative of t with respect to x). You can express this with the following equation (5.2):

$$\frac{\partial z}{\partial x} = \frac{\partial z}{\partial t}\frac{\partial t}{\partial x} \qquad (5.2)$$

You can remember equation (5.2) easily because ∂t's cancel each other out, as shown here: $\frac{\partial z}{\partial x} = \frac{\partial z}{\partial t}\frac{\partial t}{\partial x}$

Now, let's use the chain rule to obtain the derivative of equation (5.2), $\left(\frac{\partial z}{\partial x}\right)$. First, obtain the local differential (partial differential) of equation (5.1):

$$\frac{\partial z}{\partial t} = 2t$$
$$\frac{\partial t}{\partial x} = 1 \qquad (5.3)$$

As shown in equation (5.3), $\frac{\partial z}{\partial t}$ is 2t and $\frac{\partial t}{\partial x}$ is 1. This result is analytically obtained from the differentiation formula. The final result, $\frac{\partial z}{\partial x}$, can be calculated by the product of the derivatives obtained in equation (5.3):

$$\frac{\partial z}{\partial x} = \frac{\partial z}{\partial t}\frac{\partial t}{\partial x} = 2t \cdot 1 = 2(x + y) \qquad (5.4)$$

The Chain Rule and Computational Graphs

Now, let's use a computational graph to express the calculation of the chain rule in equation (5.4). When we represent a square with a node "**2", we can write a graph for it, as follows:

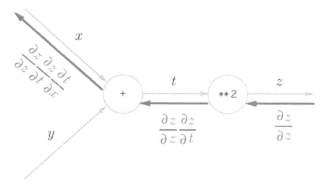

Figure 5.7: Computational graph of equation (5.4) – local derivatives are multiplied and passed in the backward direction

As shown in the preceding diagram, backward propagation in a computational graph propagates signals from right to left. Backward propagation multiplies the signal provided to a node by the local derivative (partial derivative) of the node and passes it to the next node. For example, the input to "**2" in backward propagation is $\frac{\partial z}{\partial z}$. It is multiplied by the local derivative, $\frac{\partial z}{\partial t}$ (in forward propagation, the input is t and the output is z, so the (local) derivative at this node is $\frac{\partial z}{\partial t}$) and then multiplied and passed to the next node. In the preceding diagram, the first signal in backward propagation $\frac{\partial z}{\partial z}$ did not appear in the previous equation. It was omitted there because $\frac{\partial z}{\partial z} = 1$.

What we should note from the preceding diagram is the result of backward propagation at the leftmost position. It corresponds to the "derivative of z with respect to x" because $\frac{\partial z}{\partial z}\frac{\partial z}{\partial t}\frac{\partial t}{\partial x} = \frac{\partial z}{\partial t}\frac{\partial t}{\partial x} = \frac{\partial z}{\partial x}$ due to the chain rule. What backward propagation performs is based on the principle of the chain rule.

When you assign the result of equation (5.3), as shown in the preceding diagram, the result is as follows. Thus, $\frac{\partial z}{\partial x}$ is 2(x + y):

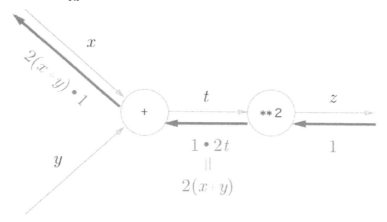

Figure 5.8: Based on the result of backward propagation in the computational graph, is 2(x + y)

Backward Propagation

The previous section described how backward propagation in a computational graph is based on the chain rule. We will now cover how backward propagation works by taking operations, such as "+" and "x", as examples.

Backward Propagation in an Addition Node

First, let's consider backward propagation in an additional node. Here, we will look at backward propagation for the equation $z = x + y$. We can obtain the derivatives of $z = x + y$ (analytically) as follows:

$$\frac{\partial z}{\partial x} = 1$$
$$\frac{\partial z}{\partial y} = 1$$

(5.5)

As equation (5.5) shows, both $\frac{\partial z}{\partial x}$ and $\frac{\partial z}{\partial y}$ are 1. Therefore, we can represent them in a computational graph, as shown in the following diagram. In backward propagation, the derivative from the upper stream—$\frac{\partial L}{\partial z}$, in this example—is multiplied by 1 and passed downstream. In short, backward propagation in an addition node multiplies 1, so it only passes the input value to the next node.

In this example, the differential value from the upper stream is expressed as $\frac{\partial L}{\partial z}$. This is because we assume a large computational graph that finally outputs L, as shown in *Figure 5.10*. The calculation, $z = x + y$, exists somewhere in the large computational graph, and the value of $\frac{\partial L}{\partial z}$ is passed from the upper stream. The values of $\frac{\partial L}{\partial x}$ and $\frac{\partial L}{\partial y}$ are propagated downstream:

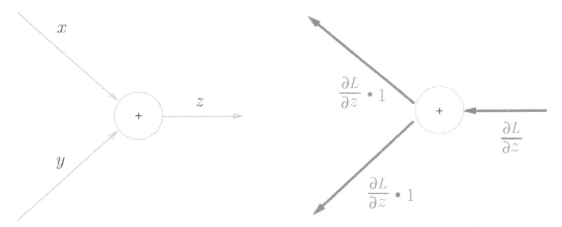

Figure 5.9: Backward propagation in an addition node – forward propagation on the left and backward propagation on the right.

As shown on the right, backward propagation in an addition node passes a value from the upper stream to the lower stream without changing it.

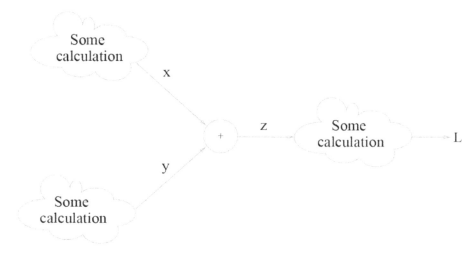

Figure 5.10: This addition node exists somewhere in the final output calculation.

In backward propagation, starting from the rightmost output, local derivatives are propagated from node to node in the backward direction

Now, let's look at an example of backward propagation. For example, say that a calculation, "10 + 5 = 15", exists and that a value of 1.3 flows from the upper stream in backward propagation. The following diagram shows this in terms of a computational graph:

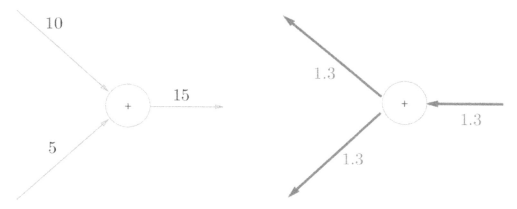

Figure 5.11: Example of backward propagation in an addition node

Because backward propagation in an addition node only outputs the input signal to the next node, it passes 1.3 to the next node.

Backward Propagation in a Multiplication Node

Let's take a look at backward propagation in a multiplication node by taking an equation, $z = xy$, as an example. The differential of this equation is expressed by the following equation (5.6):

$$\frac{\partial z}{\partial x} = y$$
$$\frac{\partial z}{\partial y} = x$$

$$(5.6)$$

Based on the preceding equation (5.6), you can write a computational graph as follows.

For the backward propagation of multiplication, the upstream value multiplied by the "reversed value" of the input signal for forward propagation is passed downstream. A reversed value means that if the signal is x in forward propagation, the value to multiply is y in backward propagation; and that if the signal is y in forward propagation, the value to multiply is x in backward propagation, as shown in the following diagram.

Let's look at an example. Assume that a calculation 10 x 5 = 50 exists and that the value of 1.3 flows from the upper stream in backward propagation. *Figure 5.13* shows this in the form of a computational graph.

In the backward propagation of multiplication, the reversed input signals are multiplied, so 1.3 x 5 = 6.5 and 1.3 x 10 = 13 are obtained. In the backward propagation of addition, the upstream value was only passed downstream. Therefore, the value of the input signal in forward propagation is not required. On the other hand, for the backward propagation of multiplication, the value of the input signal in forward propagation is required. Therefore, to implement a multiplication node, the input signal of forward propagation is retained:

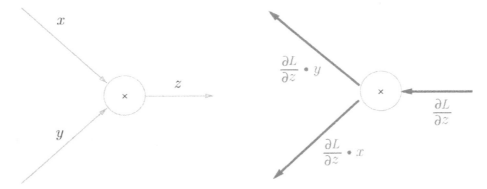

Figure 5.12: Backward propagation in a multiplication node – forward propagation on the left and backward propagation on the right

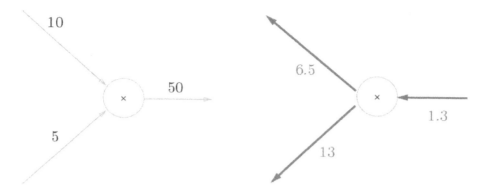

Figure 5.13: Example of backward propagation in a multiplication node

Apples Example

Let's think about the example of buying apples—two apples and consumption tax—from the beginning of this chapter again. The problem to solve here is how each of the three variables (the price of an apple, the number of apples, and consumption tax) affect the final amount paid. This corresponds to obtaining the "derivative of the amount paid with respect to the price of an apple," the "derivative of the amount paid with respect to the number of apples," and the "derivative of the amount paid with respect to consumption tax." We can solve this by using backward propagation in a computational graph, as shown in the following diagram:

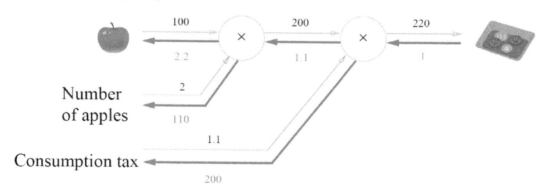

Figure 5.14: Example of backward propagation for purchasing apples

As mentioned previously, input signals are reversed and passed downstream in the backward propagation of a multiplication node. According to the result shown in the preceding diagram, the differential of the price of an apple is 2.2, there are 110 apples, and the consumption tax is 200. They indicate that when consumption tax and the price of an apple increase by the same quantity, the consumption tax affects the final amount paid in the size of 200 and that the price of an apple affects it in the size of 2.2. However, this result is brought about because the consumption tax and the price of an apple in this example are different in terms of units (1 for the consumption tax is 100%, while 1 for the price of an apple is 1 yen).

Lastly, let's solve the backward propagation of "buying apples and oranges" as an exercise. Please obtain the derivatives of individual variables and put the numbers in the squares provided in the following diagram (you can find the answer in the next section):

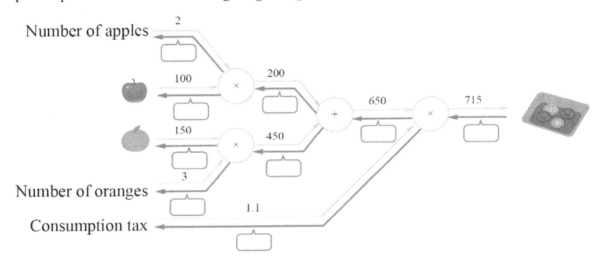

Figure 5.15: Example of backward propagation for purchasing apples and oranges – complete this calculation by putting figures in the squares

Implementing a Simple Layer

In this section, we will implement the apple example we've described in Python using the multiplication node in a computational graph as the **multiplication layer (MulLayer)** and the addition node as the **addition layer (AddLayer)**.

> **Note**
>
> In the next section, we will implement the "layers" that constitute a neural network in one class. The "layer" here is a functional unit in a neural network—the Sigmoid layer for a sigmoid function, and the Affine layer for matrix multiplication. Therefore, we will also implement multiplication and addition nodes here on a "layer" basis.

Implementing a Multiplication Layer

We will implement a layer so that it has two common methods (interfaces): `forward()` and `backward()`, which correspond to forward propagation and backward propagation, respectively. Now, you can implement a multiplication layer as a class called `MulLayer`, as follows (the source code is located at `ch05/layer_naive.py`):

```python
class MulLayer:
    def __init__ (self):
        self.x = None
        self.y = None

    def forward(self, x, y):
        self.x = x
        self.y =y
        out = x * y

        return out

    def backward(self, dout):
        dx = dout * self.y # Reverse x and y
        dy = dout * self.x

        return dx, dy
```

`__init__()` initializes the instance variables, `x`, and `y`, which are used to retain the input values in forward propagation. `forward()` takes two variables, `x` and `y`, and multiplies and outputs their product. On the other hand, `backward()` multiplies the derivative from the upper stream (`dout`) by the "reversed value" of forward propagation and passes the result downstream.

Now, use `MulLayer` to implement the "purchase of apples"–two apples and consumption tax. In the previous section, we used forward and backward propagations in a computational graph for this calculation, as shown in the following diagram:

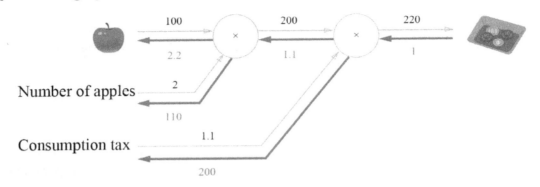

Figure 5.16: Purchasing two apples

By using the multiplication layer, we can implement forward propagation for this as follows (the source code is located at `ch05/buy_apple.py`):

```
apple = 100
apple_num = 2
tax = 1.1

# layer
mul_apple_layer = MulLayer()
mul_tax_layer = MulLayer()

# forward
apple_price = mul_apple_layer.forward(apple, apple_num)
price = mul_tax_layer.forward(apple_price, tax)

print(price) # 220
```

You can use `backward()` to obtain the differential of each variable.

```
# backward
dprice = 1
dapple_price, dtax = mul_tax_layer.backward(dprice)
dapple, dapple_num = mul_apple_layer.backward(dapple_price)
print(dapple, dapple_num, dtax) # 2.2 110 200
```

Here, the order of calling `backward()` is the opposite of that of calling `forward()`. Note that the argument of `backward()` is the "derivative with respect to the output variable in forward propagation." For example, the multiplication layer, `mul_apple_layer`, returns `apple_price` in forward propagation, while it takes the derivative value of `apple_price` (`dapple_price`) as an argument in backward propagation. The execution result of this program matches the result shown in the preceding diagram.

Implementing an Addition Layer

Now, we will implement an addition layer, which is an addition node, as follows:

```
class AddLayer:
    def __init__ (self):
        pass

    def forward(self, x, y):
        out = x + y
        return out

    def backward(self, dout):
        dx = dout * 1
        dy = dout * 1
        return dx, dy
```

An addition layer requires no initialization, so `__init__` () does nothing (the pass statement is "does nothing"). `forward()` in the addition layer takes two arguments, `x` and `y`, and adds them for output. `backward()` passes the differential (`dout`) from the upper stream to the lower stream.

Now, let's use the addition and multiplication layers to implement the purchase of two apples and three oranges, as shown in the following diagram.

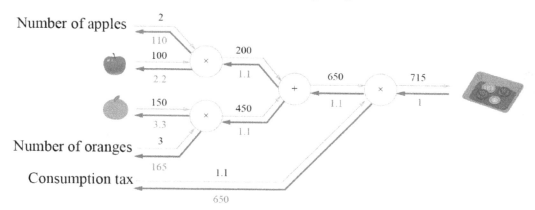

Figure 5.17: Purchasing two apples and three oranges

You can implement this computational graph in Python as follows (the source code is located at ch05/buy_apple_orange.py):

```
apple = 100
apple_num = 2
orange = 150
orange_num = 3
tax = 1.1

# layer
mul_apple_layer = MulLayer()
mul_orange_layer = MulLayer()
add_apple_orange_layer = AddLayer()
mul_tax_layer = MulLayer()

# forward
apple_price = mul_apple_layer.forward(apple, apple_num) #(1)
orange_price = mul_orange_layer.forward(orange, orange_num) #(2)
all_price = add_apple_orange_layer.forward(apple_price, orange_price) #(3)
price = mul_tax_layer.forward(all_price, tax) #(4)

# backward
dprice = 1
dall_price, dtax = mul_tax_layer.backward(dprice) #(4)
dapple_price, dorange_price = add_apple_orange_layer.backward(dall_price)
#(3)
dorange, dorange_num = mul_orange_layer.backward(dorange_price) #(2)
dapple, dapple_num = mul_apple_layer.backward(dapple_price) #(1)

print(price) # 715
print(dapple_num, dapple, dorange, dorange_num, dtax) # 110 2.2 3.3 165
650
```

This implementation is a little long, but each statement is simple. The required layers are created and the forward propagation method, **forward()**, is called in an appropriate order. Then, the backward propagation method, **backward()**, is called in the opposite order to forward propagation to obtain the desired derivatives.

In this way, implementing layers (here, the addition and multiplication layers) in a computational graph are easy, and you can use them to obtain complicated derivatives. Next, we will implement the layers that are used in a neural network.

Implementing the Activation Function Layer

Now, we will apply the idea of a computational graph to a neural network. Here, we will implement the "layers" that constitute a neural network in one class using the ReLU and Sigmoid layers, which are activation functions.

ReLU Layer

A **Rectified Linear Unit (ReLU)** is used as an activation function and is expressed by the following equation (5.7):

$$y = \begin{cases} x & (x > 0) \\ 0 & (x \leq 0) \end{cases} \tag{5.7}$$

From the preceding equation (5.7), you can obtain the derivative of y with respect to x with equation (5.8):

$$\frac{\partial y}{\partial x} = \begin{cases} 1 & (x > 0) \\ 0 & (x \leq 0) \end{cases} \tag{5.8}$$

As equation (5.8) shows, if the input in forward propagation, x, is larger than 0, backward propagation passes the upstream value downstream without changing it. Meanwhile, if x is 0 or smaller in forward propagation, the signal stops there in backward propagation. You can express this in a computational graph, as shown in the following diagram:

Figure 5.18: Computational graph of the ReLU layer

Next, let's implement the ReLU layer. When implementing a layer in a neural network, we assume that **forward()** and **backward()** take NumPy arrays as arguments. The implementation of the ReLU layer is located at **common/layers.py**:

```
class Relu:
    def __init__(self):
        self.mask = None

    def forward(self, x):
        self.mask = (x <= 0)
        out = x.copy()
        out[self.mask] = 0
```

```
        return out

    def backward(self, dout):
        dout[self.mask] = 0
        dx = dout

        return dx
```

The `Relu` class has an instance variable, `mask`. The `mask` variable is a NumPy array that consists of `True`/`False` values. If an element of the input, `x`, in forward propagation is 0 or smaller, the mask's corresponding element is `True`. Otherwise (if it is larger than 0), the element is `False`. For example, the `mask` variable contains a NumPy array that consists of `True` and `False`, as shown in the following code:

```
>>> x = np.array( [[1.0, -0.5], [-2.0, 3.0]] )
>>> print(x)
[[ 1.    -0.5]
 [-2.     3. ]]
>>> mask = (x <= 0)
>>> print(mask)
[[False True]
 [ True False]]
```

As shown in the preceding diagram, the value of backward propagation is 0 when the input value in forward propagation is 0 or smaller. Therefore, in backward propagation, the mask variable stored in forward propagation is used to set `dout` from the upper stream. If an element of the mask is `True`, the corresponding element in `dout` is set to 0.

> **Note**
>
> The ReLU layer works as a "switch" in a circuit. In forward propagation, it turns on the switch if an electric current flows through it, and turns off the switch if an electric current does not flow through it. In backward propagation, the electric current keeps on flowing if the switch is ON and does not flow any longer if the switch is OFF.

Sigmoid Layer

Next, let's implement a sigmoid function. This is expressed by equation (5.9):

$$y = \frac{1}{1 + \exp(-x)} \qquad (5.9)$$

The following diagram shows the computational graph that represents equation (5.9):

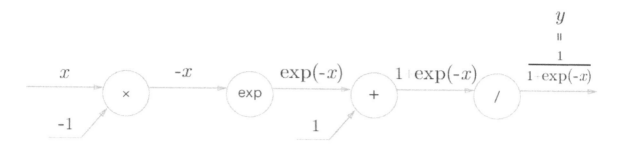

Figure 5.19: Computational graph of the Sigmoid layer (forward propagation only)

Here, the *exp* and / nodes appear in addition to the X and + nodes. The *exp* node calculates $y = exp(x)$, while the / node calculates $y = \frac{1}{x}$.

The calculation of equation (5.9) consists of the propagation of local calculations. Next, let's consider the backward propagation shown in the preceding computational graph, looking at the flow of backward propagation step by step to summarize what we have described so far.

Step 1:

The / node represents $y = \frac{1}{x}$. Its derivative is analytically expressed by the following equation:

$$\frac{\partial y}{\partial x} = -\frac{1}{x^2}$$
$$= -y^2$$

$$(5.10)$$

Based on equation (5.10), in backward propagation, the node multiplies the upstream value by $-y^2$ (the additive inverse of the square of the output in forward propagation) and passes the value to the lower stream. The following computational graph shows this:

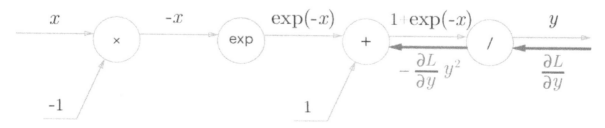

Figure 5.20: Computational graph of the Sigmoid layer (with the additive inverse of the square)

Step 2:

The + node only passes the upstream value to the lower stream. The following computational graph shows this:

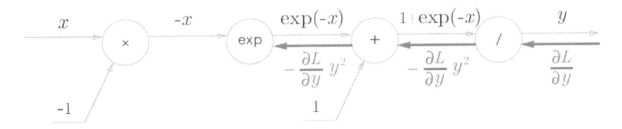

Figure 5.21: Computational graph of the Sigmoid layer (with passing upstream value)

Step 3:

The "exp" node represents $y = exp(x)$, and its derivative is expressed by the following equation:

$$\frac{\partial y}{\partial x} = \exp(x) \tag{5.11}$$

In the following computational graph, the node multiplies the upstream value by the output in forward propagation ($exp(-x)$, in this example) and passes the value to the lower stream:

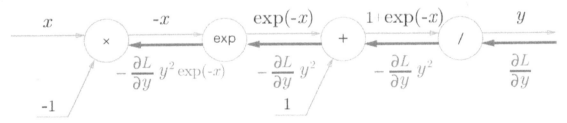

Figure 5.22: Computational graph of the Sigmoid layer

Step 4:

The X node reverses the values in forward propagation for multiplication. Therefore, –1 is multiplied here:

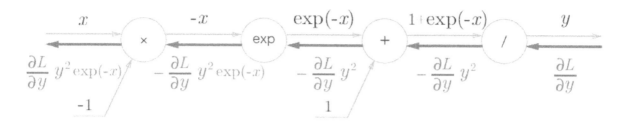

Figure 5.23: Computational graph of the Sigmoid layer (reversed values)

Thus, we can show the backward propagation of the Sigmoid layer in the computational graph shown in the preceding diagram. According to the result of the preceding computational graph, the output of backward propagation is $\frac{\partial L}{\partial y}y^2\exp(-x)$ and it is propagated to the downstream nodes. Note here that $\frac{\partial L}{\partial y}y^2\exp(-x)$ can be calculated from the input, x, and output, y, of forward propagation. Therefore, we can draw the computational graph shown in the preceding diagram as a grouped "sigmoid" node, as follows:

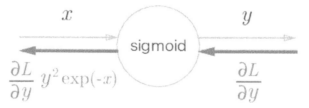

Figure 5.24: Computational graph of the Sigmoid layer (simple version)

The computational graph in *Figure* 5.23 and the simplified computational graph in *Figure* 5.24 provide the same calculation result. The simple version is more efficient because it can omit the intermediate calculation in backward propagation. It is also important to note that you can only concentrate on the input and output, without caring about the details of the Sigmoid layer, by grouping the nodes.

You can also organize $\frac{\partial L}{\partial y} y^2 \exp(-x)$ as follows:

$$
\begin{aligned}
\frac{\partial L}{\partial y} y^2 \exp(-x) &= \frac{\partial L}{\partial y} \frac{1}{(1+\exp(-x))^2} \exp(-x) \\
&= \frac{\partial L}{\partial y} \frac{1}{1+\exp(-x)} \frac{\exp(-x)}{1+\exp(-x)} \\
&= \frac{\partial L}{\partial y} y(1-y)
\end{aligned}
\tag{5.12}
$$

Therefore, you can only calculate the backward propagation in the Sigmoid layer shown in the preceding diagram from the output of forward propagation:

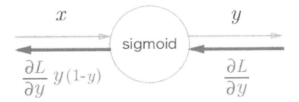

Figure 5.25: Computational graph of the Sigmoid layer – you can use the output, y, of forward propagation to calculate the backward propagation

Now, let's implement the Sigmoid layer in Python. Based on the preceding diagram, you can implement it as follows (this implementation is located at `common/layers.py`):

```python
class Sigmoid:
    def __init__ (self):
        self.out = None

    def forward(self, x):
        out = 1 / (1 + np.exp(-x))
        self.out = out

        return out

    def backward(self, dout):
        dx = dout * (1.0 - self.out) * self.out

        return dx
```

This implementation retains the output of forward propagation in the `out` instance variable, then uses the `out` variable for calculation purposes in backward propagation.

Implementing the Affine and Softmax Layers

Affine Layer

In forward propagation in a neural network, the product of matrices (`np.dot()`, in NumPy) was used to sum the weighted signals (for details, refer to the *Calculating Multidimensional Arrays* section in *Chapter 3, Neural Networks*). For example, do you remember the following implementation in Python?

```
>>> X = np.random.rand(2)  # Input values
>>> W = np.random.rand(2,3)  # Weights
>>> B = np.random.rand(3)  # Biases
>>>
>>> X.shape # (2,)
>>> W.shape # (2, 3)
>>> B.shape # (3,)
>>>
>>> Y = np.dot(X, W) + B
```

Here, assume that `X`, `W`, and `B` are multidimensional arrays of the shape `(2,)`, `(2, 3)`, and `(3,)`, respectively. With this, you can calculate the weighted sum of neurons as `Y = np.dot(X, W) + B`. `Y` is converted by the activation function and propagated to the next layer, which is the flow of forward propagation in a neural network. Note that the number of elements in corresponding dimensions must be the same for matrix multiplication. This means that in the product of `X` and `W`, the number of elements in corresponding dimensions must be the same, as shown in the following image. Here, the shape of a matrix is represented in parentheses as (2, 3) (this is for consistency with the output of NumPy's shape):

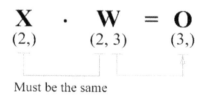

Figure 5.26: The number of elements in corresponding dimensions must be the same for matrix multiplication

> **Note**
>
> The product of matrices in forward propagation in a neural network is called an "affine transformation" in the field of geometry. Therefore, we will implement the process that performs an affine transformation as an "Affine layer."

Now, let's take a look at the calculation—the product of matrices and the sum of biases—in a computational graph. When we represent the node that calculates the product of matrices as "dot," the following computational graph can show the calculation `np.dot(X, W) + B`. Above each variable, the shape of the variable is indicated (for example, the shape of X is (2,) and that of X – W is (3,) are shown here):

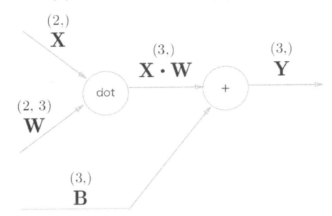

Figure 5.27: Computational graph of the Affine layer. Note that the variables are matrices. Above each variable, the shape of the variable is shown

The preceding is a relatively simple computational graph. However, note that X, W, and B are multidimensional arrays. In the computational graphs we've looked at so far, "scalar values" flow between nodes, while in this example, "multidimensional arrays" propagate between nodes.

Let's think about the backward propagation of the preceding computational graph. To obtain the backward propagation for multidimensional arrays, you can use the same procedure as the previous computational graphs used for scalar values by writing each element of the multidimensional arrays. Doing this, we can obtain the following equation (how we can obtain equation (5.13) is omitted here):

$$\frac{\partial L}{\partial \mathbf{X}} = \frac{\partial L}{\partial \mathbf{Y}} \cdot \mathbf{W}^{\mathrm{T}}$$

$$\frac{\partial L}{\partial \mathbf{W}} = \mathbf{X}^{\mathrm{T}} \cdot \frac{\partial L}{\partial \mathbf{Y}}$$

(5.13)

In equation (5.13), T in W^T indicates transpose. Transpose switches the (i, j) elements of W to the (j, i) elements, shown in the following equation:

$$\mathbf{W} = \begin{pmatrix} w_{11} & w_{12} & w_{13} \\ w_{21} & w_{22} & w_{23} \end{pmatrix}$$

$$\mathbf{W}^{\mathrm{T}} = \begin{pmatrix} w_{11} & w_{21} \\ w_{12} & w_{22} \\ w_{13} & w_{23} \end{pmatrix} \qquad (5.14)$$

As shown in equation (5.14), when the shape of W is (2, 3), the shape of W^T becomes (3, 2).

Based on equation (5.13), let's write backward propagation in the computational graph. The following diagram shows the result:

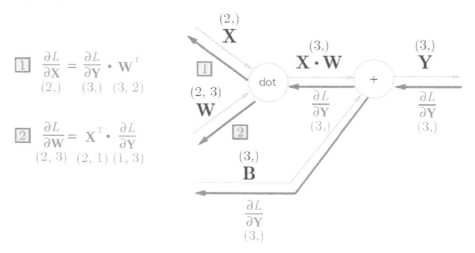

Figure 5.28: Backward propagation of the Affine layer. Note that the variables are matrices. Below each variable, the shape of the variable is shown

Let's consider the shape of each variable carefully. Please note that X and $\frac{\partial L}{\partial X}$ are the same shape, and that W and $\frac{\partial L}{\partial W}$ are the same in terms of shape because of the following equation:

$$\mathbf{X} = (x_0, x_1, \cdots, x_n)$$

$$\frac{\partial L}{\partial \mathbf{X}} = \left(\frac{\partial L}{\partial x_0}, \frac{\partial L}{\partial x_1}, \cdots, \frac{\partial L}{\partial x_n} \right) \qquad (5.15)$$

We pay attention to the shapes of matrices because the number of elements in the corresponding dimensions must be the same for matrix multiplication, and checking that they're the same can lead to equation (5.13). For example, consider the product of $\frac{\partial L}{\partial Y}$ and W so that the shape of $\frac{\partial L}{\partial X}$ becomes (2,) when the shape of $\frac{\partial L}{\partial Y}$ is (3,) and the shape of W is (2,3). Then, equation (5.13) follows. This can be seen in the following diagram:

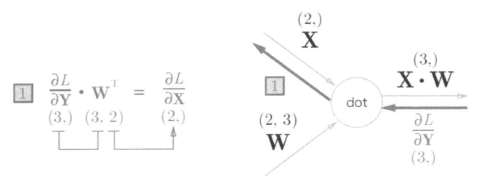

Figure 5.29: Product of matrices (you can create backward propagation of the "dot" node by configuring a product so that the number of elements in the corresponding dimensions is the same in the matrices)

Batch-Based Affine Layer

The Affine layer takes one piece of data as input, X. In this section, we will consider a batch-based Affine layer, which propagates N pieces of data collectively (a group of data is called a "batch"). Let's start by looking at the computational graph of the batch-based Affine layer (*Figure 5.30*).

The only difference from the previous explanation is that the shape of the input, X, is now (N, 2). All we have to do is to calculate the matrices in the computational graph in the same way as we did previously. For backward propagation, we must be careful regarding the shapes of the matrices. Only after that can we obtain $\frac{\partial L}{\partial X}$ and $\frac{\partial L}{\partial W}$ in the same way.

You must be careful when adding bias. When adding biases in forward propagation, a bias is added to each piece of data for X · W. For example, when N = 2 (two pieces of data), biases are added to each of the two pieces of data (to each calculation result). The following diagram shows a specific example of this:

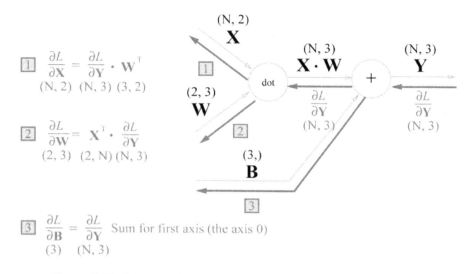

Figure 5.30: Computational graph of the batch-based Affine layer

```
>>> X_dot_W = np.array([[0, 0, 0], [10, 10, 10]])
>>> B = np.array([1, 2, 3])
>>>
>>> X_dot_W
array([[  0,    0,    0],
       [ 10,   10,  10]])
>>> X_dot_W + B
array([[  1,    2,    3],
       [11,   12,  13]])
```

In forward propagation, the biases are added to each piece of data (the first, the second, and so on). Therefore, in backward propagation, the values of each piece of data in backward propagation must be integrated into the elements of biases. The following code shows this:

```
>>> dY = np.array([[1, 2, 3,], [4, 5, 6]])
>>> dY
array([[1,   2,    3],
[4,   5,   6]])
>>>
>>> dB = np.sum(dY, axis=0)
>>> dB
array([5,   7,   9])
```

In this example, we're assuming that there are two pieces of data (N = 2). In backward propagation of biases, the derivatives with respect to the two pieces of data are summed for each piece of data. To do that, `np.sum()` sums the elements of axis 0.

Thus, the implementation of the Affine layer is as follows. The Affine implementation in `common/layers.py` is slightly different from the implementation described here because it considers the case when input data is a tensor (four-dimensional array):

```python
class Affine:
    def __init__(self, W, b):
        self.W = W
        self.b = b
        self.x = None
        self.dW = None
        self.db = None

    def forward(self, x):
        self.x = x
        out = np.dot(x, self.W) + self.b

        return out

    def backward(self, dout):
        dx = np.dot(dout, self.W.T)
        self.dW = np.dot(self.x.T, dout)
        self.db = np.sum(dout, axis=0)

        return dx
```

Softmax-with-Loss Layer

Finally, we should consider a softmax function, which is the output layer. The softmax function normalizes entered values and outputs them (as described earlier). For example, the following diagram shows the output of the Softmax layer for handwritten digit recognition.

As we can see, the Softmax layer normalizes the entered values (meaning it converts them so that the total of the output values is 1) and outputs them. The Softmax layer has 10 inputs because handwritten digit recognition classifies data into 10 classes.

Note

Neural network processing consists of two phases: **inference** and **training**. Usually, inference in a neural network does not use the Softmax layer. For example, for inference in the network shown in the following diagram, the output of the final Affine layer is used as the inference result. The unnormalized output result from a neural network (the output of the Affine layer before the Softmax layer in the following diagram) is sometimes called a "score." To obtain only one answer in neural network inference, you only need to calculate the maximum score, so you do not need a Softmax layer. However, you do need a Softmax layer in neural network training.

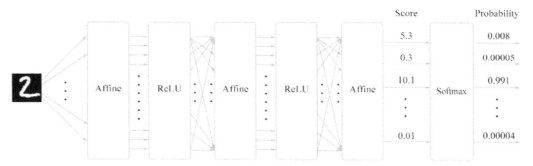

Figure 5.31: The images are converted by the Affine and ReLU layers and 10 input values are normalized by the Softmax layer

In this example, the score for "0" is 5.3, which is converted into 0.008 (0.8%) by the Softmax layer. The score for "2" is 10.1, which is converted into 0.991 (99.1%).

Now, we will implement the "Softmax-with-Loss layer," which also contains a cross-entropy error, which is a loss function. The following diagram shows the computational graph of the Softmax-with-Loss layer (the softmax function and cross-entropy error):

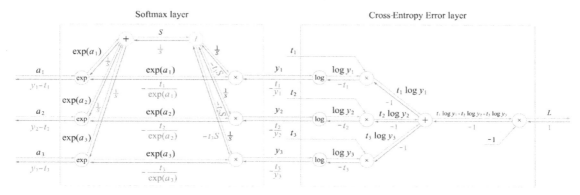

Figure 5.32: Computational graph of the Softmax-with-Loss layer

As you can see, the Softmax-with-Loss layer is slightly complicated. Only the result is shown here. If you are interested in how the Softmax-with-Loss layer is created, refer to the *Computational Graph of the Softmax-with-Loss Layer* section in the *Appendix*.

We can simplify the computational graph shown in the preceding diagram as follows:

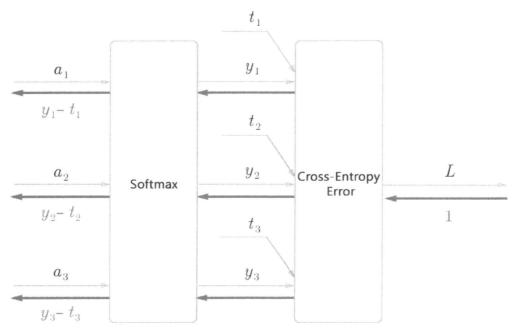

Figure 5.33: "Simplified" computational graph of the Softmax-with-Loss layer

In the preceding computational graph, the Softmax layer indicates the Softmax function, while the Cross-Entropy Error layer indicates the cross-entropy error. Here, we're assuming that the data, which is classified into three classes and three inputs (scores), is received from the previous layer. As we can see, the Softmax layer normalizes the input (a1, a2, a3) and outputs (y1, y2, and y3). The Cross-Entropy Error layer receives the output from Softmax, (y1, y2, y3), and the label, (t1, t2, t3), and outputs the loss, L, based on this data.

Backward propagation from the Softmax layer returns (y1 t1, y2 t2, y3 t3), which is a "clean" result. Because (y1, y2, y3) is the output of the Softmax layer and (t1, t2, t3) is the label, (y1 – t1, y2 – t2, y3 – t3) is the difference between the output of the Softmax layer and the label. When backward propagating a neural network, an error, which is the difference, is passed to the previous layer. This characteristic is important when training a neural network.

Note that the purpose of neural network training is to adjust weight parameters so that the neural network's output (output of Softmax) approaches the label. To do that, we need to pass the error between the neural network's output and the label to the previous layer in an efficient manner. The previous result, (y1 – t1, y2 – t2, y3 – t3), is exactly the difference between the output of the Softmax layer and the label, and clearly shows the current error between the neural network's output and the label.

When we use a "cross-entropy error" as the loss function for the "softmax function," backward propagation returns a "pretty" result, (y1 – t1, y2 – t2, y3 – t3). This "pretty" result is not accidental. A function that calls a cross-entropy error is designed to do this. In a regression problem, an "identity function" is used for the output layer, and the "sum of squared errors" is used as the loss function (refer to the *Designing the Output Layer* section of *Chapter 3, Neural Networks*) for the same reason. When we use the sum of squared errors as the loss function of an "identity function", backward propagation provides a "pretty" result, (y1 – t1, y2 – t2, y3 – t3).

Let's consider a specific example here. Say that, for one piece of data, the label is (0, 1, 0) and the output of the Softmax layer is (0.3, 0.2, 0.5). At this time, the neural network does not recognize it correctly because the probability of it being the correct label is 0.2 (20%). Here, backward propagating from the Softmax layer propagates a large error, (0.3, –0.8, 0.5). Because this large error propagates to the previous layers, the layers before the Softmax layer learn a lot from the large error.

As another example, let's assume that, for one piece of data, the label is (0, 1, 0) and the output of the Softmax layer is (0.01, 0.99, 0) (this neural network recognizes quite accurately). In this case, backward propagating from the Softmax layer propagates a small error, (0.01, –0.01, 0). This small error propagates to the previous layers. The layers before the Softmax layer learn only small pieces of information because the error is small.

Now, let's implement the Softmax-with-Loss layer. You can implement the Softmax-with-Loss layer as follows:

```
class SoftmaxWithLoss:
    def __init__(self):
        self.loss = None # Loss
        self.y = None   # Output of softmax
        self.t = None   # Label data (one-hot vector)

    def forward(self, x, t):
        self.t = t
        self.y = softmax(x)
        self.loss = cross_entropy_error(self.y, self.t)
```

```
        return self.loss

    def backward(self, dout=1):
        batch_size = self.t.shape[0]
        dx = (self.y - self.t) / batch_size

        return dx
```

This implementation uses the **softmax()** and **cross_entropy_error()** functions. They were implemented in the sub-section, *Issues when Implementing the Softmax Function*, of *Chapter 3, Neural networks* and sub-section, *Implementing Cross-Entropy Error (Using Batches)*, of *Chapter 4, Neural Network Training*. Therefore, the implementation here is very easy. Note that the error per data propagates to the previous layers in backward propagation because the value of propagation is divided by the number of batches (**batch_size**).

Implementing Backpropagation

You can build a neural network by combining the layers implemented in the previous sections as if you were assembling Lego blocks. Here, we will build a neural network by combining the layers we've implemented so far.

Overall View of Neural Network Training

Because my description was a little long, let's check the overall view of neural network training again before proceeding with its implementation. Now we will take a look at the procedure for neural network training.

Presupposition

A neural network has adaptable weights and biases. Adjusting them so that they fit the training data is called "training." Neural network training consists of the following four steps:

Step 1 (mini-batch):

Select some data at random from the training data.

Step 2 (calculating the gradients):

Obtain the gradient of the loss function for each weight parameter.

Step 3 (updating the parameters):

Update the parameters slightly in the gradient's direction.

Step 4 (repeating):

Repeat steps 1, 2, and 3.

Backpropagation occurs in *Step 2, Calculating the gradients*. In the previous chapter, we used numerical differentiation to obtain a gradient. Numerical differentiation is easy to implement, but calculation takes a lot of time. If we use backpropagation, we can obtain a gradient much more quickly and efficiently.

Implementing a Neural Network That Supports Backpropagation

In this section, we will implement a two-layer neural network called `TwoLayerNet`. First, we will look at the instance variables and methods of this class in *Tables 5.1 and 5.2*.

The implementation of this class is a little long but has many sections in common with the implementation as in the *Implementing a Training Algorithm* section, of *Chapter 4, Neural Network Training*. A large change from the previous chapter is that layers are being used here. If you use layers, you can obtain recognition results (`predict( )`) and gradients (`gradient( )`) by propagating between the layers:

Instance variable	Description
params	A dictionary variable that contains the parameters of the neural network. `params['W1']` is the weights for layer 1, while `params['b1']` is the biases for layer 1. `params['W2']` is the weights for layer 2, while `params['b2']` is the biases for layer 2.
layers	An **ordered dictionary** variable that contains the parameters of the neural network layers. An **ordered dictionary** such as `layers['Affine1']`, `layers['Relu1']`, and `layers['Affine2']` retains each layer.
lastLayer	The last layer of the neural network. In this example, it is the `SoftmaxWithLoss` layer.

Table 5.1: Instance variables in the TwoLayerNet class

Method	Description
`__init__ (self, input_size, hidden_size, output_size, weight_init_std)`	Initializes the arguments. The arguments are the numbers of neurons in the input layer, in the hidden layer, and the output layer, and the scale of the Gaussian distribution at weight initialization, in order from left to right.
`predict(self, x)`	Conducts recognition (makes a prediction). Argument **x** is the image data.
`loss(self, x, t)`	Obtains the value of the loss function. Argument **x** is the image data, while argument **t** is the label.
`accuracy(self, x, t)`	Obtains the recognition accuracy.
`numerical_gradient(self, x, t)`	Uses numerical differentiation to obtain the gradient for the weight parameters (the same as in the previous chapter).
`gradient(self, x, t)`	Uses backpropagation to obtain the gradient for the weight parameters.

Table 5.2: Methods in the TwoLayerNet class

Now, let's implement `TwoLayerNet`:

```python
import sys, os
sys.path.append(os.pardir)
import numpy as np
from common.layers import *
from common.gradient import numerical_gradient
from collections import OrderedDict

class TwoLayerNet:
    def __init__ (self, input_size, hidden_size, output_size,
            weight_init_std=0.01):
    # Initialize weights
    self.params = {}
    self.params['W1'] = weight_init_std * \
                np.random.randn(input_size, hidden_size)
    self.params['b1'] = np.zeros(hidden_size)
    self.params['W2'] = weight_init_std * \
                np.random.randn(hidden_size, output_size)
    self.params['b2'] = p.zeros(output_size)

    # Create layers
    self.layers = OrderedDict( )
```

```python
self.layers['Affine1'] = \
    Affine(self.params['W1'], self.params['b1'])
self.layers['Relu1'] = Relu( )
self.layers['Affine2'] = \
Affine(self.params['W2'], self.params['b2'])

self.lastLayer = SoftmaxWithLoss( )

def predict(self, x):
    for layer in self.layers.values( ):
        x = layer.forward(x)

    return x

# x: input data, t: label data
def loss(self, x, t):
    y = self.predict(x)
    return self.lastLayer.forward(y, t)

def accuracy (self, x, t):
    y = self.predict(x)
    y = np.argmax(y, axis=1)
    if t.ndim != 1 : t = np.argmax(t, axis=1)

    accuracy = np.sum(y == t) / float(x.shape[0])
    return accuracy

# x: input data, t: teacher data
def numerical_gradient(self, x, t):
    loss_W = lambda W: self.loss(x, t)

    grads = {}
    grads['W1'] = numerical_gradient(loss_W, self.params['W1'])
    grads['b1'] = numerical_gradient(loss_W, self.params['b1'])
    grads['W2'] = numerical_gradient(loss_W, self.params['W2'])
    grads['b2'] = numerical_gradient(loss_W, self.params['b2'])

    return grads

def gradient(self, x, t):
    # forward
```

```
        self.loss(x, t)

        # backward
        dout = 1
        dout = self.lastLayer.backward(dout)

        layers = list(self.layers.values( ))
        layers.reverse( )
        for layer in layers:
            dout = layer.backward(dout)

        # Settings
        grads = {}
        grads['W1'] = self.layers['Affine1'].dW
        grads['b1'] = self.layers['Affine1'].db
        grads['W2'] = self.layers['Affine2'].dW
        grads['b2'] = self.layers['Affine2'].db

        return grads
```

Note the code in bold here. Retaining a neural network layer as `OrderedDict` (i,e, an ordered dictionary) is especially important, as it means that the dictionary can remember the order of the elements added to it. Therefore, in forward propagation in the neural network, you can complete processing by calling the `forward()` method of the layer in the order of addition. In backward propagation, you only have to call the layers in reverse order. The Affine and ReLU layers internally process forward propagation and backward propagation properly. So, all you have to do is combine the layers in the correct order and call them in order (or in reverse order).

Thus, by implementing the components of the neural network as "layers," you can build the neural network easily. The advantage of modular implementation using "layers" is enormous. If you want to create a large network containing five, 10, or 20 layers, you can create it by adding the required layers (as if you were assembling Lego blocks). In this way, the gradients required for recognition and learning are obtained properly by forward propagation and backward propagation being implemented in each layer.

Gradient Check

So far, we have seen two methods for calculating a gradient. One of them uses numerical differentiation, while the other solves the equation analytically. The latter method enables efficient calculation by using backpropagation, even if many parameters exist. Therefore, we'll be using backpropagation instead of slow numerical differentiation to calculate a gradient from now on.

Numerical differentiation takes time to calculate. If the correct implementation of backpropagation exists, we do not need the implementation of numerical differentiation. So, what is numerical differentiation useful for? The fact is that numerical differentiation is required to check whether the implementation of backpropagation is correct.

The advantage of numerical differentiation is that it is easy to implement, making mistakes infrequent compared to the far more complicated backpropagation. So, the result of numerical differentiation is often compared with that of backpropagation to check whether the implementation of backpropagation is correct. The process of this verification is called a **gradient check**. The following code shows the implementation of a gradient check (the source code is located at ch05/**gradient_check.py**):

```python
import sys, os
sys.path.append(os.pardir)
import numpy as np
from dataset.mnist import load_mnist
from two_layer_net import TwoLayerNet

# Load data
(x_train, t_train), (x_test, t_test) = \
    load_mnist(normalize=True, one_hot_label=True)

network = TwoLayerNet(input_size=784, hidden_size=50, output_size=10)
x_batch = x_train[:3]
t_batch = t_train[:3]

grad_numerical = network.numerical_gradient(x_batch, t_batch)
grad_backprop = network.gradient(x_batch, t_batch)
```

```
# Calculate the average of the absolute errors of individual weights
for key in grad_numerical.keys( ):
    diff = np.average( np.abs(grad_backprop[key] - grad_numerical[key]) )
    print(key + ":" + str(diff))
```

Here, the MNIST dataset is loaded as usual. Next, part of the training data is used to check the error between the gradient by numerical differentiation and that of backpropagation. As the error, the absolute values of the differences between the elements in the individual weight parameters are averaged. When the preceding code is executed, the following result is returned:

```
b1:9.70418809871e-13
W2:8.41139039497e-13
b2:1.1945999745e-10
W1:2.2232446644e-13
```

The result shows that the differences between the gradients by numerical differentiation and those by backpropagation are quite small. Case in point, the error of the biases for layer 1 is `9.7e-13` `(0.00000000000097)`. This indicates that the gradient by backpropagation is also correct and improves the reliability of its accuracy.

The error between the calculation result of numerical differentiation and that of backpropagation rarely becomes 0. This is because the accuracy of the calculations that are performed by a computer is finite (for example, 32-bit floating-point numbers are used). Because the numerical precision is limited, the error is not usually 0. However, if the implementation is correct, the error is expected to be a small value near 0. If the value is large, the implementation of backpropagation is incorrect.

Training Using Backpropagation

Lastly, we will see how we can implement neural network training using backpropagation. The only difference is that gradients are calculated via backpropagation. We will only see the code and omit the description (the source code is located at **ch05/train_neuralnet.py**):

```python
import sys, os
sys.path.append(os.pardir)
import numpy as np
from dataset.mnist import load_mnist
from two_layer_net import TwoLayerNet
```

```python
# Load data
(x_train, t_train), (x_test, t_test) = \
    load_mnist(normalize=True, one_hot_label=True)
network = TwoLayerNet(input_size=784, hidden_size=50, output_size=10)

iters_num = 10000
train_size = x_train.shape[0]
batch_size = 100
learning_rate = 0.1

train_loss_list = [ ]
train_acc_list = [ ]
test_acc_list = [ ]

iter_per_epoch = max(train_size / batch_size, 1)

for i in range(iters_num):
    batch_mask = np.random.choice(train_size, batch_size)
    x_batch = x_train[batch_mask]
    t_batch = t_train[batch_mask]

    # Use backpropagation to obtain a gradient
    grad = network.gradient(x_batch, t_batch)

    # Update
    for key in ('W1', 'b1', 'W2', 'b2'):
        network.params[key] -= learning_rate * grad[key]

    loss = network.loss(x_batch, t_batch)
    train_loss_list.append(loss)

if i % iter_per_epoch == 0:
    train_acc = network.accuracy(x_train, t_train)
    test_acc = network.accuracy(x_test, t_test)
    train_acc_list.append(train_acc)
    test_acc_list.append(test_acc)
    print(train_acc, test_acc)
```

Summary

In this chapter, we learned about computational graphs, which show calculation processes visually. We looked at a computational graph that described backpropagation in a neural network and implemented processing in a neural network with layers, including the ReLU layer, Softmax-with-Loss layer, Affine layer, and Softmax layer. These layers have forward and backward methods and can calculate the gradients of weight parameters efficiently by propagating data both forward and backward in direction. By using layers as modules, you can combine them freely in a neural network so that you can build the desired network easily. The following points were covered in this chapter:

- We can use computational graphs to show calculation processes visually.

- A node in a computational graph consists of local calculations. Local calculations constitute the whole calculation.

- Performing forward propagation in a computational graph leads to a regular calculation. Meanwhile, performing backward propagation in a computational graph can calculate the differential of each node.

- By implementing components in a neural network as layers, you can calculate gradients efficiently (backpropagation).

- By comparing the results of numerical differentiation and backpropagation, you can check that the implementation of backpropagation is correct (gradient check).

6

Training Techniques

This chapter describes important ideas in neural network training, including the optimization techniques that are used to search for optimal weight parameters, the initial values of weight parameters, and the method for setting hyperparameters—all of which are important topics when it comes to neural network training. We will look at regularization methods such as weight decay and dropout to prevent overfitting and implement them. Lastly, we will look at batch normalization, which has been used in a lot of research in recent years. By using the methods described in this chapter, you will be able to promote neural network training efficiently to improve recognition accuracy.

Updating Parameters

The purpose of neural network training is to find the parameters that minimize the value of the loss function. The problem is finding the optimal parameters—a process called **optimization**. Unfortunately, the optimization is difficult because the parameter space is very complicated, and the optimal solution is difficult to find. You cannot do this by solving an equation to obtain the minimum value immediately. In a deep network, it is more difficult because the number of parameters is huge.

So far, we have depended on the gradients (derivatives) of the parameters to find the optimal parameters. By repeatedly using the gradients of the parameters to update the parameters in the gradient direction, we approach the optimal parameters gradually. This is a simple method called **stochastic gradient descent** (**SGD**), but it is a "smarter" method than searching the parameter space randomly. However, SGD is a simple method, and (for some problems) there are some methods that work better. So, let's first consider the disadvantage of SGD and introduce other optimization techniques.

Story of an Adventurer

Before moving on to the main topic, we can consider an allegory to describe the situation we are in regarding optimization.

> **Note**
>
> There is a strange adventurer. He travels through a vast dry region to find a deep valley floor every day. His goal is to reach the deepest valley bottom, which he calls the "deep place." It is the reason why he travels. In addition, he has put two strict "restrictions" on himself. One of them is to not use a map, while the other is to cover his eyes. Therefore, he does not know where the deepest valley bottom exists in the vast land, and he cannot see anything. Under these strict conditions, how can this adventurer look for the "deep place"? How can he move to find the "deep place" efficiently?

The situation we are in when searching for the optimal parameters is a world of darkness just like that of this adventurer. We must look for the "deep place" blindfolded and without a map in a vast and complicated landscape

What is important in this difficult situation is the "inclination" of the ground. The adventurer cannot see around him, but he knows the inclination of the ground due to where he stands (his feet can feel it). So, moving in the direction where the inclination is the steepest is the strategy of SGD. "By repeating this, I may be able to reach the "deep place" someday," the brave adventurer thinks.

SGD

Now that we understand the difficulty of this optimization problem, let's start by reviewing SGD. Equation 6.1 represents SGD as follows:

$$\mathbf{W} \leftarrow \mathbf{W} - \eta \frac{\partial L}{\partial \mathbf{W}} \qquad (6.1)$$

Here, the weight parameters to update are W and the gradients of the loss function for W are $\frac{\partial L}{\partial W}$. η is the learning rate. We need to predefine it as a value, such as 0.01 or 0.001. <- in the equation indicates that the value on the right-hand side is used to update the value on the left-hand side. As equation 6.1 shows, SGD is a simple method that moves a certain distance in the gradient direction. Now, we will implement SGD as a class in Python:

```
class SGD:
    def __init__ (self, lr=0.01):
        self.lr = lr

    def update(self, params, grads):
        for key in params.keys():
            params[key] -= self.lr * grads[key]
```

Here, the argument at initialization, `lr`, is the learning rate. The learning rate is retained as an instance variable. We will also define the `update(params, grads)` method, which is called repeatedly in SGD. The arguments, `params` and `grads`, are dictionary variables (as in the implementation of neural networks so far). Like `params['W1']` and `grads['W1']`, each element stores a weight parameter or a gradient. By using the SGD class, you can update the parameters in a neural network as follows (the following code is pseudocode that doesn't run):

```
network = TwoLayerNet(...)
optimizer = SGD()

for i in range(10000):
    ...
    x_batch, t_batch = get_mini_batch(...)   # Mini-batch
    grads = network.gradient(x_batch, t_batch)
    params = network.params
    optimizer.update(params, grads)
    ...
```

The name of the variable that appears here, `optimizer`, means a "person who optimizes." Here, SGD plays this role. The `optimizer` variable takes responsibility for updating the parameters. All we need to do here is pass information regarding the parameters and gradients to the optimizer.

Thus, separately implementing the class that optimizes facilitates the modularization of the features. For example, we will soon implement another optimization technique called **Momentum** so that it has a common method called `update(params, grads)`. Then, we can switch from SGD to Momentum by changing the `optimizer = SGD()` statement to `optimizer = Momentum()`.

> **Note**
>
> In many deep learning frameworks, various optimization techniques are implemented, and a mechanism is provided so that we can switch between them easily. For example, in a deep learning framework called Lasagne, optimization techniques are implemented as functions in the `updates.py` file (http://github. com/Lasagne/Lasagne/blob/master/lasagne/updates.py). The user can select the desired optimization technique from them.

Disadvantage of SGD

Although SGD is simple and easy to implement, it may be inefficient for some problems. To discuss the disadvantage of SGD, let's consider a problem that calculates the minimum value of the following function:

$$f(x, y) = \frac{1}{20}x^2 + y^2 \qquad (6.2)$$

The shape of the function represented by equation 6.2 looks like a "bowl" stretched in the x-axis direction, as shown in the following plots. Actually, the contour lines of equation 6.2 look like ellipses extended in the x-axis direction.

Now, let's look at the gradients of the function that are represented by equation 6.2. *Figure* 6.2 shows the gradients. These gradients are large in the y-axis direction and small in the x-axis direction. In other words, the inclination in the y-axis direction is steep, while in the x-axis direction, it's gradual. Note that the position of the minimum value of equation 6.2 is `(x, y) = (0, 0)` but that the gradients in *Figure* 6.2 do not point to the (0, 0) direction in many places.

Let's apply SGD to the function that has the shape shown in the following plots. It starts searching at $(x, y) = (-7.0, 2.0)$ (initial values). *Figure 6.3* shows the result:

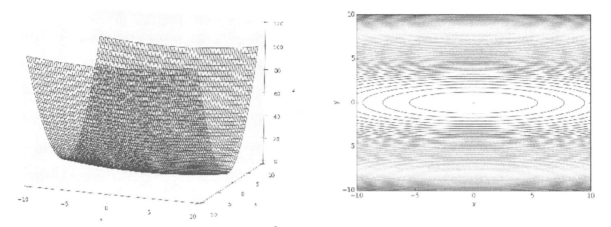

Figure 6.1: Graph of $f(x, y) = \frac{1}{20}x^2 + y^2$ (left) and its contour lines (right)

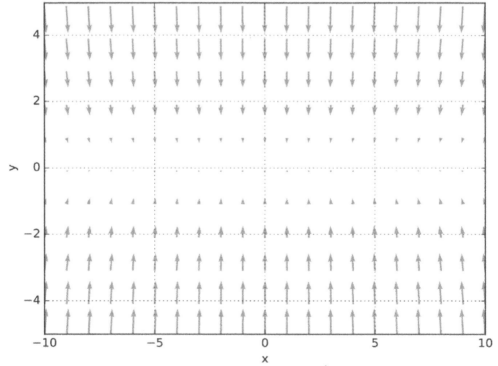

Figure 6.2: Gradients of $f(x, y) = \frac{1}{20}x^2 + y^2$

SGD moves in a zigzag, as shown in the following plot. The disadvantage of SGD is that its search path becomes inefficient if the shape of a function is not isotropic—that is, if it is elongated. So, we need a method that is smarter than SGD that moves only in the gradient direction. The root cause of SGD's search path being inefficient is that the gradients do not point to the correct minimum values:

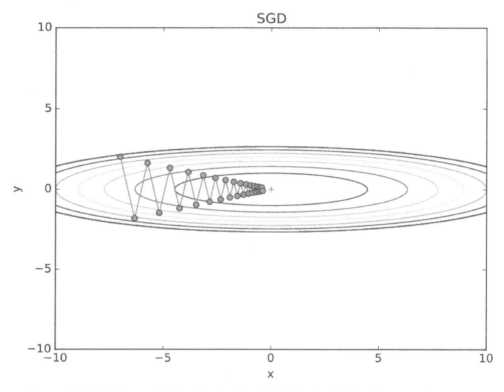

Figure 6.3: Update path of optimization by SGD – inefficient because it moves in a zigzag to the minimum value (0, 0)

To improve the disadvantage of SGD, we will introduce three alternative methods: Momentum, AdaGrad, and Adam. We will describe each of them briefly and show their equations and implementations in Python.

Momentum

Momentum is related to physics; it means the "quantity of motion." The Momentum technique is represented by the following equations:

$$\mathbf{v} \leftarrow \alpha \mathbf{v} - \eta \frac{\partial L}{\partial \mathbf{W}} \quad (6.3)$$

$$\mathbf{W} \leftarrow \mathbf{W} + \mathbf{v} \quad (6.4)$$

Just like SGD, W is the weight parameter to update, $\frac{\partial L}{\partial W}$ is the gradients of the loss function for W, and η is the learning rate. A new variable that appears here, v, is the "velocity" in physics. Equation 6.3 represents a physical law stating that an object receives a force in the gradient direction and is accelerated by this force. In Momentum, update functions are used as if a ball had been rolled on the ground, as shown in the following diagram:

Figure 6.4: Image of Momentum – a ball rolls on the slope of the ground

The term αv in equation 6.3 slows the object down gradually when it receives no force (a value such as 0.9 is set for α). This is the friction created by the ground or air resistance. The following code shows the implementation of Momentum (the source code is located at `common/optimizer.py`):

```python
class Momentum:
    def __init__(self, lr=0.01, momentum=0.9):
        self.lr = lr
        self.momentum = momentum
        self.v = None

    def update(self, params, grads):
        if self.v is None:
        self.v = {}
        for key, val in params.items():
            self.v[key] = np.zeros_like(val)

        for key in params.keys():
            self.v[key] = self.momentum*self.v[key] - self.lr*grads[key]
            params[key] += self.v[key]
```

The instance variable, **v**, retains the velocity of the object. At initialization, **v** retains nothing. When **update()** is called, it retains the data of the same structure as a dictionary variable. The remaining implementation is simple: it just implements equations 6.3 and 6.4.

Now, let's use Momentum to solve the optimization problem of equation 6.2. The following image shows the result.

As shown in the following plot, the update path moves like a ball being rolled around in a bowl. You can see that "the degree of zigzag" is reduced compared to SGD. The force in the x-axis direction is very small, but the object always receives the force in the same direction and is accelerated constantly in the same direction. On the other hand, the force in the y-axis direction is large, but the object receives the forces in the positive and negative directions alternately. They cancel each other out, so the velocity in the y-axis direction is unstable. This can accelerate the motion in the x-axis direction and reduce the zigzag motion compared to SGD:

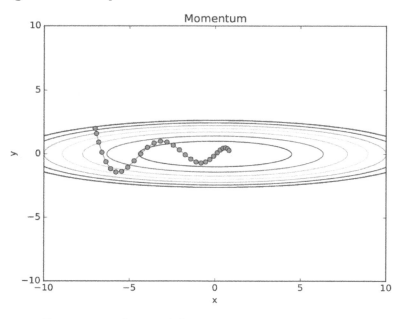

Figure 6.5: Update path for optimization by Momentum

AdaGrad

In neural network training, the value of the learning `rate--η` in the `equation--` is important. If it is too small, training takes too long. If it is too large, divergence occurs, and correct training cannot be achieved.

There is an effective technique for the learning rate called **learning rate decay**. It uses a lower learning rate as training advances. This method is often used in neural network training. A neural network learns "much" first and learns "less" gradually.

Reducing the learning rate gradually is the same as reducing the values of the learning rates for all the parameters collectively. AdaGrad (*John Duchi, Elad Hazan, and Yoram Singer (2011): Adaptive Subgradient Methods for Online Learning and Stochastic Optimization. Journal of Machine Learning Research 12, Jul (2011), 2121 – 2159.*) is an advanced version of this method. AdaGrad creates a custom-made value for each parameter.

AdaGrad adjusts the learning rate for each element of the parameter adaptively for training (the "Ada" in AdaGrad comes from "Adaptive"). Now, we will show AdaGrad's update method with equations:

$$\mathbf{h} \leftarrow \mathbf{h} + \frac{\partial L}{\partial \mathbf{W}} \odot \frac{\partial L}{\partial \mathbf{W}} \qquad (6.5)$$

$$\mathbf{W} \leftarrow \mathbf{W} - \eta \frac{1}{\sqrt{\mathbf{h}}} \frac{\partial L}{\partial \mathbf{W}} \qquad (6.6)$$

Just like SGD, W is the weight parameters to update, $\frac{\partial L}{\partial W}$ is the gradients of the loss function for W, and η is the learning rate. Here, a new variable, h, appears. The h variable stores the sum of the squared gradient values thus far, as shown in equation 6.5 ($\odot$ in equation 6.5 indicates multiplication between array elements). When updating parameters, AdaGrad adjusts the scale of learning by multiplying $\frac{1}{\sqrt{h}}$. For the parameter element that moved significantly (i.e., was updated heavily), the learning rate becomes smaller. Thus, you can attenuate the learning rate for each parameter element by gradually reducing the learning rate of the parameter that moved significantly.

> **Note**
>
> AdaGrad records all the past gradients as the sum of squares. Therefore, as learning advances, the degree of update becomes small. When learning is conducted infinitely, the degree of update becomes 0, resulting in no update. The RMSProp (*Tieleman, T., & Hinton, G. (2012): Lecture 6.5—RMSProp: Divide the gradient by a running average of its recent magnitude. COURSERA: Neural Networks for Machine Learning*) method solves this problem. It does not add all the past gradients equally. It forgets the past gradients gradually and conducts addition so that the information about new gradients is clearly reflected. This reduces the scale of the past gradients exponentially, which is called the "exponential moving average."

Now, let's implement AdaGrad. You can implement AdaGrad as follows (the source code is located at `common/optimizer.py`):

```
class AdaGrad:
    def __init__ (self, lr=0.01):
        self.lr = lr
        self.h = None

    def update(self, params, grads):
        if self.h is None:
            self.h = {}
```

```
        for key, val in params.items():
            self.h[key] = np.zeros_like(val)

    for key in params.keys():
        self.h[key] += grads[key] * grads[key]
        params[key] -= self.lr * grads[key] / (np.sqrt(self.h[key]) + 1e-7)
```

Note that a small value of `1e-7` was added in the last line. This prevents division by 0 when `self.h[key]` contains 0. In many deep learning frameworks, you can configure this small value as a parameter, but here, a fixed value, `1e-7`, is used.

Now, let's use AdaGrad to solve the optimization problem of equation 6.2. The following image shows the result:

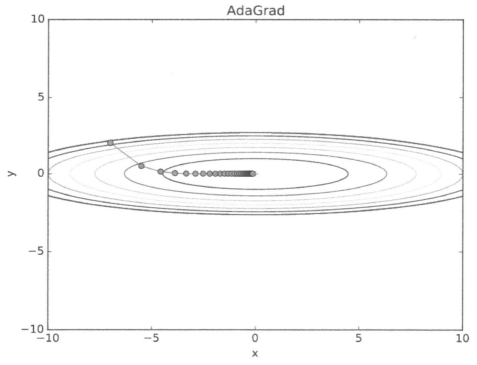

Figure 6.6: Update path for optimization by AdaGrad

The result shown in the preceding image shows that the parameters are moving efficiently to the minimum value. The parameters move a lot at first because the gradient in the y-axis direction is large. Adjustment is conducted in proportion to the large motion so that the update step becomes small. Thus, the degree of update in the y-axis direction is weakened, reducing the zigzag motion.

Adam

In Momentum, the parameters move based on physical law, such as a ball rolled in a bowl. AdaGrad adjusts the update step adaptively for each parameter element. So, what happens when the two techniques, Momentum and AdaGrad, are combined? This is the basic idea of the technique called Adam (this explanation of Adam is intuitive and lacking some of the finer technical details. For a more granular definition, please see the original article).

Adam is a new technique that was proposed in 2015. The theory is slightly complicated. Intuitively, it is like a combination of Momentum and AdaGrad. By combining the advantages of these two techniques, we can expect to search the parameter space efficiently. The "bias correction" of hyperparameters is also a characteristic of Adam. For more details, please see the original paper (*Diederik Kingma and Jimmy Ba. (2014): Adam: A Method for Stochastic Optimization. arXiv:1412.6980[cs] (December 2014)*). It is implemented in Python as the `Adam` class in `common/optimizer.py`.

Now, let's use Adam to solve the optimization problem of equation 6.2. The following figure shows the result.

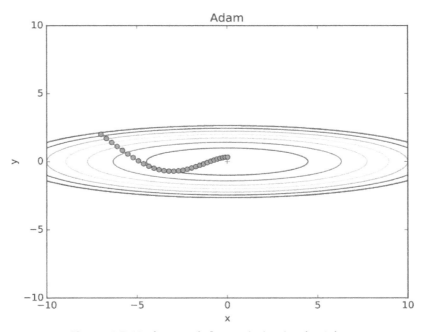

Figure 6.7: Update path for optimization by Adam

As shown in *Figure* 6.7, the update path by Adam moves as if a ball has been rolled in a bowl. The motion is similar to that in Momentum, but the left and right motions of the ball are smaller. This advantage is caused by the adaptive adjustment of the learning rate.

Note

Adam has three hyperparameters. The first is the learning rate (appearing as α in the paper). The others are the coefficient for the primary moment, β_1, and the coefficient for the secondary moment, β_2. The article states that the standard values are 0.9 for β_1 and 0.999 for β_2, which are effective in many cases.

Which Update Technique Should We Use?

We have considered four-parameter updating techniques so far. Here, we will compare their results (the source code is located at `ch06/optimizer_compare_naive.py`).

As shown in *Figure 6.8*, different techniques use different paths to update the parameters. This image seems to show that AdaGrad is the best, but note that the results vary depending on the problems being solved. Naturally, the results also vary depending on the values of the hyperparameters (such as the learning rate):

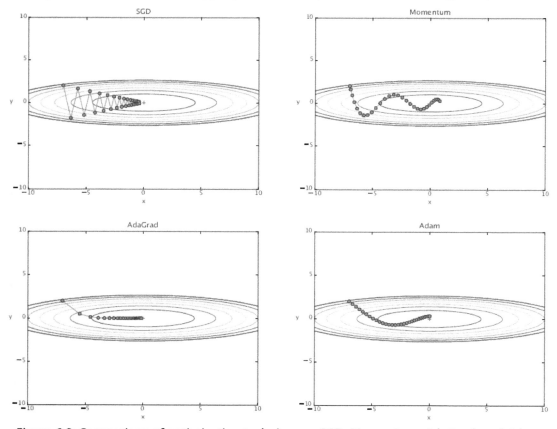

Figure 6.8: Comparison of optimization techniques – SGD, Momentum, AdaGrad, and Adam

So far, we have looked at four techniques: SGD, Momentum, AdaGrad, and Adam. But which should we use? Unfortunately, there is no one technique currently known that is good at solving all problems. Each has its own distinct characteristics and advantages, which make it better suited to certain problems over others. Therefore, it's important to know which technique works best given a specific set of circumstances.

SGD is still used in a lot of research. Momentum and AdaGrad are also worth trying. Recently, many researchers and engineers seem to prefer Adam. This book mainly uses SGD and Adam. You can try the other techniques as you like.

Using the MNIST Dataset to Compare the Update Techniques

For handwritten digit recognition, we will compare the four techniques we've described so far: SGD, Momentum, AdaGrad, and Adam. Let's explore how each technique works in the progress of training. *Figure 6.9* shows the results (the source code is located at `h06/optimizer_compare_mnist.py`):

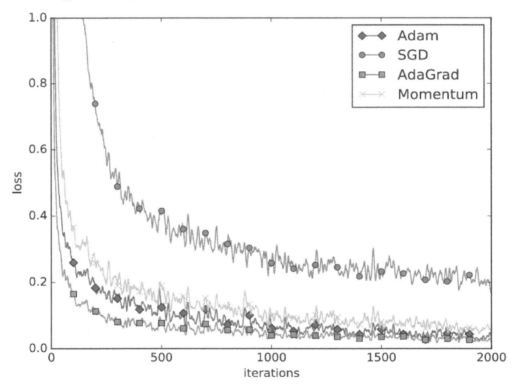

Figure 6.9: Using the MNIST dataset to compare the four update techniques – the horizontal axis indicates the iterations of learning, while the vertical axis indicates the values of the loss function

This experiment used a five-layer neural network, and each layer had 100 neurons. ReLU was used as the activation function.

The result of *Figure* 6.9 shows that other techniques learned faster than SGD. It seems that the remaining three techniques learned similarly quickly. When we look closer, it seems that AdaGrad learned a little faster. In this experiment, note that the results are different depending on the hyperparameter of the learning rate and the structure of the neural network (the number of layers). However, generally, the other three techniques can learn faster than SGD and sometimes achieve better final recognition performance.

Initial Weight Values

The initial weight values are especially important in neural network training. What values are set as the initial weight values often determines the success or failure of neural network training. In this section, we will explain the recommended initial weight values, then conduct an experiment to check that they accelerate neural network learning.

How About Setting the Initial Weight Values to 0?

Later, we will look at a technique called weight decay, which reduces overfitting and improves generalization performance. In short, weight decay is a technique that reduces the values of the weight parameters to prevent overfitting.

If we want the weights to be small, starting with the smallest possible initial values is probably a good approach. Here, we use an initial weight value such as `0.01 * np.random.randn(10, 100)`. This small value is the value generated from the Gaussian distribution multiplied by 0.01–a Gaussian distribution with a standard deviation of 0.01.

If we want the weight values to be small, how about setting all the initial weight values to 0? This is a bad idea as it prevents us from training correctly.

Why should the initial weight values not be 0? Or in other words, why should the weights not be uniform values? Well, because all weight values are updated uniformly (in the same way) in backpropagation. So, say that layers 1 and 2 have 0 as their weights in a two-layer neural network. Then, in forward propagation, the same value is propagated to all the neurons in layer 2 because the weight of the input layer is 0. When the same values are entered for all the neurons in layer 2, all the weights in layer 2 are updated similarly in backward propagation (please remember "backward propagation in a multiplication node"). Therefore, the weights are updated with the same value and become symmetrical values (duplicate values). Due to this, there is no meaning in having many weights. To prevent the weights from being uniform or breaking their symmetrical structure, random initial values are required.

Distribution of Activations in the Hidden Layers

Observing the distribution of activations (referring here to the output data after the activation function, though some literature calls the data that flows between layers an "activation") in the hidden layers provides a lot of information. Here, we will conduct a simple experiment to see how the initial weight values change the activations in the hidden layers. We will enter some randomly generated data into a five-layer neural network (using a sigmoid function as the activation function) and show the data distribution of the activations in each layer in a histogram. This experiment is based on the CS231n (*CS231n: Convolutional Neural Networks for Visual Recognition* (http://cs231n.github.io/)) course at Stanford University.

The source code for the experiment is located at `ch06/weight_init_activation_histogram.py`. The following is part of this code:

```
import numpy as np
import matplotlib.pyplot as plt

def sigmoid(x):
    return 1 / (1 + np.exp(-x))

x = np.random.randn(1000, 100) # 1000 data

node_num = 100 # Number of nodes (neurons) in each hidden layer
hidden_layer_size = 5 # Five hidden layers exist
activations = {} # The results of activations are stored here


for i in range(hidden_layer_size):
    if i != 0:
        x = activations[i-1]

    w = np.random.randn(node_num, node_num) * 1

    z = np.dot(x, w)
    a = sigmoid(z) # Sigmoid function!
    activations[i] = a
```

Here, there are five layers and that each layer has 100 neurons. As input data, 1,000 pieces of data are generated at random with Gaussian distribution and are provided to the five-layer neural network. A sigmoid function is used as the activation function, and the activation results of each layer are stored in the `activations` variable. Please note the weight scale. Here, a Gaussian distribution with a standard deviation of 1 is being used. The purpose of this experiment is to observe how the distribution of `activations` changes by changing this scale (standard deviation). Now, let's show the data of each layer that is stored in `activations` in a histogram:

```
# Draw histograms
for i, a in activations.items( ):
    plt.subplot(1, len(activations), i+1)
    plt.title(str(i+1) + "-layer")
    plt.hist(a.flatten(), 30, range=(0,1))
plt.show()
```

Executing this code creates the histograms shown in the following image.

This image shows that the activations of each layer are mainly 0 and 1. The sigmoid function that's being used here is an S-curve function. As the output of the sigmoid function approaches 0 (or 1), the value of the differential approaches 0. Therefore, when the data is mainly 0s and 1s, the values of the gradients in backward propagation get smaller until they vanish. This is a problem called **gradient vanishing**. In deep learning, where there's a large number of layers, gradient vanishing can be a more serious problem.

Next, let's conduct the same experiment, but this time with the standard deviation of the weights as 0.01. To set the initial weight values, you will need to modify the previous code, as follows:

```
# w = np.random.randn(node_num, node_num) * 1
w = np.random.randn(node_num, node_num) * 0.01
```

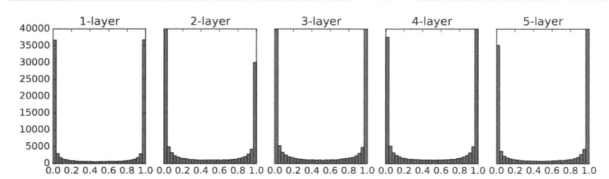

Figure 6.10: Distribution of the activations of each layer when a Gaussian distribution with a standard deviation of 1 is used for the initial weight values

Observe the results. The following image shows the distribution of the activations of each layer when a Gaussian distribution with a standard deviation of 0.01 is used:

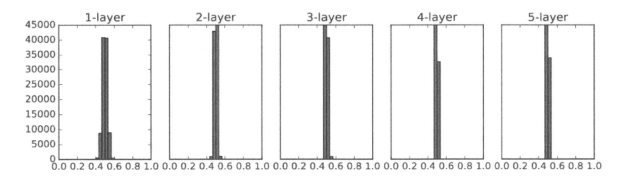

Figure 6.11: Distribution of the activations of each layer when a Gaussian distribution with a standard deviation of 0.01 is used for the initial weight values

Now, the activations concentrate around 0.5. Unlike the previous example, they are not biased toward 0 and 1. The problem of gradient vanishing does not occur. However, when activations are biased, it causes a large problem in terms of its representation. If multiple neurons output almost the same values, there is no meaning in the existence of multiple neurons. For example, when 100 neurons output almost the same values, one neuron can represent almost the same thing. Therefore, the biased activations cause a problem because representation is limited.

> **Note**
>
> The distribution of the activations in each layer needs to be spread properly. This is because, when moderately diverse data flows in each layer, a neural network learns efficiently. On the other hand, when biased data flows, training may not go well because of the gradient vanishing and "limited representation."

Next, we will use the initial weight values that were recommended in a paper by Xavier Glorot et al. (*Xavier Glorot and Yoshua Bengio (2010): Understanding the difficulty of training deep feedforward neural networks. In Proceedings of the International Conference on Artificial Intelligence and Statistics (AISTATS2010). Society for Artificial Intelligence and Statistics*). This is called "Xavier initialization." Currently, the Xavier initializer is usually used in ordinary deep learning frameworks. For example, in the Caffe framework, you can specify the `xavier` argument for the initial weight setting to use the Xavier initializer.

Xavier's paper obtained the appropriate scale of weights so that the activation of each layer was spread similarly. It concluded that distribution with a standard deviation of $\frac{1}{\sqrt{n}}$ should be used when the number of nodes in the previous layer is n (Xavier's paper suggested setting values that consider both the number of input nodes in the previous layer and the number of output nodes in the next layer. However, in framework implementations such as Caffe, the values are only calculated based on the input nodes in the previous layer for simplification, as described here). This can be seen in the following diagram:

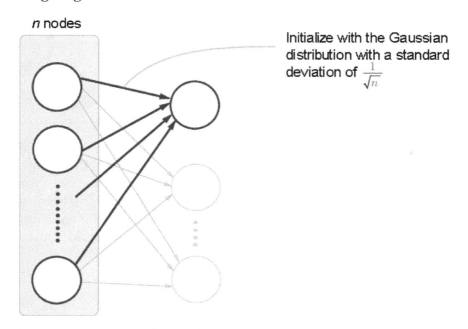

Figure 6.12: Xavier initializer – when **n** nodes in the previous layer are connected, a distribution with the standard deviation of $\frac{1}{\sqrt{n}}$ is used for initial values

When the Xavier initializer is used, since the number of nodes in the previous layer is larger, the weight scale that is set for the initial values for the target nodes is smaller. Now, let's use the Xavier initializer to complete some experiments. You only have to modify the initial weight value, as follows (the implementation is simplified here because the number of nodes is 100 in all the layers):

```
node_num = 100 # Number of nodes in the previous layer
w = np.random.randn(node_num, node_num) / np.sqrt(node_num)
```

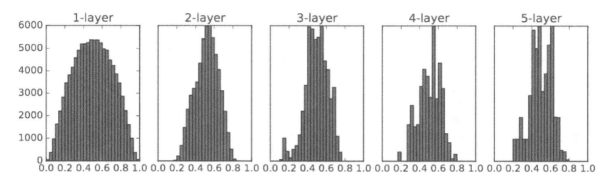

Figure 6.13: Distribution of the activations of each layer when the Xavier initializer is used as the initial weight value

The preceding image shows the results when the Xavier initializer is used. It shows that distributions are spread more widely, although a higher layer has a more distorted shape. We can expect that training is conducted efficiently because the data that flows in each layer is spread properly, and the representation of the sigmoid function is not limited.

> **Note**
>
> Also, the distributions of the upper layers are slightly distorted in terms of their shape. The distorted shape is improved when a `tanh` function (hyperbolic function) is used instead of a `sigmoid` function. Actually, when a `tanh` function is used, distributions will have a bell shape. The `tanh` function is an S-curve function, like a `sigmoid` function. The `tanh` function is symmetrical about the origin (0, 0), while the `sigmoid` function is symmetrical about `(x, y) = (0, 0.5)`. It is best to use the `tanh` function so that the activation function is symmetrical about the origin.

Initial Weight Values for ReLU

The Xavier initializer is based on the assumption that the activation function is linear. The Xavier initializer is suitable because the `sigmoid` and `tanh` functions are symmetrical and can be regarded as linear functions around their centers. Meanwhile, for ReLU, using the initial value is recommended. This is known as the He initializer and was recommended by Kaiming He and et. al. (*Kaiming He, Xiangyu Zhang, Shaoqing Ren, and Jian Sun (2015): Delving Deep into Rectifiers: Surpassing Human-Level Performance on ImageNet Classification. In 1026 – 1034*). The He initializer uses a Gaussian distribution with a standard deviation of $\sqrt{\frac{2}{n}}$ when the number of nodes in the previous layer is n. When we consider that the Xavier initializer is $\sqrt{\frac{1}{n}}$, we can assume (intuitively) that the coefficient must be doubled to provide more spread because a negative area is 0 for ReLU.

Let's look at the distribution of activations when ReLU is used as the activation function. We will consider the results of three experiments after using a Gaussian distribution with a standard deviation of 0.01 (that is, `std=0.01`), the Xavier initializer, and the He initializer, which is specifically used for ReLU (*Figure* 6.14).

The results indicate that the activations of each layer are very small (the averages of the distributions are as follows: layer 1: 0.0396, layer 2: 0.00290, layer 3: 0.000197, layer 4: 1.32e-5, and layer 5: 9.46e-7) for `std=0.01`. When small data flows through a neural network, the gradients of the weights in backward propagation are also small. This is a serious problem as training will barely advance.

Next, let's look at the results from using the Xavier initializer. This shows that the bias becomes larger little by little as the layers become deeper—as do the activations. Gradient vanishing will be a problem when it comes to training. On the other hand, for the He initializer, the spread of Gaussian distribution in each layer is similar. The spread of data is similar even when the layers are deeper. So, we can expect that appropriate values also flow for backward propagation.

In summary, when you use ReLU as the activation function, use the He initializer, and for S-curve functions such as `sigmoid` and `tanh`, use the Xavier initializer. As of the time of writing, this is the best practice.

Using the MNIST Dataset to Compare the Weight Initializers

Let's use actual data to see how neural network learning is affected by different weight initializers. We will use `std=0.01`, the Xavier initializer, and the He initializer in our experiments (the source code is located at `ch06/weight_init_compare.py`). The following image shows the results:

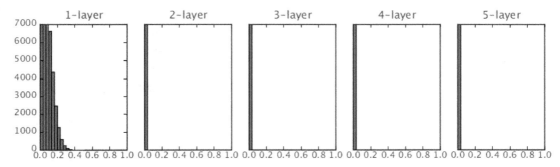

When the Gaussian distribution with the standard deviation
of 0.01 is used for the initial weight values

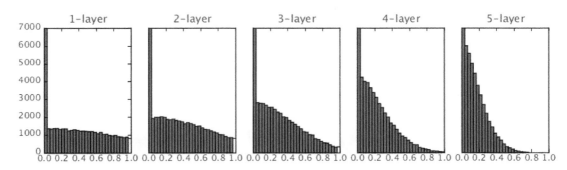

When the Xavier initializer is used

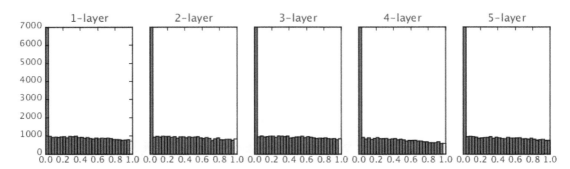

When the He initializer is used

Figure 6.14: Change of activation distribution by weight initializers when ReLU is used
as the activation function

This experiment uses a five-layer neural network (100 neurons in each layer) and ReLU as the activation function. The results shown in the following image reveal that no learning is conducted for `std=0.01`. This is because small values (data near 0) flow in forward propagation, as we observed in the distribution of activations earlier. Thus, the gradients to obtain are also small in backward propagation, resulting in few updates occurring for the weights. On the other hand, training is performed smoothly for the Xavier and He initializers. The following image also shows that training advances fast for the He initializer:

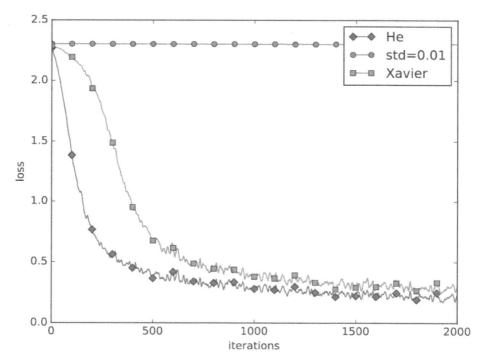

Figure 6.15: Using the MNIST dataset to compare the weight initializers – the horizontal axis indicates the iterations of training, while the vertical axis indicates the values of the loss function

As we have seen, the initial weight values are very important in neural network training. They often determine their success or failure. Although the importance of the initial weight values is sometimes overlooked, the starting (initial) value is important for everything.

Batch Normalization

In the previous section, we observed the distribution of activations in each layer. We learned that the appropriate initial weight values provide a proper spread for the distribution of activations of each layer, thus enabling smooth training. So, how about adjusting the distribution of activations "forcefully" so that there's a proper spread in each layer?

This technique is based on the idea of batch normalization (*Sergey Ioffe and Christian Szegedy (2015): Batch Normalization: Accelerating Deep Network Training by Reducing Internal Covariate Shift. arXiv:1502.03167[cs] (February 2015)*).

Batch Normalization Algorithm

Batch normalization (also known as batch norm) was first proposed in 2015. Although batch norm is a new technique, it is widely used by many researchers and engineers. In fact, in competitions surrounding machine learning, batch norm often achieves excellent results.

Batch norm attracts a lot of attention due to the following advantages:

- It can accelerate learning (it can increase the learning rate).

- It is not as dependent on the initial weight values (you do not need to be cautious about the initial values).

- It reduces overfitting (it reduces the necessity of dropout).

The first advantage is particularly attractive because deep learning takes a lot of time. With batch norm there's no need to be anxious about the initial weight values, and due to it reducing overfitting, it removes this cause of anxiety from deep learning.

As we described earlier, the purpose of batch norm is to adjust the distribution of the activations in each layer so that it has a proper spread. To do that, the layer that normalizes data distribution is inserted into a neural network as the batch normalization layer (also known as the batch norm layer), as shown in the following diagram:

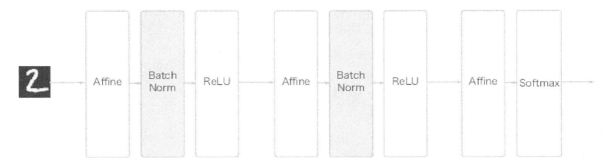

Figure 6.16: Neural network example that uses batch normalization (the batch norm layers are shown in gray)

As its name indicates, batch norm normalizes each mini-batch that is used for training. Specifically, it normalizes data so that the average is 0 and the variance is 1. The following equation shows this:

$$\mu_B \leftarrow \frac{1}{m}\sum_{i=1}^{m} x_i$$

$$\sigma_B^2 \leftarrow \frac{1}{m}\sum_{i=1}^{m}(x_i - \mu_B)^2 \qquad (6.7)$$

$$\hat{x}_i \leftarrow \frac{x_i - \mu_B}{\sqrt{\sigma_B^2 + \varepsilon}}$$

Here, a set of m input data, $b = \{x_1, x_2, \ldots, x_m\}$, is treated as a mini-batch and its average, μ_b, and variance, σ_b^2, are calculated. The input data is normalized so that its average is 0 and its variance is 1 for the appropriate distribution. In equation 6.7, ε is a small value (such as 10e-7). This prevents division by 0.

Equation 6.7 simply converts the input data for a mini-batch, $\{x_1, x_2 \ldots, x_m\}$, into data with an average of 0 and a variance of 1, $\{\hat{x}_1, \hat{x}_2, \ldots, \hat{x}_{1m}\}$. By inserting this process before (or after) the activation function (see (*Sergey Ioffe and Christian Szegedy (2015): Batch Normalization: Accelerating Deep Network Training by Reducing Internal Covariate Shift. arXiv:1502.03167[cs] (February 2015)*) and (*Dmytro Mishkin and Jiri Matas (2015): All you need is a good init. arXiv:1511.06422[cs] (November 2015)*) for a discussion (and experiments) on whether batch normalization should be inserted before or after the activation function), you can reduce the distribution bias of the data.

In addition, the batch norm layer converts the normalized data with a peculiar scale and shift. The following equation shows this conversion:

$$y_i \leftarrow \gamma\hat{x}_i + \beta \qquad (6.8)$$

Here, γ and β are parameters. They start with $\gamma = 1$ and $\beta = 0$ and will be adjusted to the appropriate values through training.

This is the algorithm of batch norm. This algorithm provides the forward propagation in a neural network. By using a computational graph, as described in *Chapter 5, Backpropagation*, we can represent batch norm as follows.

We won't go into detail about how to derive backward propagation in batch norm here because it is a little complicated. When you use a computational graph, such as the one shown in the following image, you can derive the backward propagation of batch norm relatively easily. Frederik Kratzert's blog, *Understanding the Backward Pass through the Batch Normalization Layer* (https://kratzert.github.io/2016/02/12/understanding-the-gradient-flow-through-the-batch-normalization-layer.html), provides a detailed description of this. Please refer to it if you are interested:

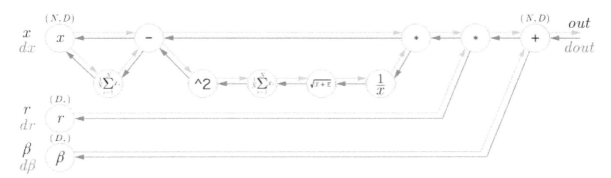

Figure 6.17: Computational graph of batch normalization

> **Note**
>
> *Figure 6.17* is cited from reference, *Frederik Kratzert's blog "Understanding the backward pass through Batch Normalization Layer"* (https://kratzert.github.io/2016/02/12/understanding-the-gradient-flow-through-the-batch-normalization-layer.html).

Evaluating Batch Normalization

Now, let's use the batch norm layer to conduct some experiments. First, we will use the MNIST dataset to see how the progress of learning changes with and without the batch norm layer (the source code can be found at `ch06/batch_norm_test.py`). *Figure 6.18* shows the result.

Figure 6.18 shows that batch norm accelerates training. Next, let's see how the progress of training changes when various scales for the initial values are used. *Figure 6.19* contains graphs that show the progress of training when the standard deviations of the initial weight values are changed.

This indicates that batch norm accelerates training in almost all cases. In fact, when batch norm is not used, training does not advance at all without a good scale of initial values.

As we have seen, using batch norm can accelerate training and provides robustness to the initial weight values ("robustness to the initial values" means having a little dependence on them). Batch norm will play an active part in many situations because it has such wonderful characteristics.

Regularization

Overfitting often creates difficulties in machine learning problems. In overfitting, the model fits the training data too well and cannot properly handle other data that is not contained in the training data. Machine learning aims at generalizing performance. It is desirable for the model to properly recognize unknown data that is not contained in the training data. While you can create a complicated and representative model this way, reducing overfitting is also important:

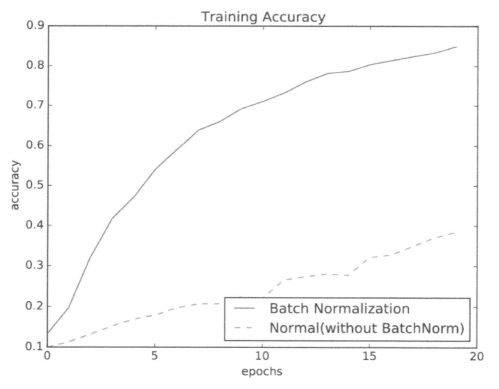

Figure 6.18: Effect of batch norm – batch norm accelerates learning

Overfitting

The main two causes of overfitting are as follows:

- The model has many parameters and is representative.
- The training data is insufficient.

Here, we will generate overfitting by providing these two causes. Out of 60,000 pieces of training data in the MNIST dataset, only 300 are provided, and a seven-layer network is used to increase the network's complexity. It has 100 neurons in each layer. ReLU is used as the activation function:

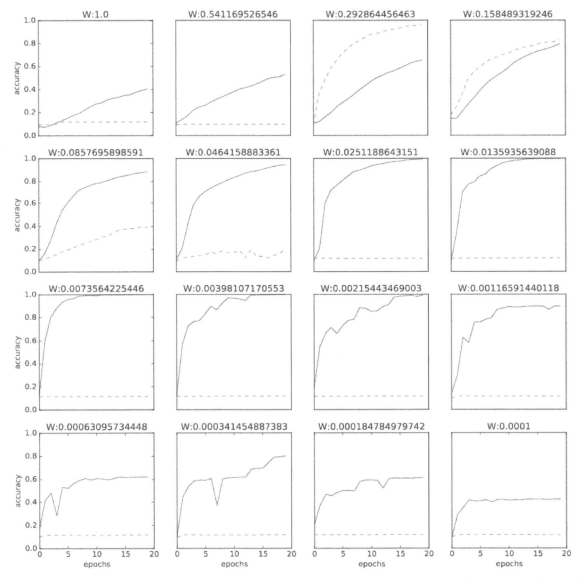

Figure 6.19: The solid lines show the results of using batch norm, while the dotted lines show the results without it – the title of each graph indicates the standard deviation of the initial weight values

The following is part of the code for this experiment (the source file is at ch06/overfit_weight_decay.py). First, the code loads the data:

```
(x_train, t_train), (x_test, t_test) = load_mnist(normalize=True)
# Reduce learning data to reproduce overfitting
x_train = x_train[:300]
t_train = t_train[:300]
```

The following code conducts training. Here, the recognition accuracy is calculated for each epoch for all the training data and all the test data:

```
network = MultiLayerNet(input_size=784, hidden_size_list=[100, 100, 100,
100, 100, 100], output_size=10)
optimizer = SGD(lr=0.01) # Use SGD with the learning rate of 0.01 to
update the parameters

max_epochs = 201
train_size = x_train.shape[0]
batch_size = 100

train_loss_list = []
train_acc_list = []
test_acc_list = []

iter_per_epoch = max(train_size / batch_size, 1)
epoch_cnt = 0

for i in range(1000000000):
    batch_mask = np.random.choice(train_size, batch_size)
    x_batch = x_train[batch_mask]
    t_batch = t_train[batch_mask]

    grads = network.gradient(x_batch, t_batch)
    optimizer.update(network.params, grads)

    if i % iter_per_epoch == 0:
        train_acc = network.accuracy(x_train, t_train)
        test_acc = network.accuracy(x_test, t_test)
        train_acc_list.append(train_acc)
        test_acc_list.append(test_acc)

        epoch_cnt += 1
        if epoch_cnt >= max_epochs:
            break
```

The `train_acc_list` and `test_acc_list` lists store the recognition accuracies for each epoch. An epoch indicates that all the training data has been used. Let's draw graphs based on these lists (`train_acc_list` and `test_acc_list`). The following plot shows the results.

The recognition accuracies that were measured using the training data reached almost 100% after 100 epochs, but the recognition accuracies on the test data are far below 100%. These large differences are caused by overfitting the training data. This graph shows that the model cannot handle general data (test data) that was not used in training properly:

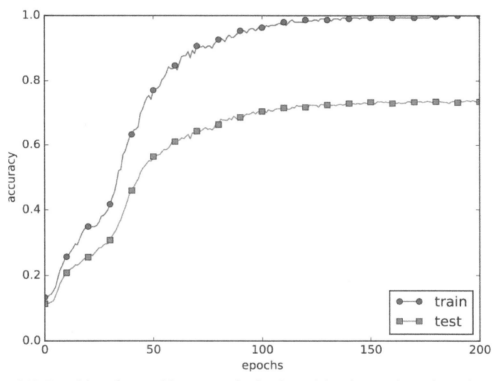

Figure 6.20: Transition of recognition accuracies for the training data (train) and test data (test)

Weight Decay

The **weight decay** technique has often been used to reduce overfitting. It avoids overfitting by imposing a penalty on large weights during training. Overfitting often occurs when a weight parameter takes a large value.

As described earlier, the purpose of neural network training is to reduce the value of the loss function. For example, you can add the squared norm (L2 norm) of the weight to the loss function. Then, you could prevent the weight from being large. When the weights are W, the L2 norm of the weight decay is $\frac{1}{2}\lambda W^2$. This $\frac{1}{2}\lambda W^2$ is added to the loss function. Here, λ is the hyperparameter that controls the strength of regularization. If you set a larger value to λ, you can impose a stronger penalty on a large weight. $\frac{1}{2}$ at the beginning of $\frac{1}{2}\lambda W^2$ is a constant for adjustment so that the differential of $\frac{1}{2}\lambda W^2$ is λW.

Weight decay adds $\frac{1}{2}\lambda W^2$ to the loss function for all weights. Therefore, the differential of the regularization term, λW, is added to the result of backpropagation when calculating the gradient of a weight.

The L2 norm is the sum of squares of each element. In addition to the L2 norm, L1 and L ∞ norms also exist. The L1 norm is the sum of absolute values, that is, $|w_1| + |w_2| + \ldots + |w_n|$. The L ∞ norm is also called the max norm. It is the largest among the absolute values of all the elements. You can use any of these norms as a regularization term. Each has its own characteristics, but we will only implement the L2 norm here since it's the most commonly used.

Now, let's conduct an experiment. We will apply the weight decay of $\lambda = 0.1$ to the preceding experiment. The following plot shows the results (the network that supports weight decay is located at `common/multi_layer_net.py` and the code for the experiment is located at `ch06/overfit_weight_decay.py`):

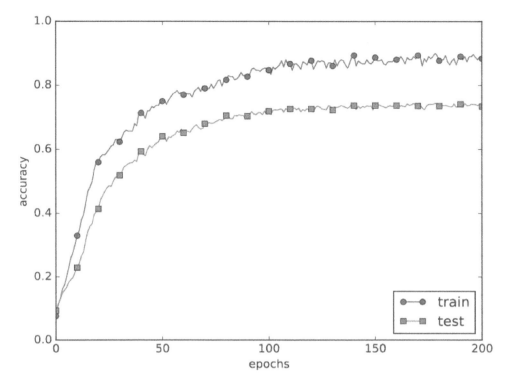

Figure 6.21: Transition of recognition accuracies for the training data (train) and test data (test) when weight decay is used

The preceding image shows that the recognition accuracies of the training data and test data are different, but that the difference is smaller than in the one shown in *Figure 6.20* where weight decay was not used. This indicates that overfitting was reduced. Note that the recognition accuracies of the training data have not reached 100% (1.0).

Dropout

The previous section described the weight decay technique. It adds the L2 norm of the weights to the loss function to reduce overfitting. Weight decay is easy to implement and can reduce overfitting to some extent. However, as a neural network model becomes more complicated, weight decay is often insufficient. This is when the dropout technique (*N. Srivastava, G. Hinton, A. Krizhevsky, I. Sutskever, and R. Salakhutdinov* (2014): *Dropout: A simple way to prevent neural networks from overfitting. The Journal of Machine Learning Research, pages 1929 – 1958, 2014*) is often used.

Dropout erases neurons at random during training. During training, it selects neurons in a hidden layer at random to erase them. As shown in the following image, the erased neurons do not transmit signals. During training, the neurons to be erased are selected at random each time data flows. During testing, the signals of all the neurons are propagated. The output of each neuron is multiplied by the rate of the erased neurons during training:

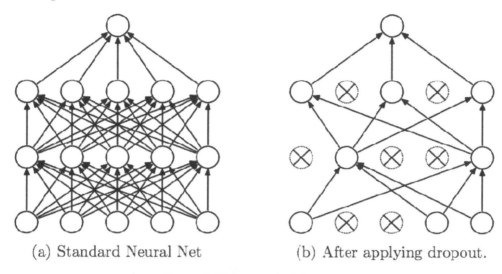

(a) Standard Neural Net   (b) After applying dropout.

Figure 6.22: Concept of dropout

Note

Figure 6.22 is cited from reference, N. Srivastava, G. Hinton, A. Krizhevsky, I. Sutskever, and R. Salakhutdinov (2014): Dropout: A simple way to prevent neural networks from overfitting. The Journal of Machine Learning Research pages 1929–1958, 2014.

The left-hand image shows an ordinary neural network, while the right-hand image shows a network that dropout has been applied to. Dropout selects neurons at random and erases them to stop the transmission of subsequent signals.

Now, let's implement dropout. Simplicity is emphasized in the implementation here. If appropriate calculation is conducted during training, we only have to flow data through forward propagation (without multiplying the rate of the erased neurons). Such an implementation is conducted in deep learning frameworks. For efficient implementation, the dropout implemented in the Chainer framework, for example, may be useful:

```
class Dropout:
    def __init__ (self, dropout_ratio=0.5):
```

```
        self.dropout_ratio = dropout_ratio
        self.mask = None

    def forward(self, x, train_flg=True):
        if   train_flg:
            self.mask = np.random.rand(*x.shape) > self.dropout_ratio
            return x * self.mask
        else:
            return x * (1.0 - self.dropout_ratio)

    def backward(self, dout):
        return dout * self.mask
```

Please note that, in each forward propagation, the neurons to erase are stored as `False` in `self.mask`. `self.mask` generates an array of the same shape as `x` at random and sets the elements to `True` when their values are larger than `dropout_ratio`. The behavior in backward propagation is the same as that in ReLU. If a neuron is passed a signal in forward propagation, it passes the received signal without changing it in backward propagation. If a neuron doesn't pass a signal in forward propagation, it stops the received signal in backward propagation.

We will use the MNIST dataset to validate the effect of dropout. The source code can be found in `ch06/overfit_dropout.py`. It uses the `Trainer` class to simplify implementation.

The `Trainer` class is implemented in `common/trainer.py`. It conducts network training that has been conducted so far in this chapter. For details, please see `common/trainer.py` and `ch06/overfit_dropout.py`.

To experiment with dropout, we'll use a seven-layer network (where 100 neurons exist in each layer and ReLU is used as the activation function), as in the previous experiment. One of the experiments will use dropout, while the other won't. The following image shows the results.

As we can see, using dropout reduces the difference between the recognition accuracies of training data and test data. It also indicates that the recognition accuracy of the training data has not reached 100%. Due to this, you can use dropout to reduce overfitting, even in a representative network:

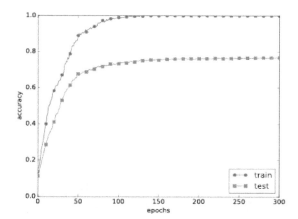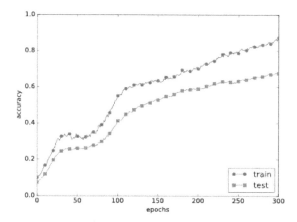

Figure 6.23: The left-hand image shows the experiment without dropout, while the right-hand image shows the experiment with dropout (dropout_rate=0.15)

Note

In machine learning, ensemble learning is often used in which multiple models learn separately, and their multiple outputs are averaged through prediction. For example, when we use it in a neural network, we prepare five networks with the same (or similar) structure and train each of them. Then, we average the five outputs during testing to obtain the result. Experiments have shown that ensemble learning improves a neural network's recognition accuracy by several percent.

Ensemble learning is close to dropout. Erasing neurons at random while training in dropout can be interpreted as providing a different model to learn data each time. While predicting, the output from the neurons is multiplied by the rate of the erasures (0.5, for example) to average the models. Thus, we can say that dropout simulates ensemble learning in one network.

Validating Hyperparameters

A neural network uses many hyperparameters, as well as parameters such as weights and biases. The hyperparameters here include the number of neurons in each layer, batch size, the learning rate for updating parameters, and weight decay. Setting the hyperparameters to inappropriate values deteriorates the performance of the model. The values of these hyperparameters are very important, but determining them usually requires a lot of trial and error. This section describes how to search for hyperparameter values as efficiently as possible.

Validation Data

In the dataset we've used so far, the training data and test data are separate. The training data is used to train a network, while the test data is used to evaluate generalization performance. Thus, you can determine whether or not the network conforms too well only to the training data (that is, whether overfitting occurs) and how large the generalization performance is.

We will use various hyperparameter settings for validation. Please note that you must not use test data to evaluate the performance of hyperparameters. This is very important but is often overlooked.

So, why can't we use test data to evaluate the performance of hyperparameters? Well, if we use test data to adjust hyperparameters, the hyperparameter values will overfit the test data. In other words, it uses test data to check that the hyperparameter values are "good," so the hyperparameter values are adjusted so that they only fit the test data. Here, the model may provide low generalization performance and cannot fit other data.

Therefore, we need to use verification data (called **validation data**) to adjust them. This validation data is used to evaluate the quality of our hyperparameters.

Training data is used for learning parameters (weights and biases). Validation data is used to evaluate the performance of hyperparameters. Test data is used (once, ideally) at the end of training to check generalization performance.

Some datasets provide training data, validation data, and test data separately. Some provide only training data and test data, while some provide only one type of data. In that case, you must separate the data manually. For the MNIST dataset, the simplest way to obtain the validation data is to separate 20% of the training data beforehand and use that as validation data. The following code shows this:

```
(x_train, t_train), (x_test, t_test) = load_mnist()

# Shuffle training data
x_train, t_train = shuffle_dataset(x_train, t_train)
```

```
# Separate validation data
validation_rate = 0.20
validation_num = int(x_train.shape[0] * validation_rate)

x_val = x_train[:validation_num]
t_val = t_train[:validation_num]
x_train = x_train[validation_num:]
t_train = t_train[validation_num:]
```

Here, the input data and labeled data are shuffled before separating the training data. This is because some datasets may have biased data (for example, numbers "0" to "10" are arranged in this order). The `shuffle_dataset` function uses `np.random.shuffle` and is contained in `common/util.py`.

Next, let's use validation data to look at the technique that's used for optimizing hyperparameters.

Optimizing Hyperparameters

What is important when optimizing hyperparameters is to gradually narrow down the range where "good" hyperparameter values exist. To do this, we will set a broad range initially, select hyperparameters at random from the range (sampling), and use the sampled values to evaluate the recognition accuracy. Next, we will repeat these steps several times and observe the result of the recognition accuracy. Based on the result, we will narrow down the range of "good" hyperparameter values. By repeating this procedure, we can gradually limit the range of appropriate hyperparameters.

It has been reported that random sampling before a search provides better results than a systematic search, such as a grid search, to optimize hyperparameters in a neural network (*James Bergstra and Yoshua Bengio (2012): Random Search for Hyper-Parameter Optimization. Journal of Machine Learning Research 13, Feb (2012), 281 – 305*). This is because the degree by which the final recognition accuracy will be affected is different among different hyperparameters.

Specifying a "broad" range of hyperparameters is effective. We will specify the range in "powers of 10," such as from 0.001 (10^{-3}) to 1,000 (10^3) (this is also called "specifying on a log scale").

Please note that when optimizing hyperparameters, deep learning takes a lot of time (even a few days or weeks). Therefore, any hyperparameters that seem inappropriate must be abandoned while searching for them. When optimizing hyperparameters, it is effective to reduce the size of epoch for training to shorten the time that one evaluation takes. We discussed the optimization of hyperparameters previously. The following summarizes this discussion:

Step 0

Specify the range of the hyperparameters.

Step 1

Sample the hyperparameters from the range at random.

Step 2

Use the hyperparameter values sampled in *Step 1* for training and use the validation data to evaluate the recognition accuracy (set small epochs).

Step 3

Repeat *steps* 1 and 2 a certain number of times (such as 100 times) and narrow down the range of hyperparameters based on the result of the recognition accuracy. When the range is narrowed down to some extent, select one hyperparameter value from it. This is one practical approach to optimizing hyperparameters.

> **Note**
>
> However, you may feel that this approach is the "wisdom" of engineers rather than science. If you need a more refined technique for optimizing hyperparameters, you can use **Bayesian optimization**. It makes good use of mathematical theories such as Bayes' theorem to provide stricter and more efficient optimization. For details, please see the paper *Practical Bayesian Optimization of Machine Learning Algorithms (Jasper Snoek, Hugo Larochelle, and Ryan P. Adams (2012): Practical Bayesian Optimization of Machine Learning Algorithms. In F. Pereira, C. J. C. Burges, L. Bottou, & K. Q. Weinberger, eds. Advances in Neural Information Processing Systems 25. Curran Associates, Inc., 2951 – 2959).*

Implementing Hyperparameter Optimization

Now, let's use the MNIST dataset to optimize some hyperparameters. We will look for two hyperparameters: the learning rate and the weight decay rate. The weight decay rate controls the strength of weight decay. This problem and solution are based on the CS231n (CS231: *Convolutional Neural Networks for Visual Recognition* (http://cs231n.github.io/)) course at Stanford University.

As described earlier, hyperparameters are validated by sampling them at random from the range on a log scale, such as from 0.001 (10^{-3}) to 1,000 (10^3). We can write this as 10 `** np.random.uniform(-3, 3)` in Python. This experiment will start with a range from 10^{-8} to 10^{-4} for the weight decay rate and from 10^{-6} to 10^{-2} for the learning rate. In this case, we can write the random sampling of the hyperparameters as follows:

```
weight_decay = 10 ** np.random.uniform(-8, -4)
lr = 10 ** np.random.uniform(-6, -2)
```

Here, the hyperparameters were sampled at random, and the sampled values were used for training. Then, training is repeated several times by using various hyperparameter values to find where the appropriate hyperparameters exist. Here, the details of implementation have been omitted, and only the result has been shown. The source code for optimizing hyperparameters is located at `ch06/hyperparameter_optimization.py`.

When we have a range of 10^{-8} to 10^{-4} for the weight decay rate and a range of 10^{-6} to 10^{-2} for the learning rate, we get the following results. Here, we can see the transitions in learning the validation data in descending order of high-recognition accuracies:

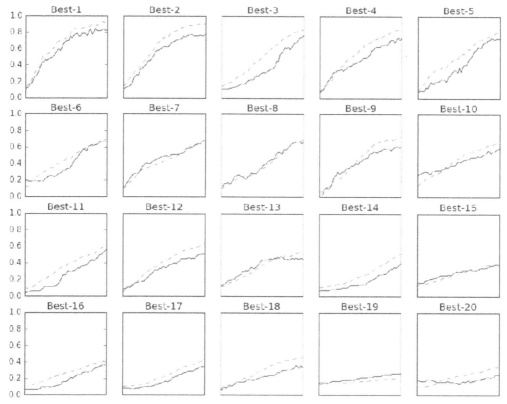

Figure 6.24: The solid lines show the recognition accuracies of the validation data, while the dotted lines show the recognition accuracies of the training data

This indicates that the training advanced smoothly from `Best-1` to `Best-5`. Let's check the hyperparameter values (that is, the learning rate and weight decay rate) of `Best-1` to `Best-5`. These are the results:

```
Best-1 (val acc:0.83) | lr:0.0092, weight decay:3.86e-07
Best-2 (val acc:0.78) | lr:0.00956, weight decay:6.04e-07
Best-3 (val acc:0.77) | lr:0.00571, weight decay:1.27e-06
Best-4 (val acc:0.74) | lr:0.00626, weight decay:1.43e-05
Best-5 (val acc:0.73) | lr:0.0052, weight decay:8.97e-06
```

Here, we can see that when the learning rate was 0.001 to 0.01 and the weight decay rate was 10^{-8} to 10^{-6}, learning advanced well. Due to this, the range of the hyperparameters where training is likely to succeed is observed to narrow the range of values. You can repeat the same procedure in the narrowed range. Thus, you can narrow the range where appropriate hyperparameters exist and select each of the final hyperparameters at a certain stage.

Summary

This chapter described some important techniques that are used for neural network training. How to update parameters, how to specify initial weight values, batch normalization, and dropout are all essential techniques that are used in modern neural networks. The techniques described here are often used in state-of-the-art deep learning. In this chapter, we learned about the following:

- Four famous methods for updating parameters: Momentum, AdaGrad, Adam, and SGD.

- How to specify initial weight values, which is very important if we wish to train correctly.

- The Xavier initializer and He initializer, which are effective as initial weight values.

- Batch normalization accelerates training and provides robustness to the initial weight values.

- Weight decay and dropout are regularization techniques that are used to reduce overfitting.

- To search for good hyperparameters, gradually narrowing down the range where appropriate values exist is an efficient method.

Convolutional Neural Networks

This chapter describes **convolutional neural networks (CNNs)**. CNNs are used everywhere in AI, including image recognition and speech recognition. This chapter will detail the mechanisms of CNNs and how to implement them in Python.

Overall Architecture

First, let's look at the network architecture of CNNs. You can create a CNN by combining layers, much in the same way as the neural networks that we have seen so far. However, CNNs have other layers as well: a convolution layer and a pooling layer. We will look at the details of the convolution and pooling layers in the following sections. This section describes how layers are combined to create a CNN.

In the neural networks that we have seen so far, all the neurons in adjacent layers are connected. These layers are called **fully connected** layers, and we implemented them as Affine layers. You can use Affine layers to create a neural network consisting of five fully connected layers, for example, as shown in *Figure 7.1*.

As *Figure 7.1* shows, the ReLU layer (or the Sigmoid layer) for the activation function follows the Affine layer in a fully connected neural network. Here, after four pairs of **Affine – ReLU** layers, comes the Affine layer, which is the fifth layer. And finally, the Softmax layer outputs the final result (probability):

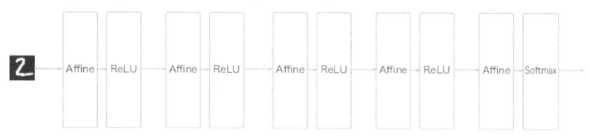

Figure 7.1: Sample network consisting of fully connected layers (Affine layers)

So, what architecture does a CNN have? *Figure 7.2* shows a sample CNN:

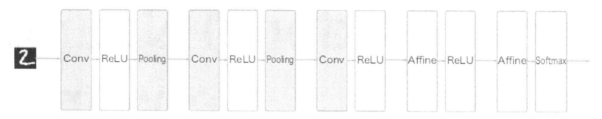

Figure 7.2: Sample CNN – convolution and pooling layers are added
(they are shown as gray rectangles)

As shown in *Figure 7.2*, CNN has additional convolution and pooling layers. In the CNN, layers are connected in the order of **Convolution – ReLU – (Pooling)** (a pooling layer is sometimes omitted). We can consider the previous **Affine – ReLU** connection as being replaced with "Convolution – ReLU – (Pooling)."

In the CNN of *Figure 7.2*, note that the layers near the output are the previous "Affine – ReLU" pairs, while the last output layers are the previous "Affine – Softmax" pairs. This is the structure often seen in an ordinary CNN.

The Convolution Layer

There are some CNN-specific terms, such as padding and stride. The data that flows through each layer in a CNN is data with shape (such as three-dimensional data), unlike in previous fully connected networks. Therefore, you may feel that CNNs are difficult when you learn about them for the first time. Here, we will look at the mechanism of the convolution layer used in CNNs.

Issues with the Fully Connected Layer

The fully connected neural networks that we have seen so far used fully connected layers (Affine layers). In a fully connected layer, all the neurons in the adjacent layer are connected, and the number of outputs can be determined arbitrarily.

The issue with a fully connected layer, though, is that the shape of the data is *ignored*. For example, when the input data is an image, it usually has a three-dimensional shape, determined by the height, the width, and the channel dimension. However, three-dimensional data must be converted into one-dimensional flat data when it is provided to a fully connected layer. In the previous examples that we used for the MNIST dataset, the input images had the shape of 1, 28, 28 (1 channel, 28 pixels in height, and 28 pixels in width), but the elements were arranged in a line, and the resulting 784 pieces of data were provided to the first Affine layer.

Let's say an image has a three-dimensional shape and that the shape contains important spatial information. Essential patterns to recognize this information may hide in three-dimensional shapes. Spatially close pixels have similar values, the RBG channels are closely related to each other, and the distant pixels are not related. However, a fully connected layer ignores the shape and treats all the input data as equivalent neurons (neurons with the same number of dimensions), so it cannot use the information regarding the shape.

On the other hand, a convolution layer maintains the shape. For images, it receives the input data as three-dimensional data and outputs three-dimensional data to the next layer. Therefore, CNNs can understand data with a shape, such as images, properly.

In a CNN, the input/output data for a convolution layer is sometimes called a **feature map**. The input data for a convolution layer is called an **input feature map**, while the output data for a convolution layer is called an **output feature map**. In this book, *input/output data* and *feature map* will be used interchangeably.

Convolution Operations

The processing performed in a convolution layer is called a "convolution operation" and is equivalent to the "filter operation" in image processing. Let's look at example (*Figure* 7.3) to understand a convolution operation:

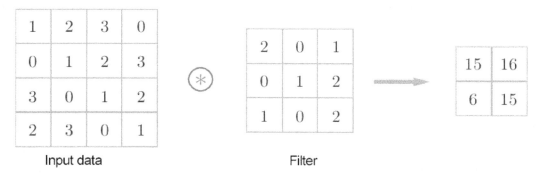

Input data   Filter

Figure 7.3: Convolution operation – the ⊛ symbol indicates a convolution operation

As shown in *Figure* 7.3, a convolution operation applies a filter to input data. In this example, the shape of the input data has a height and width, and so does the shape of the filter. When we indicate the shape of the data and filter as (height, width), the input size is (4, 4), the filter size is (3, 3), and the output size is (2, 2) in this example. Some literature uses the word "kernel" for the term "filter."

Now, let's break down the calculation performed in the convolution operation shown in *Figure* 7.3. *Figure* 7.4 shows the calculation procedure of the convolution operation.

A convolution operation is applied to the input data while the filter window is shifted at a fixed interval. The window here indicates the gray 3x3 section shown in *Figure* 7.4. As shown in *Figure* 7.4, the element of the filter and the corresponding element of the input are multiplied and summed at each location (this calculation is sometimes called a **multiply-accumulate operation**). The result is stored in the corresponding position of the output. The output of the convolution operation can be obtained by performing this process at all locations.

A fully connected neural network has biases as well as weight parameters. In a CNN, the filter parameters correspond to the previous "weights." It also has biases. The convolution operation of *Figure* 7.3 shows the stage when a filter was applied. *Figure* 7.5 shows the processing flow of a convolution operation, including biases:

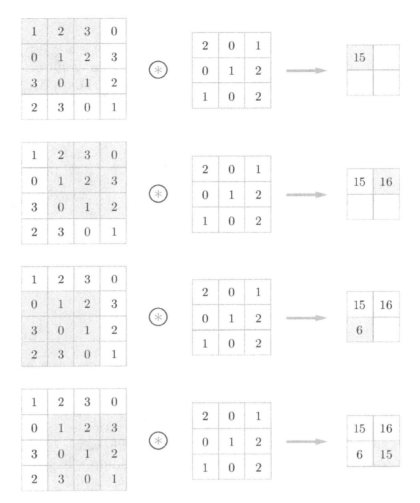

Figure 7.4: Calculation procedure of a convolution operation

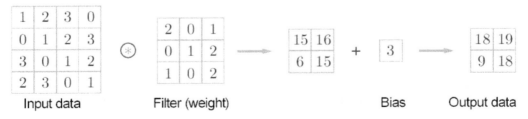

Input data	Filter (weight)	Bias	Output data

Figure 7.5: Bias in a convolution operation – a fixed value (bias) is added to the element after the filter is applied

As shown in *Figure 7.5*, a bias term is added to the data after the filter is applied. Here, the bias is always only one (1x1) where one bias exists for the four pieces of data after the filter is applied. This one value is added to all the elements after the filter is applied.

Padding

Before a convolution layer is processed, fixed data (such as 0) is sometimes filled around the input data. This is called **padding** and is often used in a convolution operation. For example, in *Figure 7.6*, padding of 1 is applied to the (4, 4) input data. The padding of 1 means filling the circumference with zeros with the width of one pixel:

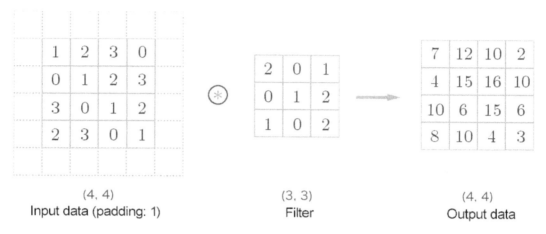

(4, 4)
Input data (padding: 1)
      (3, 3)
Filter
      (4, 4)
Output data

Figure 7.6: Padding in a convolution operation – add zeros around the input data (padding is shown by dashed lines here, and the zeros are omitted)

As shown in *Figure 7.6*, padding converts the (4, 4) input data into (6, 6) data. After the (3, 3) filter is applied, (4, 4) output data is generated. In this example, the padding of 1 was used. You can set any integer, such as 2 or 3, as the padding value. If the padding value was 2, the size of the input data would be (8, 8). If the padding was 3, the size would be (10, 10).

> **Note**
>
> Padding is used mainly for adjusting the output size. For example, when a (3, 3) filter is applied to (4, 4) input data, the output size is (2, 2). The output size is smaller than the input size by two elements. This causes a problem in deep networks, where convolution operations are repeated many times. If each convolution operation spatially reduces the size, the output size will reach 1 at a certain time, and no more convolution operations will be available. To avoid such a situation, you can use padding. In the previous example, the output size (4, 4) remains the same as the input size (4, 4) when the width of padding is 1. Therefore, you can pass the data of the same spatial size to the next layer after performing a convolution operation.

Stride

The interval of the positions for applying a filter is called a **stride**. In all previous examples, the stride was 1. When the stride is 2, for example, the interval of the window for applying a filter will be two elements, as shown in *Figure 7.7*.

In *Figure 7.7*, a filter is applied to the (7, 7) input data with the stride of 2. When the stride is 2, the output size becomes (3, 3). Thus, the stride specifies the interval for applying a filter.

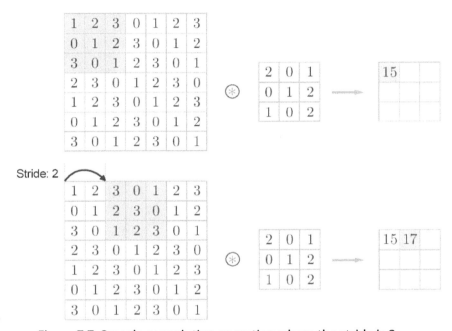

Figure 7.7: Sample convolution operation where the stride is 2

As we have seen so far, the larger the stride, the smaller the output size, and the larger the padding, the larger the output size. How can we represent such relations in equations? Let's see how the output size is calculated based on padding and stride.

Here, the input size is (H, W), the filter size is (FH, FW), the output size is (OH, OW), the padding is P, and the stride is S. In this case, you can calculate the output size with the following equation—that is, equation (7.1):

$$OH = \frac{H + 2P - FH}{S} + 1$$

$$OW = \frac{W + 2P - FW}{S} + 1 \tag{7.1}$$

Now, let's use this equation to do some calculations:

1. **Example 1: Example is shown in Figure 7.6**

   Input size: (4, 4), padding: 1, stride: 1, filter size: (3, 3):

   $$OH = \frac{4 + 2 \cdot 1 - 3}{1} + 1 = 4$$

   $$OW = \frac{4 + 2 \cdot 1 - 3}{1} + 1 = 4$$

2. **Example 2: Example is shown in Figure 7.7**

   Input size: (7, 7), padding: 0, stride: 2, filter size: (3, 3):

   $$OH = \frac{7 + 2 \cdot 0 - 3}{2} + 1 = 3$$

   $$OW = \frac{7 + 2 \cdot 0 - 3}{2} + 1 = 3$$

3. **Example 3**

   Input size: (28, 31), padding: 2, stride: 3, filter size:(5, 5):

   $$OH = \frac{28 + 2 \cdot 2 - 5}{3} + 1 = 10$$

   $$OW = \frac{31 + 2 \cdot 2 - 5}{3} + 1 = 11$$

As these examples show, you can calculate the output size by assigning values to equation (7.1). You can only obtain the output size by assignment, but note that you must assign values so that $\frac{W+2P-FW}{S}$ and $\frac{H+2P-FH}{S}$ in equation (7.1) are divisible. If the output size is not divisible (i.e., the result is a decimal), you must handle that by generating an error. Some deep learning frameworks advance this process without generating an error; for example, they round the value to the nearest integer when it is not divisible.

Performing a Convolution Operation on Three-Dimensional Data

The examples we've looked at so far targeted two-dimensional shapes that have a height and a width. For images, we must handle three-dimensional data that has a channel dimension, as well as a height and a width. Here, we will look at an example of a convolution operation on three-dimensional data using the same technique we used in the previous examples.

Figure 7.8 shows an example of convolution operation, while *Figure* 7.9 shows the calculation procedure. Here, we can see the result of performing a convolution operation on three-dimensional data. You can see that the feature maps have increased in depth (the channel dimension) compared to the two-dimensional data (the example shown in *Figure* 7.3). If there are multiple feature maps in the channel dimension, a convolution operation using the input data and the filter is performed for each channel, and the results are added to obtain one output:

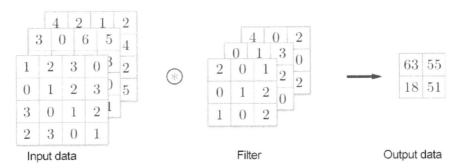

Input data Filter Output data

Figure 7.8: Convolution operation for three-dimensional data

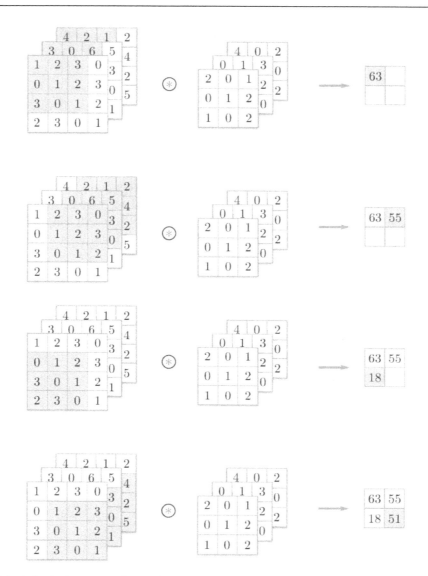

Figure 7.9: Calculation procedure of the convolution operation for three-dimensional data

> **Note**
>
> In a three-dimensional convolution operation, as shown in this example, the input data and the filter must be the same in terms of the number of channels they have. In this example, the number of channels in the input data and the filter are the same; there are three. On the other hand, you can set the filter size to whatever you like. In this example, the filter size is (3, 3). You can set it to any size, such as (2, 2), (1, 1), or (5,5). However, as mentioned earlier, the number of channels must be the same as that of the input data. In this example, there must be three.

Thinking in Blocks

In a three-dimensional convolution operation, you can consider the data and filter as rectangular blocks. A block here is a three-dimensional cuboid, as shown in *Figure 7.10*. We will represent three-dimensional data as a multidimensional array in the order channel, height, width. So, when the number of channels is C, the height is H, and the width is W for shape, it is represented as (C, H, W). We will represent a filter in the same order so that when the number of channels is C, the height is **FH (Filter Height)**, and the width is **FW (Filter Width)** for a filter, it is represented as (C, FH, FW):

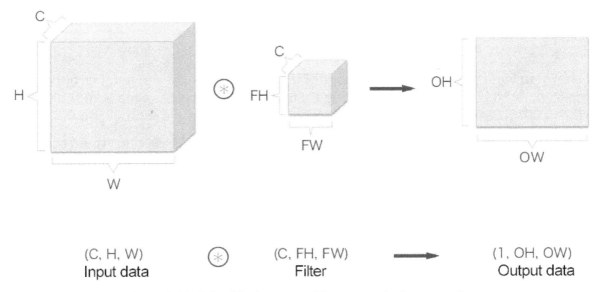

(C, H, W)
Input data
⊛
(C, FH, FW)
Filter
⟶
(1, OH, OW)
Output data

Figure 7.10: Using blocks to consider a convolution operation

In this example, the data's output is one feature map. One feature map means that the size of the output channel is one. So, how can we provide multiple outputs of convolution operations in the channel dimension? To do that, we use multiple filters (weights). *Figure 7.11* shows this graphically:

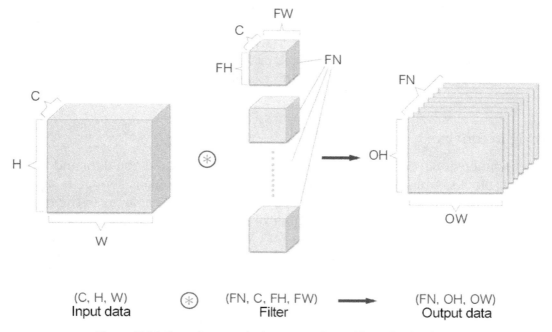

(C, H, W)
Input data
(FN, C, FH, FW)
Filter
(FN, OH, OW)
Output data

Figure 7.11: Sample convolution operation with multiple filters

As shown in *Figure 7.11*, when the number of filters applied is FN, the number of output maps generated is also FN. By combining FN maps, you can create a block of the shape (FN, OH, OW). Passing this completed block to the next layer is the process a CNN.

You must also consider the number of filters in a convolution operation. To do that, we will write the filter weight data as four-dimensional data (output_channel, input_channel, height, width). For example, when there are 20 filters with three channels where the size is 5 x 5, it is represented as (20, 3, 5, 5).

A convolution operation has biases (like a fully connected layer). *Figure 7.12* shows the example provided in *Figure 7.11* when you add biases.

As we can see, each channel has only one bias data. Here, the shape of the bias is (FN, 1, 1), while the shape of the filter output is (FN, OH, OW). Adding these two blocks adds the same bias value to each channel in the filter output result, (FN, OH, OW). NumPy's broadcasting facilitates blocks of different shapes (please refer to *Broadcasting* section in *Chapter 1, Introduction to Python*):

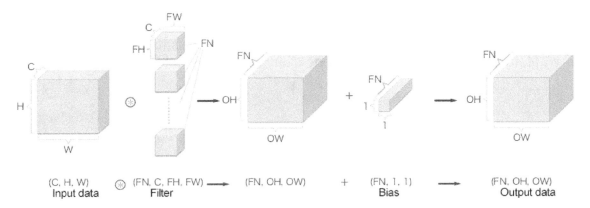

Figure 7.12: Process flow of a convolution operation (the bias term is also added)

Batch Processing

Input data is processed in batches in neural network processing. The implementations we've looked at so far for fully connected neural networks have supported batch processing, which enables more efficient processing and supports mini-batches in the training process.

We can also support batch processing in a convolution operation by storing the data that flows through each layer as four-dimensional data. Specifically, the data is stored in the order (batch_num, channel, height, width). For example, when the processing shown in *Figure 7.12* is conducted for N data in batches, the shape of the data becomes as follows.

In the data flow for batch processing shown here, the dimensions for the batches are added at the beginning of each piece of data. Thus, the data passes each layer as four-dimensional data. Please note that four-dimensional data that flows in the network indicates that a convolution operation is performed for N data; that is, N processes are conducted at one time:

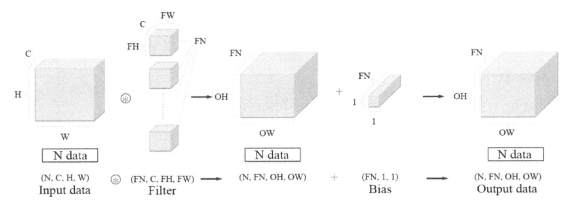

Figure 7.13: Process flow of a convolution operation (batch processing)

The Pooling Layer

A pooling operation makes the space of the height and width smaller. As shown in *Figure 7.14*, it converts a 2 x 2 area into one element to reduce the space's size:

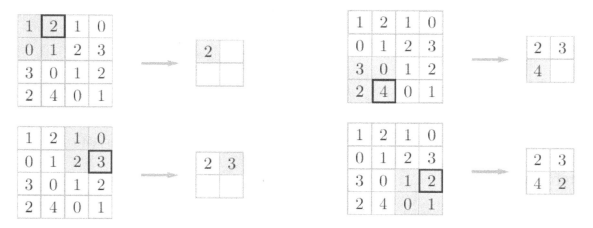

Figure 7.14: Procedure of max pooling

This example shows this procedure when 2 x 2 max-pooling is conducted with a stride of 2. "Max pooling" takes the maximum value of a region, while "2 x 2" indicates the size of the target region. As we can see, it takes the maximum element in a 2 x 2 region. The stride is 2 in this example, so the 2 x 2 window moves by two elements at one time. Generally, the same value is used for the pooling window size and the stride. For example, the stride is 3 for a 3 x 3 window, and the stride is 4 for a 4 x 4 window.

> **Note**
>
> In addition to max pooling, average pooling can also be used. Max pooling takes the maximum value in the target region, while average pooling averages the values in the target region. In image recognition, max pooling is mainly used. Therefore, a "pooling layer" in this book indicates max pooling.

Characteristics of a Pooling Layer

A pooling layer has various characteristics, described below.

There are no parameters to learn

Unlike a convolution layer, a pooling layer has no parameters to learn. Pooling has no parameters to learn because it only takes the maximum value (or averages the values) in the target region.

The number of channels does not change

In pooling, the number of channels in the output data is the same as that in the input data. As shown in *Figure 7.15*, this calculation is performed independently for each channel:

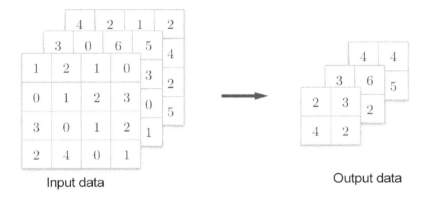

Input data   Output data

Figure 7.15: Pooling does not change the number of channels

It is robust to a tiny position change

Pooling returns the same result, even when the input data is shifted slightly. Therefore, it is robust to a tiny shift of input data. For example, in 3 x 3 pooling, pooling absorbs the shift of input data, as shown in *Figure 7.16*:

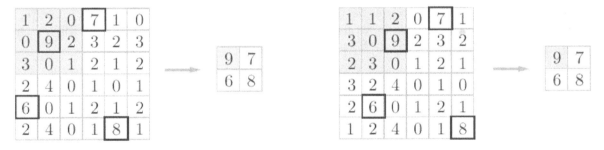

Figure 7.16: Even when the input data is shifted by one element in terms of width, the output is the same (it may not be the same, depending on the data)

Implementing the Convolution and Pooling Layers

So far, we have seen convolution and pooling layers in detail. In this section, we will implement these two layers in Python. As described in *Chapter 5, Backpropagation*, the class that will be implemented here also provides forward and backward methods so that it can be used as a module.

You may feel that implementing convolution and pooling layers is complicated, but you can implement them easily if you use a certain "trick." This section describes this trick and makes the task at hand easy. Then, we will implement a convolution layer.

Four-Dimensional Arrays

As described earlier, four-dimensional data flows in each layer in a CNN. For example, when the shape of the data is (10, 1, 28, 28), it indicates that ten pieces of data with a height of 28, width of 28, and 1 channel exist. You can implement this in Python as follows:

```
>>> x = np.random.rand(10, 1, 28, 28) # Generate data randomly
>>> x.shape
(10, 1, 28, 28)
```

To access the first piece of data, you can write `x[0]` (the index begins at 0 in Python). Similarly, you can write `x[1]` to access the second piece of data:

```
>>> x[0].shape # (1, 28, 28)
>>> x[1].shape # (1, 28, 28)
```

To access the spatial data in the first channel of the first piece of data, you can write the following:

```
>>> x[0, 0] # or x[0][0]
```

You can handle four-dimensional data in this way in a CNN. Therefore, implementing a convolution operation may be complicated. However, a "trick" called `im2col` makes this task easy.

Expansion by im2col

To implement a convolution operation, you normally need to nest `for` statements several times. Such an implementation is slightly troublesome and `for` statements in NumPy slow down the processing speed (in NumPy, it is desirable that you do not use any `for` statements to access elements). Here, we will not use any `for` statements. Instead, we will use a simple function called `im2col` for a simple implementation.

The `im2col` function expands input data conveniently for a filter (weight). As shown in *Figure 7.17*, `im2col` converts three-dimensional input data into a two-dimensional matrix (to be exact, it converts four-dimensional data, including the number of batches, into two-dimensional data).

`im2col` expands the input data conveniently for a filter (weight). Specifically, it expands the area that a filter will be applied to in the input data (a three-dimensional block) into a row, as shown in *Figure 7.18*. `im2col` expands all the locations to apply a filter to.

In *Figure 7.18*, a large stride is used so that the filter areas do not overlap. This is done for visibility reasons. In actual convolution operations, the filter areas will overlap in most cases, in which case, the number of elements after expansion by `im2col` will be larger than that in the original block. Therefore, an implementation using `im2col` has the disadvantage of consuming more memory than usual. However, putting data into a large matrix is beneficial to perform calculations with a computer. For example, matrix calculation libraries (linear algebra libraries) highly optimize matrix calculations so that they can multiply large matrices quickly. Therefore, you can use a linear algebra library effectively by converting input data into a matrix:

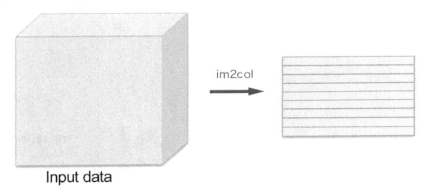

Figure 7.17: Overview of im2col

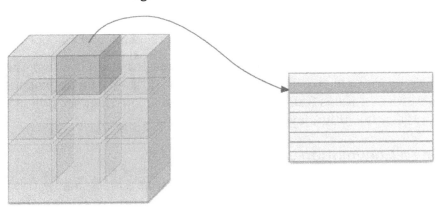

Figure 7.18: Expanding the filter target area from the beginning in a row

> **Note**
>
> The name `im2col` is an abbreviation of "image to column," meaning the conversion of images into matrices. Deep learning frameworks such as Caffe and Chainer provide the `im2col` function, which is used to implement a convolution layer.

After using `im2col` to expand input data, all you have to do is expand the filter (weight) for the convolution layer into a row and multiply the two matrices (see *Figure 7.19*). This process is almost the same as that of a fully connected Affine layer:

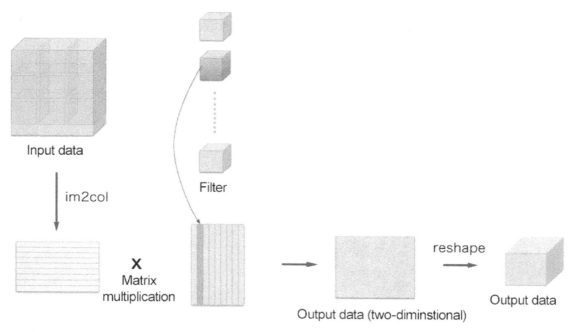

Figure 7.19: Details of filtering in a convolution operation – expand the filter into a column and multiply the matrix by the data expanded by im2col. Lastly, reshape the result of the size of the output data.

As shown in *Figure 7.19*, the output of using the `im2col` function is a two-dimensional matrix. You must transform two-dimensional output data into an appropriate shape because a CNN stores data as four-dimensional arrays. The next section covers the flow of implementing a convolution layer.

Implementing a Convolution Layer

This book uses the `im2col` function, and we will use it as a black box without considering its implementation. The `im2col` implementation is located at `common/util.py`. It is a simple function that is about 10 lines in length. Please refer to it if you are interested.

This `im2col` function has the following interface:

```
im2col (input_data, filter_h, filter_w, stride=1, pad=0)
```

- **`input_data`**: Input data that consists of arrays of four dimensions (amount of data, channel, height, breadth)
- **`filter_h`**: Height of the filter

- `filter_w`: Width of the filter

- `stride`: Stride

- `pad`: Padding

The `im2col` function considers the "filter size," "stride," and "padding" to expand input data into a two-dimensional array, as follows:

```
import sys, os
sys.path.append(os.pardir)
from common.util import im2col

x1 = np.random.rand(1, 3, 7, 7)
col1 = im2col(x1, 5, 5, stride=1, pad=0)
print(col1.shape) # (9, 75)

x2 = np.random.rand(10, 3, 7, 7)
col2 = im2col(x2, 5, 5, stride=1, pad=0)
print(col2.shape) # (90, 75)
```

The preceding code shows two examples. The first one uses 7x7 data with a batch size of 1, where the number of channels is 3. The second one uses data of the same shape with a batch size of 10. When we use the `im2col` function, the number of elements in the second dimension is 75 in both cases. This is the total number of elements in the filter (3 channels, size 5x5). When the batch size is 1, the result from `im2col` is (9, 75) in size. On the other hand, it is (90, 75) in the second example because the batch size is 10. It can store 10 times as much data.

Now, we will use `im2col` to implement a convolution layer as a class called `Convolution`:

```
class Convolution:
    def __init__(self, W, b, stride=1, pad=0):
        self.W = W
        self.b = b
        self.stride = stride
        self.pad = pad

    def forward(self, x):
        FN, C, FH, FW = self.W.shape
        N, C, H, W = x.shape
        out_h = int(1 + (H + 2*self.pad - FH) / self.stride)
        out_w = int(1 + (W + 2*self.pad - FW) / self.stride)

        col = im2col(x, FH, FW, self.stride, self.pad)
```

```
col_W = self.W.reshape(FN, -1).T # Expand the filter
out = np.dot(col, col_W) + self.b

out = out.reshape(N, out_h, out_w, -1).transpose(0, 3, 1, 2)

return out
```

The initialization method of the convolution layer takes the filter (weight), bias, stride, and padding as arguments. The filter is four-dimensional, (FN, C, FH, and FW). FN stands for filter number (number of filters), C stands for a channel, FH stands for filter height, and FW stands for filter width.

In the implementation of a convolution layer, an important section has been shown in bold. Here, im2col is used to expand the input data, while reshape is used to expand the filter into a two-dimensional array. The expanded matrices are multiplied.

The section of code that expands the filter (the section in bold in the preceding code) expands the block of each filter into one line, as shown in *Figure 7.19*. Here, -1 is specified as reshape (FN, -1), which is one of the convenient features of reshape. When -1 is specified for reshape, the number of elements is adjusted so that it matches the number of elements in a multidimensional array. For example, an array with the shape of (10, 3, 5, 5) has 750 elements in total. When reshape(10, -1) is specified here, it is reshaped into an array with the shape of (10, 75).

The forward function adjusts the output size appropriately at the end. NumPy's transpose function is used there. The transpose function changes the order of axes in a multidimensional array. As shown in *Figure 7.20*, you can specify the order of indices (numbers) that starts at 0 to change the order of axes.

Thus, you can implement the forward process of a convolution layer in almost the same way as a fully connected Affine layer by using im2col for expansion (see *Implementing the Affine and Softmax Layers* section in *Chapter 5, Backpropagation*). Next, we will implement backward propagation in the convolution layer. Note that backward propagation in the convolution layer must do the reverse of im2col. This is handled by the col2im function, which is provided in this book (located at common/util.py). Except for when col2im is used, you can implement backward propagation in the convolution layer in the same way as the Affine layer. The implementation of backward propagation in the convolution layer is located at common/layer.py.

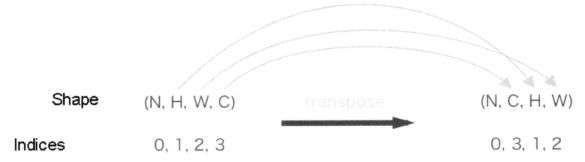

Shape	(N, H, W, C)	transpose	(N, C, H, W)
Indices	0, 1, 2, 3		0, 3, 1, 2

Figure 7.20: Using NumPy's transpose to change the order of the axes – specifying the indices (numbers) to change the order of axes

Implementing a Pooling Layer

You can use `im2col` to expand the input data when implementing a pooling layer, as in the case of a convolution layer. What is different is that pooling is independent of the channel dimension, unlike a convolution layer. As shown in *Figure 7.21*, the target pooling area is expanded independently for each channel.

After this expansion, you have only to take the maximum value in each row of the expanded matrix and transform the result into an appropriate shape (*Figure 7.22*).

This is how the forward process in a pooling layer is implemented. The following shows a sample implementation in Python:

```python
class Pooling:
    def __init__(self, pool_h, pool_w, stride=1, pad=0):
        self.pool_h = pool_h
        self.pool_w = pool_w
        self.stride = stride
        self.pad = pad

    def forward(self, x):
        N, C, H, W = x.shape
        out_h = int(1 + (H - self.pool_h) / self.stride)
        out_w = int(1 + (W - self.pool_w) / self.stride)
        # Expansion (1)

        col = im2col(x, self.pool_h, self.pool_w, self.stride, self.pad)
        col = col.reshape(-1, self.pool_h*self.pool_w)

        # Maximum value (2)
```

```
out = np.max(col, axis=1)
# Reshape (3)
out = out.reshape(N, out_h, out_w, C).transpose(0, 3, 1, 2)

    return out
```

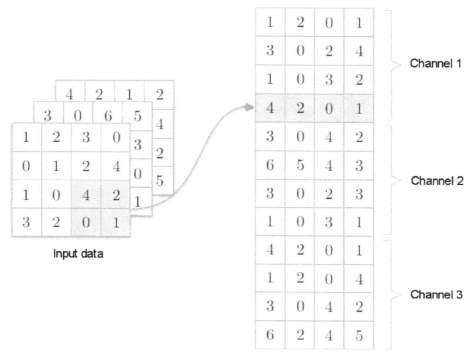

Figure 7.21: Expanding the target pooling area of the input data (pooling of 2x2)

As shown in *Figure* 7.22, there are three steps when it comes to implementing a pooling layer:

1. Expand the input data.

2. Take the maximum value in each row.

3. Reshape the output appropriately.

The implementation of each step is simple and is only one or two lines in length:

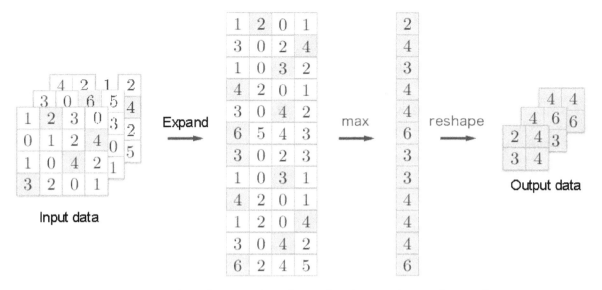

Figure 7.22: Flow of implementation of a pooling layer – the maximum elements in the pooling area are shown in gray

> **Note**
>
> You can use NumPy's `np.max` method to take the maximum value. By specifying the axis argument in np.max, you can take the maximum value along the specified axis. For example, `np.max(x, axis=1)` returns the maximum value of **x** on each axis of the first dimension.

That's all for the forward process in a pooling layer. As shown here, after expanding the input data into a shape that's suitable for pooling, subsequent implementations of it are very simple.

For the backward process in a pooling layer, backward propagation of `max` (used in the implementation of the ReLU layer in the *ReLU Layer* sub-section in *Chapter 5, Backpropagation*), provides more information on this. The implementation of a pooling layer is located at `common/layer.py`.

Implementing a CNN

So far, we have implemented convolution and pooling layers. Now, we will combine these layers to create a CNN that recognizes handwritten digits and implement it, as shown in *Figure 7.23*.

As shown in *Figure 7.23*, the network consists of "Convolution – ReLU – Pooling – Affine – ReLU – Affine – Softmax" layers. We will implement this as a class named `SimpleConvNet`:

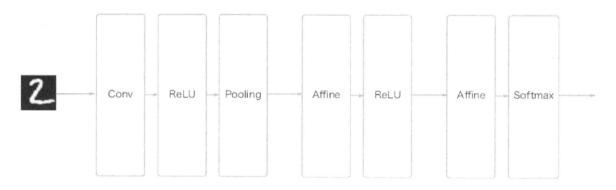

Figure 7.23: Network configuration of a simple CNN

Now, let's look at the initialization of `SimpleConvNet` (`__init__`). It takes the following arguments:

- `input_dim`: Dimensions of the input data (**channel**, **height**, **width**).

- `conv_param`: Hyperparameters of the convolution layer (dictionary). The following are the dictionary keys:

- `filter_num`: Number of filters

- `filter_size`: Size of the filter

- `stride`: Stride

- `pad`: Padding

- `hidden_size`: Number of neurons in the hidden layer (fully connected)

- `output_size`: Number of neurons in the output layer (fully connected)

- `weight_init_std`: Standard deviation of the weights at initialization

Here, the hyperparameters of the convolution layer are provided as a dictionary called `conv_param`. We assume that the required hyperparameter values are stored using `{'filter_num':30, 'filter_size':5, 'pad':0, 'stride':1}`.

The implementation of the initialization of `SimpleConvNet` is a little long, so here it's divided into three parts to make this easier to follow. The following code shows the first part of the initialization process:

```
class SimpleConvNet:
    def __init__(self, input_dim=(1, 28, 28),
                 conv_param={'filter_num':30, 'filter_size':5,
                     'pad':0, 'stride':1},
                 hidden_size=100, output_size=10, weight_init_std=0.01):
        filter_num = conv_param['filter_num']
        filter_size = conv_param['filter_size']
        filter_pad = conv_param['pad']
        filter_stride = conv_param['stride']
        input_size = input_dim[1]
        conv_output_size = (input_size - filter_size + 2*filter_pad) / \
                       filter_stride + 1
        pool_output_size = int(filter_num * (conv_output_size/2) *(conv_
output_size/2))
```

Here, the hyperparameters of the convolution layer that are provided by the initialization argument are taken out of the dictionary (so that we can use them later). Then, the output size of the convolution layer is calculated. The following code initializes the weight parameters:

```
        self.params = {}
        self.params['W1'] = weight_init_std * \
        np.random.randn(filter_num, input_dim[0],
        filter_size, filter_size)
        self.params['b1'] = np.zeros(filter_num)
        self.params['W2'] = weight_init_std * \
        np.random.randn(pool_output_size,hidden_size)
        self.params['b2'] = np.zeros(hidden_size)
        self.params['W3'] = weight_init_std * \
        np.random.randn(hidden_size, output_size)
        self.params['b3'] = np.zeros(output_size)
```

The parameters required for training are the weights and biases of the first (convolution) layer and the remaining two fully connected layers. The parameters are stored in the instance dictionary variable, **params**. The **W1** key is used for the weight, while the **b1** key is used for the bias of the first (convolution) layer. In the same way, the **W2** and **b2** keys are used for the weight and bias of the second (fully connected) layer and the **W3** and **b3** keys are used for the weight and bias of the third (fully connected) layer, respectively. Lastly, the required layers are generated, as follows:

```
self.layers = OrderedDict( )
self.layers['Conv1'] = Convolution(self.params['W1'],
                                   self.params['b1'],
                                   conv_param['stride'],
                                   conv_param['pad'])
self.layers['Relu1'] = Relu( )
self.layers['Pool1'] = Pooling(pool_h=2, pool_w=2, stride=2)
self.layers['Affine1'] = Affine(self.params['W2'],
                                self.params['b2'])
self.layers['Relu2'] = Relu( )
self.layers['Affine2'] = Affine(self.params['W3'],
                                self.params['b3'])

self.last_layer = SoftmaxWithLoss( )
```

Layers are added to the ordered dictionary (**OrderedDict**) in an appropriate order. Only the last layer, **SoftmaxWithLoss**, is added to another variable, **last-layer**.

This is the initialization of **SimpleConvNet**. After the initialization, you can implement the **predict** method for predicting and the **loss** method for calculating the value of the loss function, as follows:

```
def predict(self, x):
    for layer in self.layers.values( ):
        x = layer.forward(x)
    return x

def loss(self, x, t):
    y = self.predict(x)
    return self.lastLayer.forward(y, t)
```

Here, the **x** argument is the input data and the **t** argument is the label. The **predict** method only calls the added layers in order from the top, and passes the result to the next layer. In addition to forward processing in the **predict** method, the **loss** method performs forward processing until the last layer, **SoftmaxWithLoss**.

The following implementation obtains the gradients via backpropagation, as follows:

```
def gradient(self, x, t):
    # forward
    self.loss(x, t)

    # backward
    dout = 1
    dout = self.lastLayer.backward(dout)

    layers = list(self.layers.values( ))
    layers.reverse( )
    for layer in layers:
        dout = layer.backward(dout)
    # Settings
    grads = {}
    grads['W1'] = self.layers['Conv1'].dW
    grads['b1'] = self.layers['Conv1'].db
    grads['W2'] = self.layers['Affine1'].dW
    grads['b2'] = self.layers['Affine1'].db
    grads['W3'] = self.layers['Affine2'].dW
    grads['b3'] = self.layers['Affine2'].db

    return grads
```

Backpropagation is used to obtain the gradients of the parameters. To do that, forward propagation and backward propagation are conducted one after the other. Because the forward and backward propagation are implemented properly in each layer, we have only to call them in an appropriate order here. Lastly, the gradient of each weight parameter is stored in the grads dictionary. Thus, you can implement SimpleConvNet.

Now, let's train the SimpleConvNet class using the MNIST dataset. The code for training is almost the same as that described in the *Implementing a Training Algorithm* section in *Chapter 4, Neural Network Training*. Therefore, the code won't be shown here (the source code is located at ch07/train_convnet.py).

When SimpleConvNet is used to train the MNIST dataset, the recognition accuracy of the training data is 99.82%, while the recognition accuracy of the test data is 98.96% (the recognition accuracies are slightly different from training to training). 99% is a very high recognition accuracy for the test data for a relatively small network. In the next chapter, we will add layers to create a network where the recognition accuracy of the test data exceeds 99%.

As we have seen here, convolution and pooling layers are indispensable modules in image recognition. A CNN can read the spatial characteristics of images and achieve high accuracy in handwritten digit recognition.

Visualizing a CNN

What does the convolution layer used in a CNN "see"? Here, we will visualize a convolution layer to explore what happens in a CNN.

Visualizing the Weight of the First Layer

Earlier, we conducted simple CNN training for the MNIST dataset. The shape of the weight of the first (convolution) layer was (30, 1, 5, 5). It was 5x5 in size, had 1 channel, and 30 filters. When the filter is 5x5 in size and has 1 channel, it can be visualized as a one-channel gray image. Now, let's show the filters of the convolution layer (the first layer) as images. Here, we will compare the weights before and after training. *Figure* 7.24 shows the results (the source code is located at `ch07/visualize_filter.py`):

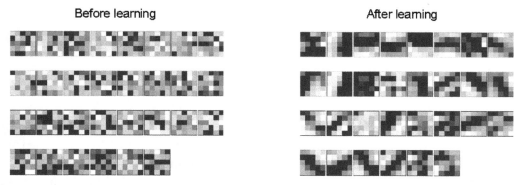

Figure 7.24: Weight of the first (convolution) layer before and after training. The elements of the weight are real numbers, but they are normalized between 0 and 255 to show the images so that the smallest value is black (0) and the largest value is white (255)

As shown in *Figure* 7.24, the filters before training are initialized randomly. Black-and-white shades have no pattern. On the other hand, the filters after training are images with a pattern. Some filters have gradations from white to black, while some filters have small areas of color (called "blobs"), which indicates that training provided a pattern to the filters.

The filters with a pattern on the right-hand side of *Figure* 7.24 "see" edges (boundaries of colors) and blobs. For example, when a filter is white in the left half and black in the right half, it reacts to a vertical edge, as shown in *Figure* 7.25.

Figure 7.25 shows the results when two learned filters are selected, and convolution processing is performed on the input image. You can see that "filter 1" reacted to a vertical edge and that "filter 2" reacted to a horizontal edge:

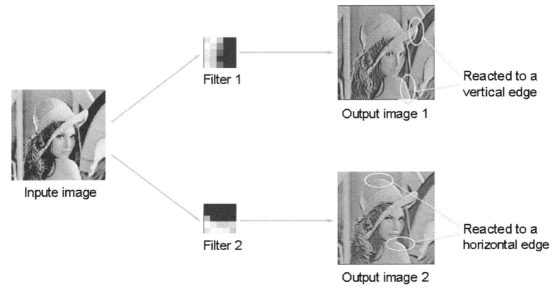

Figure 7.25: Filters reacting to horizontal and vertical edges. White pixels appear at a vertical edge in output image 1. Meanwhile, many white pixels appear at a horizontal edge in output image 2.

Thus, you can see that the filters in a convolution layer extract primitive information such as edges and blobs. The CNN that was implemented earlier passes such primitive information to subsequent layers.

Using a Hierarchical Structure to Extract Information

The preceding result comes from the first (convolution) layer. It extracts low-level information such as edges and blobs. So, what type of information does each layer in a CNN with multiple layers extract? Research on visualization in deep learning [(*Matthew D. Zeiler and Rob Fergus (2014): Visualizing and Understanding Convolutional Networks. In David Fleet, Tomas Pajdla, Bernt Schiele, & Tinne Tuytelaars, eds. Computer Vision – ECCV 2014. Lecture Notes in Computer Science. Springer International Publishing, 818 – 833*) and (*A. Mahendran and A. Vedaldi (2015): Understanding deep image representations by inverting them. In the 2015 IEEE Conference on Computer Vision and Pattern Recognition (CVPR). 5188 – 5196. DOI:* (http://dx.doi.org/10.1109/CVPR.2015.7299155)] has stated that the deeper a layer, the more abstract the extracted information (to be precise, neurons that react strongly).

Typical CNNs

CNNs of various architectures have been proposed so far. In this section, we will look at two important networks. One is LeNet (*Y. Lecun, L. Bottou, Y. Bengio, and P. Haffner (1998): Gradient-based learning applied to document recognition. Proceedings of the IEEE 86, 11 (November 1998), 2278 – 2324. DOI:* (http://dx.doi.org/10.1109/5.726791)). It was one of the first CNNs and was first proposed in 1998. The other is AlexNet (*Alex Krizhevsky, Ilya Sutskever, and Geoffrey E. Hinton (2012): ImageNet Classification with Deep Convolutional Neural Networks. In F. Pereira, C. J. C. Burges, L. Bottou, & K. Q. Weinberger, eds. Advances in Neural Information Processing Systems 25. Curran Associates, Inc., 1097 – 1105*). It was proposed in 2012 and drew attention to deep learning.

LeNet

LeNet is a network for handwritten digit recognition that was proposed in 1998. In the network, a convolution layer and a pooling layer (i.e., a subsampling layer that only "thins out elements") are repeated, and finally, a fully connected layer outputs the result.

There are some differences between LeNet and the "current CNN." One is that there's an activation function. A sigmoid function is used in LeNet, while ReLU is mainly used now. Subsampling is used in the original LeNet to reduce the size of intermediate data, while max pooling is mainly used now:

In this way, there are some differences between LeNet and the "current CNN," but they are not significant. This is surprising when we consider that LeNet was the "first CNN" to be proposed almost 20 years ago.

AlexNet

AlexNet was published nearly 20 years after LeNet was proposed. Although AlexNet created a boom in deep learning, its network architecture hasn't changed much from LeNet:

AlexNet stacks a convolution layer and a pooling layer and outputs the result through a fully connected layer. Its architecture is not much different from LeNet, but there are some differences, as follows:

- ReLU is used as the activation function

- A layer for local normalization called **Local Response Normalization** (**LRN**) is used

- Dropout is used (see *Dropout* sub-section in *Chapter 6, Training Techniques*)

LeNet and AlexNet are not very different in terms of their network architectures. However, the surrounding environment and computer technologies have advanced greatly. Now, everyone can obtain a large quantity of data, and widespread GPUs that are good at large parallel computing enable massive operations at high speed. Big data and GPUs greatly motivated the development of deep learning.

> **Note**
>
> Many parameters often exist in deep learning (a network with many layers). Many calculations are required for training, and a large quantity of data is required to "satisfy" these parameters. We can say that GPUs and big data cast light on these challenges.

Summary

In this chapter, we learned about CNNs. Specifically, we covered convolution layers and pooling layers (the basic modules that constitute CNNs) in great detail in order to understand them at the implementation level. CNNs are mostly used when looking at data regarding images. Please ensure that you understand the content of this chapter before moving on.

In this chapter, we learned about the following:

- In a CNN, convolution, and pooling layers are added to the previous network, which consists of fully connected layers.

- You can use `im2col` (a function for expanding images into arrays) to implement convolution and pooling layers simply and efficiently.

- Visualizing a CNN enables you to see how advanced information is extracted as the layer becomes deeper.

- Typical CNNs include LeNet and AlexNet.

- Big data and GPUs contribute significantly to the development of deep learning.

8

Deep Learning

Deep learning is a machine learning method based on deep neural networks. You can create a deep network by adding layers to the networks we've described so far. However, a deep network has problems. This chapter will describe the characteristics, problems, and possibilities of deep learning, as well as an overview of current deep learning practices.

Making a Network Deeper

Throughout this book, we have learned a lot about neural networks, including the various layers that constitute a neural network, effective techniques used in training, CNNs that are especially effective for handling images, and how to optimize parameters. These are all important techniques in deep learning. Here, we will integrate the techniques we have learned so far to create a deep network. Then, we will try our hand at handwritten digit recognition using the MNIST dataset.

Deeper Networks

First, we will create a CNN that has the network architecture shown in *Figure* 8.1. This network is based on the VGG network, which will be described in the next section.

As shown in *Figure* 8.1, the network is deeper than the networks that we have implemented so far. All the convolution layers used here are small 3x3 filters. Here, the number of channels becomes larger as the network deepens (as the number of channels in a convolution layer increases from 16 in the first layer to 16, 32, 32, 64, and 64). As you can see, pooling layers are inserted to reduce the spatial size of intermediate data gradually, while dropout layers are used for the latter fully connected layers:

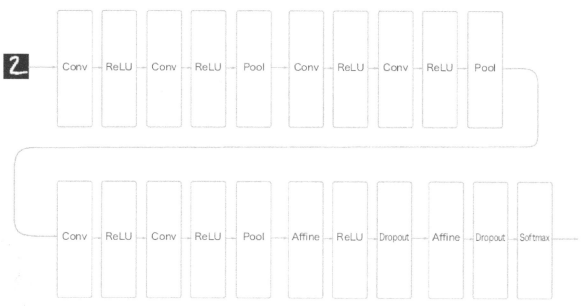

Figure 8.1: Deep CNN for handwritten digit recognition

This network uses the "He initializer" to initialize the weights, and Adam to update the weight parameters, resulting in the following characteristics:

- Convolution layers which use small 3×3 filters
- ReLU as the activation function
- A dropout layer used after a fully connected layer
- Optimization is done by Adam
- "He initializer" for initial weight values

As these characteristics indicate, the network in *Figure 8.1* uses many neural network techniques that we have learned so far. Now, let's use this network for training. The result shows that the recognition accuracy of this network is 99.38% (final recognition accuracies vary slightly, but this network will generally exceed 99%).

> **Note**
>
> The source code that implemented the network shown in *Figure 8.1* is located at `ch08/deep_convnet.py`. The code for training is provided at `ch08/train_deepnet.py`. You can use this code to reproduce the training that will be conducted here. Training in a deep network takes a lot of time (probably more than half a day). This book provides trained weight parameters in `ch08/deep_conv_net_params.pkl`. The `deep_convnet.py` code file provides a feature for loading trained parameters. You can use it as required.

The error rate of the network shown in *Figure 8.1* is only 0.62%. Here, we can see what images were incorrectly recognized. *Figure 8.2* shows the recognition error examples:

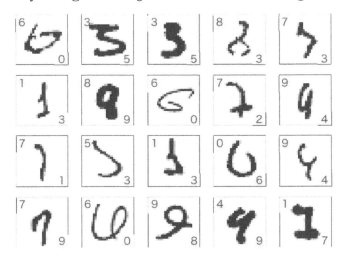

Figure 8.2: Sample images that were recognized incorrectly – the upper left of each image shows the correct label, while the lower right shows the result of prediction by this network

As shown in *Figure 8.2*, these images are difficult even for us humans to recognize. The upper-left image looks like a "0" (the correct answer is "6"), and the one next to it certainly seems to be a "5" (the correct answer is "3"). Generally, the distinctions between "1" and "7", "0" and "6", and "3" and "5" are difficult. These examples explain why they were recognized incorrectly.

While this deep CNN is very precise, it recognized images incorrectly in the same way as humans would. This also shows us the large potential of a deep CNN.

Improving Recognition Accuracy

The website called "What is the class of this image?" (*Rodrigo Benenson's blog* "*Classification datasets results*" (http://rodrigob.github.io/are_we_there_yet/build/classification_datasets_results.html)) ranks the recognition accuracies for various datasets by the techniques published in the related literature (*Figure 8.3*):

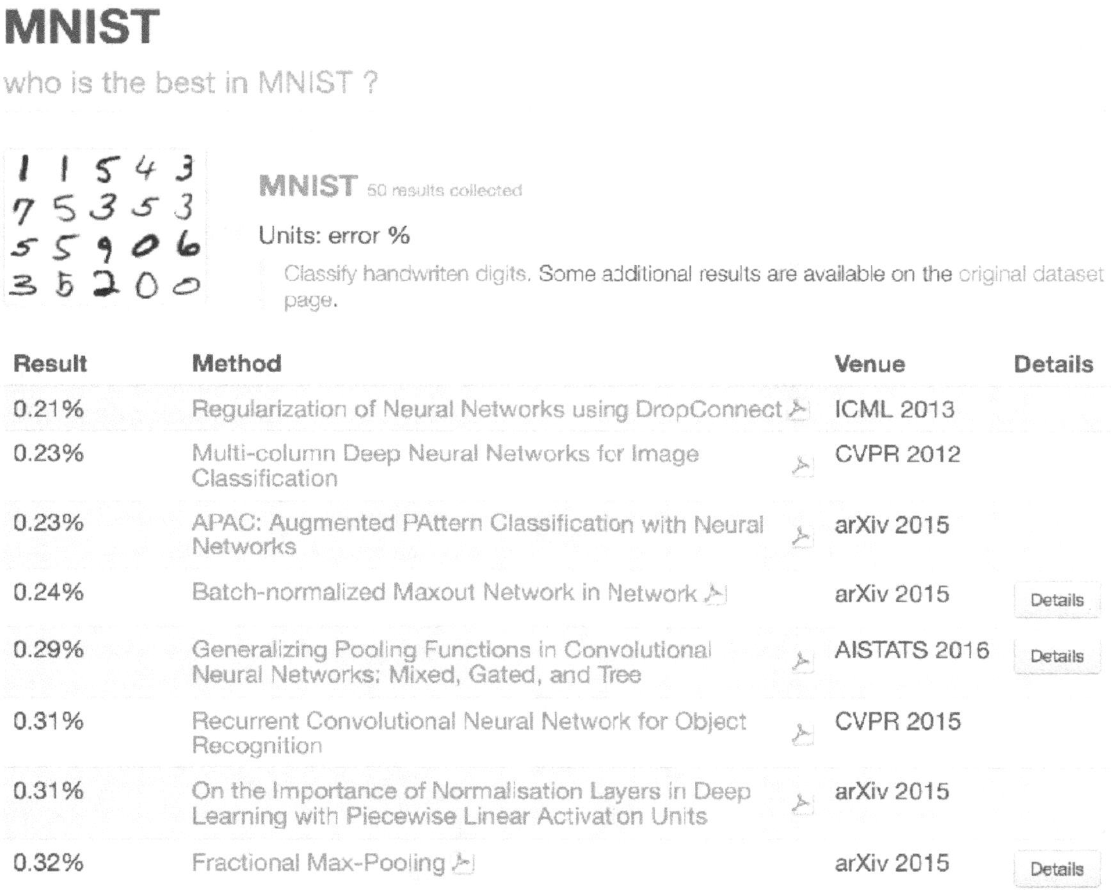

MNIST

who is the best in MNIST ?

1 1 5 4 3 *7 5 3 5 3* *5 5 9 0 6* *3 5 2 0 0*	**MNIST** 50 results collected Units: error % Classify handwriten digits. Some additional results are available on the original dataset page.

Result	Method	Venue	Details
0.21%	Regularization of Neural Networks using DropConnect	ICML 2013	
0.23%	Multi-column Deep Neural Networks for Image Classification	CVPR 2012	
0.23%	APAC: Augmented PAttern Classification with Neural Networks	arXiv 2015	
0.24%	Batch-normalized Maxout Network in Network	arXiv 2015	Details
0.29%	Generalizing Pooling Functions in Convolutional Neural Networks: Mixed, Gated, and Tree	AISTATS 2016	Details
0.31%	Recurrent Convolutional Neural Network for Object Recognition	CVPR 2015	
0.31%	On the Importance of Normalisation Layers in Deep Learning with Piecewise Linear Activation Units	arXiv 2015	
0.32%	Fractional Max-Pooling	arXiv 2015	Details

Figure 8.3: Ranking techniques for the MNIST dataset

> **Note**
>
> *Figure 8.3* is cited from reference, *Rodrigo Benenson's blog "Classification datasets results*" (http://rodrigob.github.io/are_we_there_yet/build/classification_datasets_results.html) as of June 2016.

In the ranking shown in *Figure* 8.3, keywords such as "neural networks," "deep," and "convolutional" are noticeable. Many high-ranked techniques are CNN-based. As of June 2016, the highest recognition accuracy for the MNIST dataset is 99.79% (an error rate of 0.21%), and the technique is also CNN-based (*Li Wan, Matthew Zeiler, Sixin Zhang, Yann L. Cun, and Rob Fergus (2013): Regularization of Neural Networks using DropConnect. In Sanjoy Dasgupta & David McAllester, eds. Proceedings of the 30th International Conference on Machine Learning (ICML2013). JMLR Workshop and Conference Proceedings, 1058 – 1066*). The CNN that is used there is not very deep (two convolution layers and two fully connected layers).

> **Note**
>
> For the MNIST dataset, the highest accuracy can be obtained immediately, even if the network is not very deep. For a relatively simple problem such as handwritten digit recognition, the representation of the network does not need to be very high. Therefore, adding layers is not very beneficial. In the large-scale general object recognition process, adding layers greatly improves recognition accuracy because it is a complicated problem.

By examining the aforementioned high-ranked techniques, we can find techniques and tips for further improving recognition accuracy. For example, we can see that ensemble learning, learning rate decay, and **data augmentation** contribute to the improvement of recognition accuracy. Data augmentation is a simple but particularly effective method for improving recognition accuracy.

Data augmentation uses an algorithm to expand input images (training images) artificially. As shown in *Figure* 8.4, it adds the images by slightly changing the input images with rotation or vertical/horizontal movement. This is especially effective when the number of images in the dataset is limited:

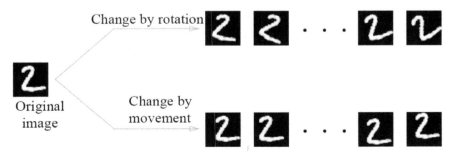

Figure 8.4: Sample data augmentation

You can use data augmentation to expand images in various ways, other than the modifications shown in *Figure 8.4*. For example, you can cut out part of an image (or crop) or reverse an image horizontally (called flipping, though this is only effective when the symmetry of the image does not need to be considered). For ordinary images, changing their appearance (e.g., by adding brightness and scaling them up or down, is also effective. If you can use data augmentation to increase the number of training images, you can improve the recognition accuracy by using deep learning. This may seem a simple trick, but it often brings good results. We will not implement data augmentation here. Since implementing this is easy, please try it for yourself if you are interested.

Motivation for a Deeper Network

There is still much that is not known about the importance of making a network deeper. Although theoretical findings are insufficient now, past research and experiments can explain some things (rather intuitively). This section will provide some data and explanations that support the importance of "making a network deeper."

First, the results from competitions surrounding large-scale image recognition such as ILSVRC show the importance of "making a network deeper" (please see the next section for details). They indicate that many of the recent high-ranked techniques are based on deep learning and that the networks tend to go deeper. The deeper the network, the better the recognition performance.

One of the advantages of this is that you can reduce the number of parameters in the network. When a network is deeper, it can achieve similar (or higher) representation with fewer parameters. This is easy to understand when you consider the filter size in a convolution operation. *Figure 8.5* shows a convolution layer with a 5x5 filter.

Please note the area of the input data each node of the output data is calculated in. Of course, each output node is based on the 5x5 area of the input data in the example shown in *Figure 8.5*. Now, let's think about a case where 3x3 convolution operations are repeated twice, as shown in *Figure 8.6*. In this case, intermediate data is based on a 3x3 area for each output node. So, which area of the previous input data is the 3x3 area of intermediate data based on? When you look at *Figure 8.6* carefully, you will notice that it is based on a 5×5 area. Thus, the output data of *Figure 8.6* "looks at" a 5×5 area of input data for calculation:

Input data   Output data

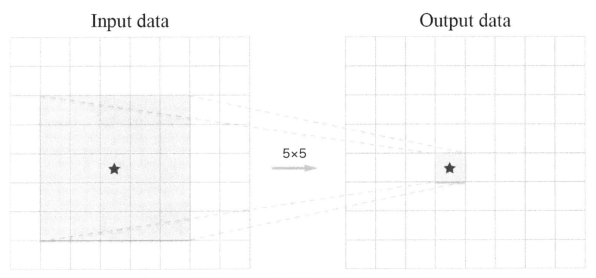

Figure 8.5: Example of a 5x5 convolution operation

Input data   Intermediate data   Output data

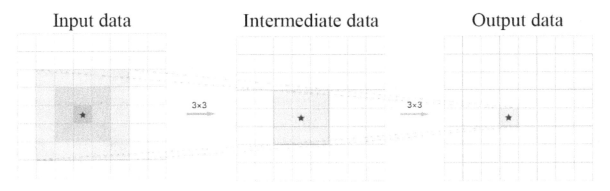

Figure 8:6: Example of when 3x3 convolution operations are repeated twice

The area of one 5x5 convolution operation is equivalent to that of two 3x3 convolution operations. The former uses 25 parameters (5x5), while the latter uses 18 parameters (2x3x3) in total. Thus, multiple convolution layers reduce the number of parameters. As the network gets deeper, the reduced number of parameters becomes larger. For example, when 3x3 convolution operations are repeated three times, the number of parameters is 27 in total. To "look at" the same area with one convolution operation, a 7x7 filter is required, which means that the number of parameters goes up to 49.

> **Note**
>
> The advantage of making a network deeper by applying a small filter several times is that it can reduce the number of parameters and expand the **receptive field** (a local space area that changes neurons). When you add layers, an activation function, such as ReLU, is placed between convolution layers, resulting in an improved network representation. This is because the activation function applies a "nonlinear" force to the network. Multiple nonlinear functions enable more complicated expressions.

Training efficiency is another advantage of making a network deeper. A deeper network can reduce training data and conduct training quickly. You can understand this intuitively by remembering the description provided in *Visualizing a CNN* section in *Chapter 7, Convolutional Neural Networks*. In that section, you learned that the convolution layers in a CNN extract information hierarchically. In the front convolution layer, neurons react to simple shapes such as edges. As a layer becomes deeper, neurons react to hierarchically more complicated shapes, such as textures and object parts.

With such a hierarchical structure of a network in mind, consider the problem of recognizing a "dog." To solve this problem in a shallow network, convolution layers must "understand" many characteristics of a dog at one time. There are various types of dogs, and what they look like varies, depending on the environment in which the image was shot. Therefore, understanding the characteristics of a dog requires varied training data and a lot of time in training.

However, you can divide the problem to learn hierarchically by making a network deeper. Then, the problem for each layer to learn becomes simpler. For example, the first layer can concentrate on learning edges. Thus, the network can learn efficiently with a small amount of training data. This is because the number of images that contain edges is larger than that of images of a dog, and the pattern of an edge is simpler than that of a dog.

It is also important that you can pass information hierarchically by making a network deeper. For example, the layer next to the one that extracted edges can use edge information, so we can expect it to learn more advanced patterns efficiently. In short, by making a network deeper, you can divide the problem for each layer to learn into "simple problems that are easy to solve" so that you can expect efficient training.

This is the explanation that supports the importance of "making a network deeper." Please note that deeper networks in recent years have been provided by new techniques and environments, such as big data and computer power, which enable correct training in a deep network.

A Brief History of Deep Learning

It is said that deep learning started to draw a lot of attention in the competition of large-scale image recognition due to the **ImageNet Large Scale Visual Recognition Challenge (ILSRVC)**, which was held in 2012. In the competition, a deep learning technique called AlexNet achieved an overwhelming win, overturning the traditional approaches to image recognition. Since deep learning launched a counterattack in 2012, it has always played the leading role in subsequent competitions. Here, we will look at the current trend of deep learning around the competition of large-scale image recognition, known as ILSVRC.

ImageNet

ImageNet (*J. Deng, W. Dong, R. Socher, L.J. Li, Kai Li, and Li Fei-Fei (2009): ImageNet: A large-scale hierarchical image database.* In IEEE Conference on *Computer Vision and Pattern Recognition, 2009. CVPR 2009. 248 – 255. DOI:* (http://dx.doi.org/10.1109/CVPR.2009.5206848)) is a dataset that contains more than 1 million images. As shown in *Figure* 8.7, it contains various types of images, and each image is associated with a label (class name). An image recognition competition called ILSVRC is held every year using this huge dataset:

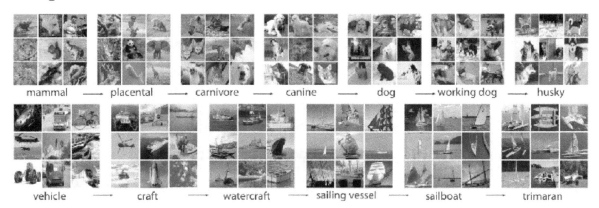

Figure 8.7: Sample data in the large-scale ImageNet dataset

Note

Figure 8.7 is cited from reference, *J. Deng, W. Dong, R. Socher, L.J. Li, Kai Li, and Li Fei-Fei (2009): ImageNet: A large-scale hierarchical image database.* In IEEE Conference on *Computer Vision and Pattern Recognition, 2009. CVPR 2009. 248 – 255. DOI:* (http://dx.doi.org/10.1109/CVPR.2009.5206848).

The ILSVRC competition provides some test items, and one of them is "classification" (in the "classification" division, 1,000 classes are classified to compete in recognition accuracy). *Figure 8.8* shows the results of the winning teams for ILSVRC's classification division since 2010. Here, a classification is regarded as "correct" if the top 5 predictions contain the correct class. The following bar graphs show the error rates:

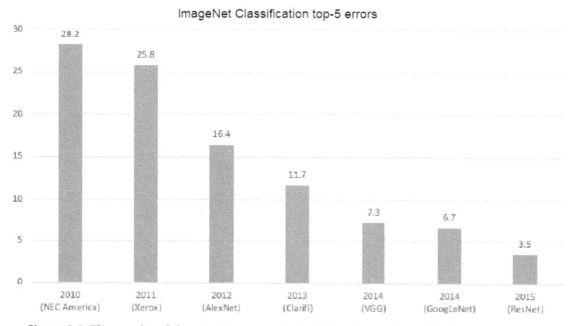

Figure 8.8: The results of the winning teams in ILSVRC – the vertical axis shows error rates, while the horizontal axis shows years. Team names or technique names are shown in the parentheses on the horizontal axis.

Please note from the preceding graph that deep learning techniques have always been on top since 2012. Actually, we can see that, in 2012, AlexNet significantly reduced the error rate. Since then, deep learning techniques have steadily improved in terms of accuracy. This was especially apparent with ResNet in 2015, which was a deep network with more than 150 layers and had reduced the error rate to 3.5%. It is even said that this result exceeded the recognition capability of ordinary humans.

Among the deep learning networks that have achieved great results for the past several years, VGG, GoogLeNet, and ResNet are the most famous. You will come across them at various places relevant to deep learning. I will introduce these three famous networks briefly next.

VGG

VGG is a "basic" CNN that consists of convolution layers and pooling layers. As shown in *Figure 8.9*, it can have as many as 16 (or 19) layers with weights (convolution layers and fully connected layers) to make itself deep and is sometimes called "VGG16" or "VGG19" based on the number of layers:

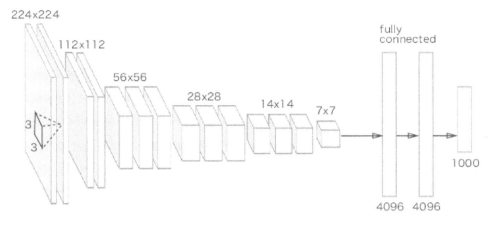

Figure 8.9: VGG

> **Note**
>
> *Figure 8.9* is cited from reference, *Karen Simonyan and Andrew Zisserman (2014): Very Deep Convolutional Networks for Large-Scale Image Recognition. arXiv:1409.1556[cs] (September 2014).*

VGG contains consecutive convolution layers with a small 3x3 filter. As shown in the preceding image, two or four consecutive convolution layers and a pooling layer halve the size, and this process is repeated. Finally, the result is provided via fully connected layers.

> **Note**
>
> VGG won second prize in the 2014 competition (GoogLeNet, which is described next, won in 2014). Its performance was not as good as the first-place network, but many engineers prefer to use VGG-based networks because they are very simple in structure and versatile.

GoogLeNet

Figure 8.10 shows the network architecture for GoogLeNet. The rectangles represent the various layers, such as convolution and pooling layers:

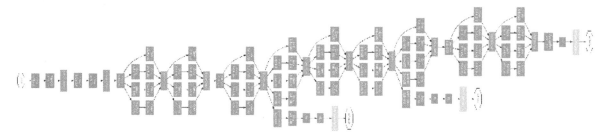

Figure 8.10: GoogLeNet

> **Note**
>
> *Figure 8.10* and *Figure 8.11* are cited from *Christian Szegedy et al. (2015): Going Deeper With Convolutions. In The IEEE Conference on Computer Vision and Pattern Recognition (CVPR).*

Its network architecture seems very complicated when you look at it, but it is basically the same as that of a CNN. What is distinctive about GoogLeNet is that the network not only has depth in the vertical direction but also in the horizontal direction (spread).

GoogLeNet has "width" in the horizontal direction. It is called an "inception architecture" and is based on the structure shown in *Figure 8.11*:

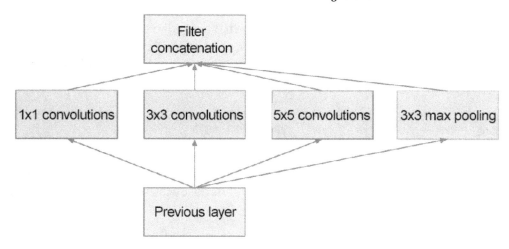

Figure 8.11: Inception architecture of GoogLeNet

As shown in *Figure 8.11*, the inception architecture applies multiple filters of different sizes (and pooling) and combines the results. Using this inception architecture as one building block (component) is the main characteristic of GoogLeNet.

GoogLeNet uses convolution layers with a 1x1 filter in many places. This 1x1 convolution operation reduces the size in the channel direction to reduce the number of parameters and accelerate processing.

ResNet

ResNet (*Kaiming He, Xiangyu Zhang, Shaoqing Ren, and Jian Sun (2015): Deep Residual Learning for Image Recognition. arXiv:1512.03385[cs] (December 2015)*) is a network developed by a team at Microsoft. It is characterized by a "mechanism" that can make the network deeper than ever.

Making a network deeper is important to improve its performance. However, when a network becomes too deep, deep learning fails and the final performance is often poor. To solve this problem, ResNet introduced a "skip architecture" (also called "shortcut" or "bypass"). By introducing this skip architecture, performance can be improved as the network becomes deeper (though there is a limit to permissible depth).

The skip architecture skips convolution layers in the input data to add the input data to the output, as shown in *Figure 8.12*:

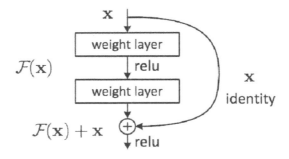

Figure 8.12: Components of ResNet – the "weight layer" here indicates a convolution layer

> **Note**
>
> *Figure 8.12* and *Figure 8.13* are cited from reference, *Kaiming He, Xiangyu Zhang, Shaoqing Ren, and Jian Sun (2015): Deep Residual Learning for Image Recognition. arXiv:1512.03385[cs] (December 2015).*

In *Figure 8.12*, the input, x, is connected to the output by skipping two consecutive convolution layers. The output of two convolution layers is originally F(x), while the skip architecture changes it to F(x) + x.

Adopting this skip architecture enables efficient learning, even when the network is deep. This is because the skip architecture transmits signals without decay during backward propagation.

> **Note**
>
> The skip architecture only passes input data "as it is." In backward propagation, it also passes the gradients from the upper stream "as they are" to the lower stream without them being changed. Therefore, you don't need to be worried about the gradients becoming small (or too large) with the skip architecture. You can expect "meaningful gradients" to be transmitted to the front layers. You can also expect the skip architecture to alleviate a traditional gradient vanishing problem that reduces gradients as the network becomes deeper.

ResNet is based on the VGG network we described earlier and adopts the skip architecture to make the network deeper. *Figure 8.13* shows the result of this:

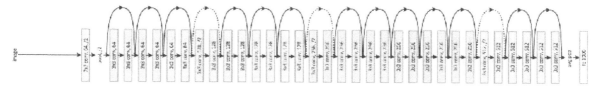

Figure 8.13: ResNet – blocks support 3x3 convolution layers. Its characteristic is the skip architecture, which skips layers.

As shown in *Figure 8.13*, ResNet skips two convolution layers to make the network deeper. Experiments have shown that recognition accuracy continues to improve, even when the network contains 150 or more layers. In the ILSVRC competition, it achieved an amazing result of 3.5% in terms of error rate (the percentage of correct classes that were not included in the top 5 predictions).

> **Note**
>
> Weight data that's trained by using the huge ImageNet dataset is often used effectively. This is called **transfer learning**. Part of the trained weights is copied to another neural network for fine-tuning. For example, a network that has the same structure as VGG is provided. Trained weights are used as initial values, and fine-tuning is conducted for a new dataset. Transfer learning is especially effective when you have a few datasets at hand.

Accelerating Deep Learning

Big data and large-scale networks require massive operations in deep learning. We have used CPUs for calculations so far, but CPUs alone are not sufficient to tackle deep learning. In fact, many deep learning frameworks support **Graphics Processing Units (GPUs)** to process a large number of operations quickly. Recent frameworks are starting to support distributed learning by using multiple GPUs or machines. This section describes accelerating calculations in deep learning. Our implementations of deep learning ended in section 8.1. We will not implement the acceleration (such as support of GPUs) described here.

Challenges to Overcome

Before discussing the acceleration of deep learning, let's see what processes take time in deep learning. The pie charts in *Figure 8.14* show the time spent on each class in the forward processing of AlexNet:

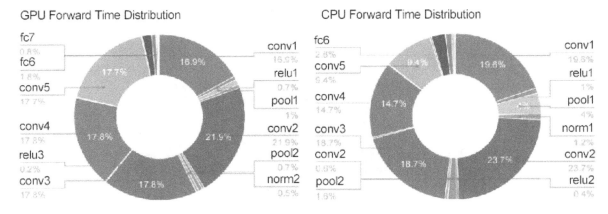

Figure 8.14: Percentage of time that each layer spends in the forward processing of AlexNet – the left-hand chart shows GPU time, while the right-hand one shows CPU time

Here, "conv" indicates a convolution layer, "pool" indicates a pooling layer, "fc" indicates a fully connected layer, and "norm" indicates a normalization layer (cited from *Jia Yangqing (2014): Learning Semantic Image Representations at a Large Scale. PhD thesis, EECS Department, University of California, Berkeley, May 2014, (*http://www.eecs.berkeley.edu/Pubs/TechRpts/2014/EECS-2014-93.html*))*.

As you can see, convolution layers spend a lot of time in AlexNet. Actually, the total processing time in convolution layers reaches 95% of GPU time and 89% of CPU time! Therefore, conducting fast and efficient operations in convolution layers is the main challenge of deep learning. *Figure 8.14* shows the results in the inference phase, but convolution layers spend a lot of time in the training phase as well.

> **Note**
>
> As explained in the *Convolution Layers* topic in *Chapter 7, Convolutional Neural Networks*, operations in convolution layers are basically "multiply-accumulate operations." Therefore, accelerating deep learning depends on how massive "multiply-accumulate operations" are calculated quickly and efficiently.

Using GPUs for Acceleration

Originally, GPUs were exclusively used for graphics. Recently, they have been used for general numerical calculations, as well as graphics processing. Because GPUs can conduct parallel arithmetic operations quickly, GPU computing uses its overwhelming power for various purposes.

Deep learning requires massive multiply–accumulate operations (or products of large matrices). GPUs are good at such massive parallel operations, while CPUs are good at continuous and complicated calculations. You can use a GPU to accelerate deep learning operations surprisingly compared to using only a CPU. *Figure 8.15* compares the time that AlexNet took for learning between a CPU and a GPU:

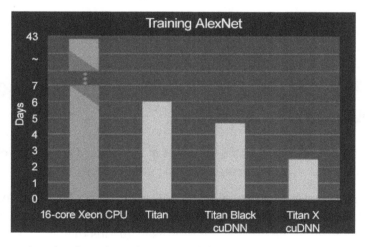

Figure 8.15: Comparing the time that AlexNet took for learning between a "16-core Xeon CPU" and a "Titan series" GPU

> **Note**
>
> *Figure 8.15* is cited from reference, *NVIDIA blog "NVIDIA Propels Deep Learning with TITAN X, New DIGITS Training System and DevBox"* (https://blogs.nvidia.com/blog/2015/03/17/digits-devbox/).

As you can see, the CPU took more than 40 days, while the GPU took only 6 days. We can also see that using the cuDNN library, which is optimized for deep learning, accelerates the training further.

GPUs are mainly provided by two companies, NVIDIA and AMD. Although you can use both of their GPUs for general arithmetic operations, NVIDIA's GPUs are more "familiar" with deep learning. Actually, many deep learning frameworks can benefit only from NVIDIA's GPUs. This is because CUDA, which is an integrated development environment for GPU computing provided by NVIDIA, is used in deep learning frameworks. cuDNN, which can be seen in *Figure 8.15*, is a library that runs on CUDA in which the functions optimized for deep learning are implemented.

> **Note**
>
> We used `im2col` to convert the operations in a convolution layer into the products of large matrices. Implementing this `im2col` method is suitable for GPUs. GPUs are good at calculating a large batch at a stretch rather than calculating small batches one by one. Using `im2col` to calculate the products of huge matrices makes it easy to exhibit a GPU's real power.

Distributed Training

You can accelerate deep learning operations by using a GPU, but a deep network still requires several days or weeks for training. As we have seen so far, deep learning involves lots of trial and error. You must try many things to create a good network. Naturally, you want to reduce the time required for training as much as possible. Then, scaling deep learning out or "distributed training" becomes important.

To further accelerate the calculations required for deep learning, you may want to distribute them among multiple GPUs or machines. Now, some deep learning frameworks support distributed training by multiple GPUs or machines. Among them, Google's TensorFlow and Microsoft's **Computational Network Toolkit (CNTK)** have been developed to focus on distributed training. Based on low-delay and high-throughput networks in huge data centers, distributed training by these frameworks achieves surprising results.

How much can distributed training accelerate deep learning? The answer is that the larger the number of GPUs, the faster the training speed. In fact, 100 GPUs (a total of 100 GPUs installed on multiple machines) achieves a 56-fold speedup compared with one GPU. This means that training that usually takes 7 days is completed in only 3 hours, for example, and indicates the surprising effect of distributed training.

"How to distribute calculations" in distributed training is a very difficult problem. It contains many problems that are not easy to solve, such as communication and data synchronization between machines. You can leave such difficult problems to excellent frameworks such as TensorFlow. Here, we will not discuss the details of distributed training. For the technical details of distributed training, please see the technical paper (white paper) about TensorFlow (*Mart í n Abadi et al. (2016): TensorFlow: Large-Scale Machine Learning on Heterogeneous Distributed Systems. arXiv:1603.04467[cs] (March 2016)*).

Reducing the Bit Number for Arithmetic Precision

Memory space and bus bandwidth, as well as computational complexity, can be bottlenecks in accelerating deep learning. For memory space, a large number of weight parameters and intermediate data must be stored in memory. For bus bandwidth, a bottleneck occurs when the data that flows through the GPU (or CPU) bus increases, exceeding a limit. In these cases, you want the bit number of the data flowing in the network to be as small as possible.

A computer mainly uses 64- or 32-bit floating-point numbers to represent real numbers. Using many bits to represent a number reduces the influence of the error at numerical calculation but increases the processing cost and memory usage, placing a load on the bus bandwidth.

From what we know about deep learning regarding numerical precision (how many bits are used to represent a numeric value), it does not need very high precision. This is one of the most important characteristics of a neural network due to its robustness. The robustness here means that, for example, the output result will not change in a neural network, even if the input images contain a small amount of noise. Think of it as a small influence on the output result because of the robustness, even if the data flowing in a network is "deteriorated."

A computer usually uses 32-bit single-precision floating-point representations or 64-bit double-precision floating-point representations to represent a decimal. Experiments have shown that 16-bit **half-precision floating-point representations** (half `float`) are sufficient in deep learning (*Suyog Gupta, Ankur Agrawal, Kailash Gopalakrishnan, and Pritish Narayanan (2015): Deep learning with limited numerical precision. CoRR, abs/1502.02551 392 (2015)*). Actually, the Pascal architecture used for NVIDIA's generation GPUs supports the operation of half-precision floating-point numbers. It is thought that the half format will be used as the standard in the future.

> **Note**
>
> NVIDIA's Maxwell generation of GPUs supported the storage of half-accuracy floating-point numbers (to maintain data), but it did not conduct 16-bit operations. The next-generation Pascal architecture conducts 16-bit operations as well. We can expect that only using half-accuracy floating-point numbers for calculations will accelerate processing so that it's around twice as fast as a previous-generation GPU.

We haven't covered numerical precision in the preceding implementations of deep learning. Python generally uses 64-bit floating-point numbers. NumPy provides a 16-bit half-accuracy floating-point data type (however, it is used only for storage, not for operations). We can easily show that using NumPy's half-accuracy floating-point numbers do not reduce recognition accuracy. If you are interested, please see `ch08/half_float_network.py`.

Some research has been conducted into reducing the bit number in deep learning. In recent research, a technique called a "binarized neural network" was proposed (*Matthieu Courbariaux and Yoshua Bengio (2016): Binarized Neural Networks: Training Deep Neural Networks with Weights and Activations Constrained to +1 or -1. arXiv preprint arXiv:1602.02830 (2016)*). It represents the weights and intermediate data by 1 bit. Reducing the number of bits to accelerate deep learning is a topic we should keep our eyes on. It is especially important when we're thinking of using deep learning for embedded devices.

Practical Uses of Deep Learning

As an example of using deep learning, we have mainly discussed image classification, such as handwritten digit recognition, which is called "object recognition." However, we can apply deep learning to many problems other than object recognition. Deep learning demonstrates excellent performance for many problems, such as image recognition, sound (speech recognition), and natural language processing. This section will introduce what deep learning can do (its applications) in the computer vision field.

Object Detection

Object detection identifies the positions of objects in images and classifies them. Object detection is more difficult than object recognition. While object recognition targets the entire image, object detection must identify the positions of classes in an image, and multiple objects may exist.

Some CNN-based techniques have been proposed for object detection. They demonstrate excellent performance, which indicates that deep learning is also effective for object detection.

Among CNN-based object detection techniques, a technique called R-CNN (*Ross Girshick, Jeff Donahue, Trevor Darrell, and Jitendra Malik (2014): Rich Feature Hierarchies for Accurate Object Detection and Semantic Segmentation. In 580 – 587*) is famous. *Figure 8.16* shows the process flow of R-CNN:

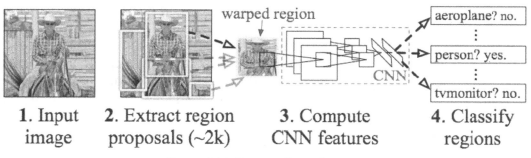

Figure 8.16: Process flow of R-CNN

> **Note**
>
> *Figure 8.16 is cited from reference, Ross Girshick, Jeff Donahue, Trevor Darrell, and Jitendra Malik (2014): Rich Feature Hierarchies for Accurate Object Detection and Semantic Segmentation. In 580 – 587.*

In *Figure 8.16*, note the 2. *Extract region proposals* and 3. *Compute* CNN *features* sections. The first technique detects the areas that seem to be objects (in some way) and then applies a CNN to the extracted areas to classify them. R-CNN converts an image into squares and uses **support vector machines** (**SVMs**) for classification. Its actual process flow is slightly complicated but mainly consists of the aforementioned processes: the extraction of candidate regions and to compute CNN features.

In the "Extract region proposals" process of R-CNN, candidates for objects are detected, and this is where various techniques that have been developed in computer vision can be used. In the paper about R-CNN, a technique called selective search is used. Recently, a technique called "Faster R-CNN" (*Shaoqing Ren, Kaiming He, Ross Girshick, and Jian Sun (2015): Faster R-CNN: Towards Real-Time Object Detection with Region Proposal Networks. In C. Cortes, N. D. Lawrence, D. D. Lee, M. Sugiyama, & R. Garnett, eds. Advances in Neural Information Processing Systems 28. Curran Associates, Inc., 91 – 99*) has been proposed. It even uses CNNs to extract region proposals. Faster R-CNN uses one CNN for the entire process, which enables fast processing.

Segmentation

Segmentation classifies an image on a pixel basis. It learns by using training data where objects are colored on a pixel basis and classifies all the pixels of an input image during inference. The neural networks we've implemented so far classify the entire image. So, how can we classify it on a pixel basis?

The simplest method of performing segmentation with a neural network is to make a prediction for each pixel. For example, you can provide a network that classifies a pixel at the center of a rectangular area to make a prediction for all the pixels. As you can see, this requires as many forward processes as the number of pixels, thus taking a lot of time to complete (the problem being that convolution operations re-calculate many areas uselessly). To reduce such useless calculations, a technique called a **Fully Convolutional Network** (**FCN**) has been proposed (*Jonathan Long, Evan Shelhamer, and Trevor Darrell (2015): Fully Convolutional Networks for Semantic Segmentation. In The IEEE Conference on Computer Vision and Pattern Recognition (CVPR)*). It classifies all the pixels in one forward process (see *Figure 8.20*).

A FCN is a network that consists only of convolution layers. While an ordinary CNN contains fully connected layers, a FCN replaces fully connected layers with *convolution layers that play the same role*. In fully connected layers in a network that's used in object recognition, the space volume of the intermediate data is processed as nodes arranged in a line. On the other hand, in a network that consists only of convolution layers, the space volume can be maintained during processing until the last output.

The main characteristic of a FCN is that the space size is expanded at the end. This expansion can enlarge shrunk intermediate data so that it's the same size as the input image all at once. The expansion at the end of an FCN is an expansion by bi-linear interpolation (bi-linear expansion). An FCN uses deconvolution to conduct the bi-linear expansion (for details, see the paper (*Jonathan Long, Evan Shelhamer, and Trevor Darrell (2015): Fully Convolutional Networks for Semantic Segmentation. In The IEEE Conference on Computer Vision and Pattern Recognition (CVPR)* about FCN).

> **Note**
>
> In a fully connected layer, the output is connected to all the inputs. You can also create a connection that's the same structure in a convolution layer. For example, a fully connected layer whose input data size is 32x10x10 (the number of channels is 32, the height is 10, and the width is 10) can be replaced with a convolution layer whose filter size is 32x10x10. If the fully connected layer has 100 output nodes, the convolution layer can achieve completely the same processing by providing 100 of the 32x10x10 filters. In this way, a fully connected layer can be replaced with a convolution layer that conducts equivalent processing.

Generating Image Captions

There is some interesting research being conducted that combines natural language and computer vision. When an image is provided, the text explaining the image (the image caption) is automatically generated.

For example, an image of a motorcycle from a dirt bike competition could include the caption: "A person riding a motorcycle on a dirt road" (this text is automatically generated from the image). It is surprising that the system even "understands" that it is on a dirt road and that a person is riding a motorcycle.

A model called **Neural Image Caption (NIC)** is typically used to generate image captions for deep learning. NIC consists of a deep CNN and a **Recurrent Neural Network (RNN)** for handling natural language. An RNN has recursive connections and is often used for sequential data such as natural language and time-series data.

NIC uses CNN to extract the features from an image and passes them to the RNN. The RNN uses the features extracted by the CNN as initial values to generate a text "recursively." We will not discuss the technical details here. Basically, NIC has a simple architecture that combines two neural networks: a CNN and an RNN. It can generate surprisingly precise image captions. Handling various types of information, such as images and natural language, is called **multi-modal processing**. Multi-modal processing has gained a lot of attention in recent years:

> **Note**
>
> The R in RNN stands for recurrent. "Recurrent" indicates a neural network's recurrent network architecture. Because of the recurrent architecture, the RNN is affected by the information generated before it – in other words, it remembers past information. This is the main characteristic of an RNN. For example, after generating the word "I," it is affected by the word and generates the next word "am." Then, it is affected by the words "I am" that were previously generated and generates the word "sleeping." For continuous data such as natural language and time-series data, the RNN behaves as if it remembered past information.

The Future of Deep Learning

Deep learning is now being used in various fields, as well as in the traditional fields. This section describes the possibilities of deep learning and some research that shows the future of deep learning.

Converting Image Styles

There is research being conducted that uses deep learning to "draw" a picture as an artist would. One popular use case of neural networks is to create a new image based on two provided images. One of them is called a "content image," while the other is called a "style image." A new image is created based on these two images.

In one example, you can specify Van Gogh's painting style as the style that will be applied to the content image, deep learning draws a new picture, as specified. This research was published in the paper "A Neural Algorithm of Artistic Style" (*Leon A. Gatys, Alexander S. Ecker, and Matthias Bethge (2015): A Neural Algorithm of Artistic Style. arXiv:1508.06576[cs, q-bio] (August 2015)*) and received a lot of attention all over the world as soon as it was published.

Roughly speaking, in the technique, the intermediate data in the network learn so that it approaches the intermediate data of the "content image." By doing so, the input image can be converted so that it is similar in shape to the content image. To absorb a style from the "style image," the concept of a style matrix is introduced. By training so that the gap of the style matrix is small, the input image can approach Van Gogh's style.

Generating Images

The preceding example of image style transfer required two images to generate a new image. On the other hand, some research has tried to generate new images without requiring any images (the technique trains by using many images beforehand but needs no images to "draw" a new image.) For example, you can use deep learning to generate the image of a "bedroom" from scratch

They may seem to be real photographs, but they were newly generated by a DCGAN. The images that were generated by the DCGAN are images that nobody has ever seen (those that do not exist in the training data) and were newly created from scratch.

When a DCGAN generates images that look like real ones, it creates a model of the process where the images were generated. The model learns by using many images (such as those of bedrooms). After training finishes, you can use the model to generate new images.

DCGANs use deep learning. The main point of the DCGAN technique is that it uses two neural networks: a generator and a discriminator. The generator generates an image that seems real, while the discriminator determines whether it is real, that is, whether it was generated by the generator or whether it was really photographed. In this way, two networks are trained by making them compete against each other.

The generator learns a more elaborate technique of creating fake images, while the discriminator grows like an appraiser who can detect fakes with higher precision. What is interesting is that in a technology called a **Generative Adversarial Network (GAN)**, both of them grow through competition. Finally, the generator that has grown through competition can draw images that look real (or may grow even more).

> **Note**
>
> The machine learning problems that we have seen so far are called **supervised learning** problems. They use a dataset that contains image data and labels in pairs, such as in handwritten digit recognition. Meanwhile, label data is not provided in the problem here. Only images (a set of images) are provided. This is called **unsupervised learning**. Unsupervised learning has been studied for a relatively long time (**Deep Belief Networks** and **Deep Boltzmann Machines** are famous), but it seems that these days, it is not being researched very actively. Since techniques using deep learning, such as DCGANs, are attracting more and more attention, it is expected that unsupervised learning will be developed further in the future.

Automated Driving

"Automated driving" technology, in which a computer drives a car instead of a human, is likely to be realized soon. IT companies, universities, and research institutions, as well as car manufacturers, are competing to realize automated driving. This can only happen when various technologies such as path plan technology, which determines a traffic route, and sensing technology, including cameras and lasers, are combined. It is said that the technology used to recognize the surrounding environment properly is the most important. It is very difficult to recognize an environment that changes every moment of every day, as well as the cars and people that move around freely.

If the system can properly recognize the travel area robustly and reliably, even in various environments, automated driving may be realized in the near future—a task for which deep learning should prove invaluable.

For example, a CNN-based network called SegNet (*Vijay Badrinarayanan, Kendall, and Roberto Cipolla (2015): SegNet: A Deep Convolutional Encoder-Decoder Architecture for Image Segmentation. arXiv preprint arXiv:1511.00561 (2015)*) can recognize the road environment accurately, as shown in *Figure 8.17*:

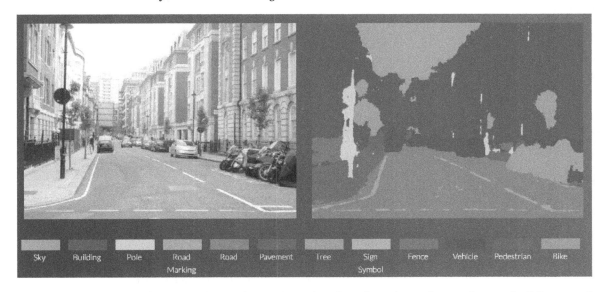

Figure 8.17: Example of segmenting an image by using deep learning – the road, cars, buildings, and sidewalks are recognized accurately

> **Note**
>
> *Figure 8.17* is cited from reference, *SegNet Demo page* (http://mi.eng.cam.ac.uk/projects/segnet/).

Segmentation (pixel-level evaluation) is conducted for the input image, as shown in *Figure 8.17*. The result indicates that the road, buildings, sidewalks, trees, cars, and motorcycles are distinguished somewhat accurately. If deep learning improves the accuracy and speed of these recognition technologies from now on, automated driving may be put into practical use in the not too distant future.

Deep Q-Networks (Reinforcement Learning)

There is a research field called **reinforcement learning** in which computers learn independently through trial and error, just as humans learn how to ride a bicycle, for example. This is different from "supervised learning," where a "supervisor" teaches face to face.

The basic framework of reinforcement learning is that an agent selects actions, depending on the situation of the environment, and its actions change the environment. After taking an action, the environment offers the agent some reward. The purpose of reinforcement learning is to determine the action policy of the agent so that it can obtain a better reward, as shown here:

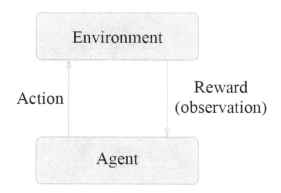

Figure 8.18: Basic framework of reinforcement learning – the agent learns independently to obtain a better reward

The diagram in *Figure 8.18* shows the basic framework of reinforcement learning. Note that the reward is not labeled data, as it is in supervised learning. For example, in the video game "Super Mario Brothers," the exact quantity of rewards you gain by moving Mario to the right is not necessarily clear. In that case, the "prospective" reward must be determined by clear indicators such as the game scores (obtaining coins, defeating enemies, and so on) and game-over logic. In supervised learning, each action can be evaluated correctly by the "supervisor."

A **Deep Q-Network (DQN)** is a reinforcement learning technique (*Volodymyr Mnih et al (2015): Human-level control through deep reinforcement learning. Nature 518, 7540 (2015), 529 – 533*) that uses deep learning. It is based on the algorithm of reinforcement learning called Q-learning. Q-learning determines a function called the optimal action-value function to determine the optimal action. A DQN uses deep learning (CNNs) to approximate the function.

Some research has shown that DQNs can learn video games automatically to achieve more successful play than humans. As shown in *Figure 8.19*, a CNN, when used in a DQN, receives four consecutive frames of game images as input and outputs the "value" of the motion of the game controller (the movement of the joystick and the button operation).

Traditionally, when a video game was learned by the network, the state of the game (such as the positions of the characters) was usually extracted and provided in advance. Meanwhile, the DQN receives only the images of a video game as input data, as shown in *Figure 8.19*. This is what is noteworthy in a DQN and highly improves its applicability. This is because you do not need to change the settings for each game, and you only need to provide game images to the DQN. In fact, DQNs have learned many games, such as "Pac-Man" and "Atari 2600" with the same configuration and achieved better results than humans:

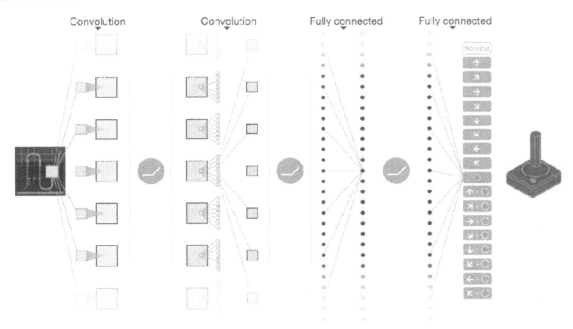

Figure 8.19: Using a Deep Q-Network to learn the operations of a video game. Here, the network receives the images of a video game as an input and learns the operation of the game controller (joystick) through trial and error

Note

Figure 8.17 is cited from reference, *Volodymyr Mnih et al. (2015): Human-level control through deep reinforcement learning. Nature 518, 7540 (2015), 529 – 533.*

> **Note**
>
> The news that an AI called AlphaGo (*David Silver et al. (2016): Mastering the game of Go with deep neural networks and tree search. Nature 529, 7587 (2016), 484 – 489*) beat the Go champion attracted much attention. Deep learning and reinforcement learning are also used in AlphaGo. It learned from 30 million game records created by professionals and played against itself many times to accumulate sufficient knowledge. Both AlphaGo and DQNs have been researched by Google's DeepMind. We must keep an eye on their activities in the future.

Summary

In this chapter, we implemented a deep CNN and achieved an excellent recognition result exceeding 99% for handwritten digit recognition. We also discussed the motivation for making a network deeper and the current tendency toward deeper networks. We also looked at the trends and applications of deep learning, and the research is accelerating it, which will advance this technology into the future.

In the field of deep learning, there is much that is still unknown, and new research is being published all the time. Researchers and engineers around the world continue to research actively and will realize technologies that we cannot even imagine yet.

The following points were covered in this chapter:

- Making a network deeper will improve performance for many deep learning problems.

- In image recognition competitions, techniques using deep learning get a high ranking, and current networks are deeper than their predecessors

- Famous networks include VGG, GoogLeNet, and ResNet.

- GPUs, distributed training, and the reduction of bit accuracy can accelerate deep learning.

- Deep learning (neural networks) can be used for object detection and segmentation, as well as for object recognition.

- Applications that use deep learning include the generation of image captions, the generation of images, and reinforcement learning. These days, the use of deep learning for automated driving is also expected.

Thank you for reading this book. We hope that you've gained a better understanding of deep learning and have found it an interesting journey.

Appendix A

About

This section is included to assist the students to perform the activities present in the book. It includes detailed steps that are to be performed by the students to complete and achieve the objectives of the activity.

Computational Graph of the Softmax-with-Loss Layer

The following figure is the computational graph of the Softmax-with-Loss layer and obtains backward propagation. We will call the softmax function the Softmax layer, the cross-entropy error the **Cross-Entropy Error** layer, and the layer where these two are combined the Softmax-with-Loss layer. You can represent the Softmax-with-Loss layer with the computational graph provided in *Figure* A.1: Entropy:

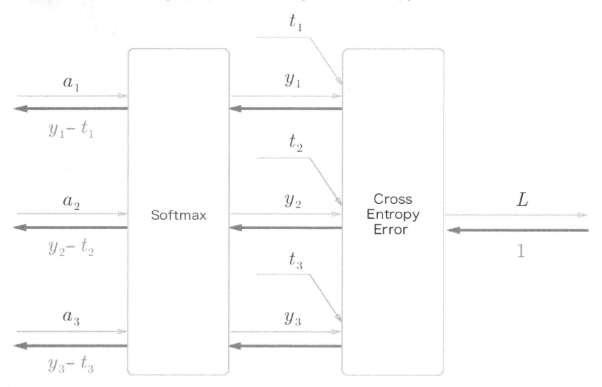

Figure A.1: Computational graph of the Softmax-with-Loss layer

The computational graph shown in *Figure* A.1 assumes that there is a neural network that classifies three classes. The input from the previous layer is (a_1, a_2, a_3), and the Softmax layer outputs (y_1, y_2, y_3). The label is (t_1, t_2, t_3) and the Cross-Entropy Error layer outputs the loss, L.

This appendix shows that the result of backward propagation of the Softmax-with-Loss layer will be $(y_1 - t_1, y_2 - t_2, y_3 - t_3)$, as shown in *Figure* A.1.

Forward Propagation

The computational graph shown in *Figure* A.1 does not show the details of the Softmax layer and the Cross-Entropy Error layer. Here, we will start by describing the details of the two layers.

First, let's look at the Softmax layer. We can represent the softmax function with the following equation:

$$y_k = \frac{\exp(a_k)}{\displaystyle\sum_{i=1}^{n} \exp(a_i)} \tag{A.1}$$

Therefore, we can show the Softmax layer with the computational graph provided in *Figure* A.2. Here, S stands for the sum of exponentials, which is the denominator in equation (A.1). The final output is (y_1, y_2, y_3).

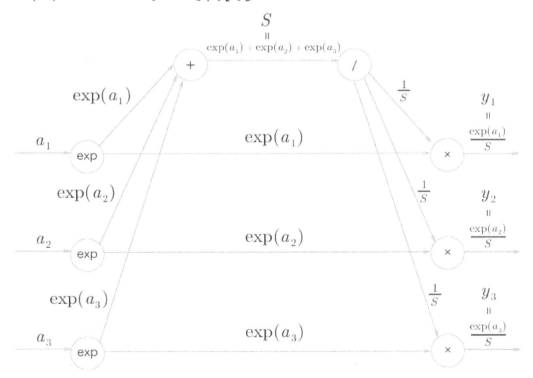

Figure A.2: Computational graph of the Softmax layer (forward propagation only)

Next, let's look at the Cross-Entropy Error layer. The following equation shows the cross-entropy error:

$$L = -\sum_k t_k \log y_k \qquad (A.2)$$

Based on equation (A.2), we can draw the computational graph of the Cross-Entropy Error layer as shown in *Figure* A.3.

The computational graph shown in *Figure* A.3 just shows equation (A. 2) as a computational graph. Therefore, I think that there is nothing particularly difficult about this.

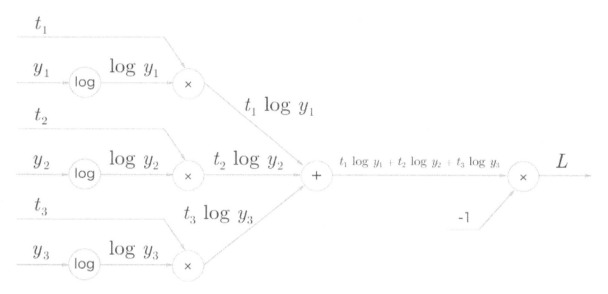

Figure A.3: Computational graph of the Cross-Entropy Error layer (forward propagation only)

Now, let's look at backward propagation:

Backward Propagation

First, let's look at backward propagation of the Cross-Entropy Error layer. We can draw backward propagation of the Cross-Entropy Error layer as follows:

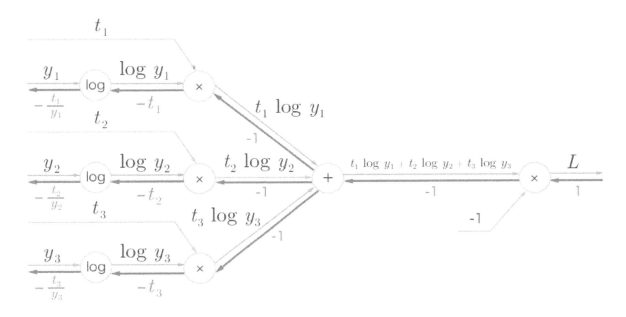

Figure A.4: Backward propagation of the Cross-Entropy Error layer

Please note the following to obtain backward propagation of this computational graph:

- The initial value of backward propagation (the rightmost value of backward propagation in *Figure* A.4) is 1 (because $\frac{\partial L}{\partial L} = 1$).

- For backward propagation of the "x" node, the "reversed value" of the input signal for forward propagation multiplied by the derivative from the upper stream is passed downstream.

- For the "+" node, the derivative from the upper stream is passed without changing it.

- The backward propagation of the "log" node observes the following equations:

$$y = \log x$$

$$\frac{\partial y}{\partial x} = \frac{1}{x}$$

Based on this, we can obtain backward propagation of the Cross-Entropy Error layer easily. As a result, the value $\left(-\frac{t_1}{y_1}, -\frac{t_2}{y_2}, -\frac{t_3}{y_3}\right)$ will be the input to the backward propagation of the Softmax layer.

Next, let's look at backward propagation of the Softmax layer. Because the Softmax layer is a little complicated, I want to check its backward propagation step by step:

Step 1:

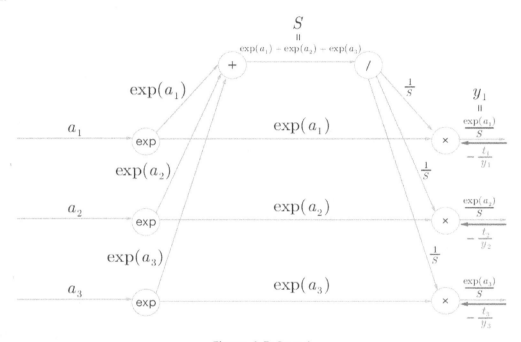

Figure A.5: Step 1

The values of the backward propagation arrive from the previous layer (Cross-Entropy Error layer).

Step 2:

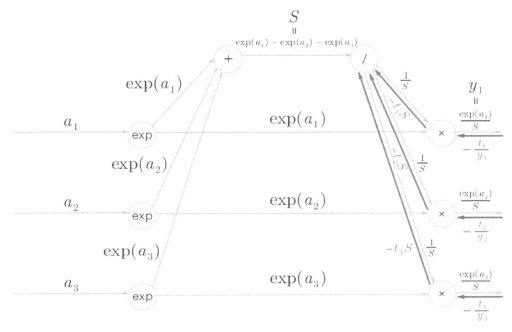

Figure A.6: Step 2

The "x" node "reverses" the values of forward propagation for multiplication. Here, the following calculation is performed:

$$-\frac{t_1}{y_1}\exp(a_1) = -t_1\frac{S}{\exp(a_1)}\exp(a_1) = -t_1 S \qquad (\text{A.3})$$

Step 3:

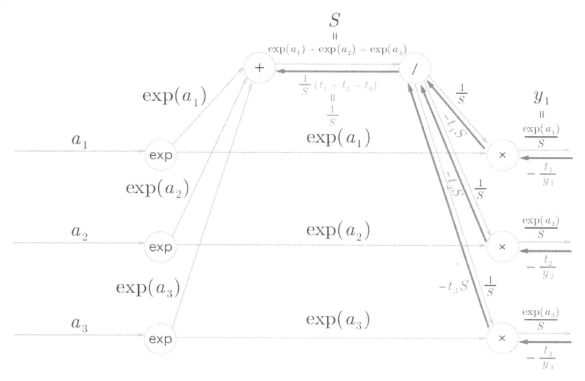

Figure A.7: Step 3

If the flow branches into multiple values in forward propagation, the separated values are added in backward propagation. Therefore, three separate values of backward propagation, $(-t_1S, -t_2S, -t_3S)$, are added here. The backward propagation of $/$ is conducted for the added values, resulting in $\frac{1}{S}(t_1 + t_2 + t_3)$. Here, (t_1, t_2, t_3) is the label and a "one-hot vector." A one-hot vector means that one of (t_1, t_2, t_3) is 1 and the others are all 0s. Therefore, the sum of (t_1, t_2, t_3) is 1.

Step 4:

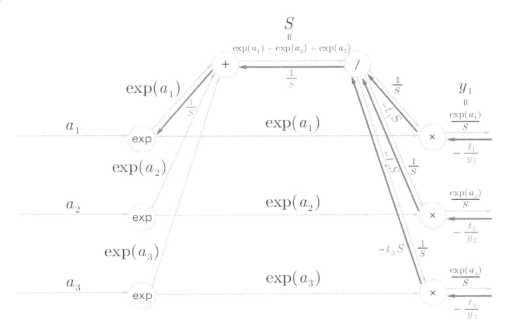

Figure A.8: Step 4

The "+" node only passes the value without changing it.

Step 5:

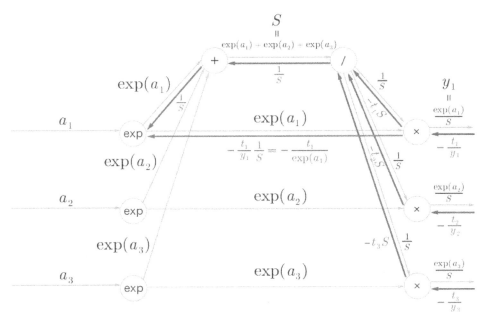

Figure A.9: Step 5

The "x" node "reverses" the values for multiplication. Here, $y_1 = \frac{\exp(a_1)}{S}$ is used to transform the equation.

Step 6:

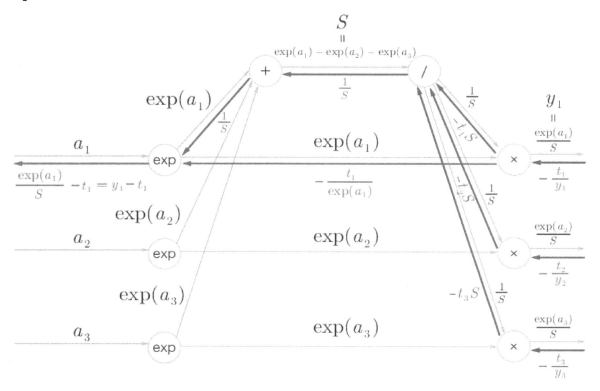

Figure A.10: Step 6

In the "exp" node, the following equations hold true:

$$y = \exp(x)$$

$$\frac{\partial y}{\partial x} = \exp(x) \quad \text{(A.4)}$$

Thus, the sum of the two separate inputs, which are multiplied by $\exp(a_1)$, is the backward propagation to obtain. We can write this as $(\frac{1}{S} - \frac{t_1}{\exp(a_1)})\exp(a_1)$ and obtain $y_1 - t_1$ after transformation. Thus, in the node where the input of forward propagation is a_1, backward propagation is $y_1 - t_1$. For a_2 and a_3, we can use the same procedure (the results are $y_2 - t_2$ and $y_3 - t_3$, respectively). With this, it is easy to show that we can achieve the same result even if we want to classify n classes instead of three classes.

Summary

Here, the computational graph of the Softmax-with-Loss layer was shown in detail, and its backward propagation was obtained. *Figure* A.11 shows the complete computational graph of the Softmax-with-Loss layer:

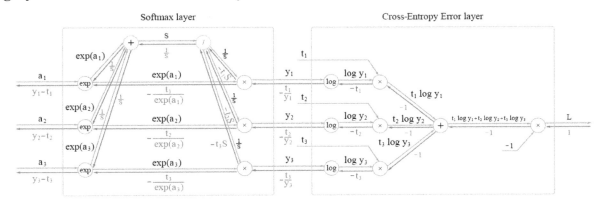

Figure A.11: Computational graph of the Softmax-with-Loss layer

The computational graph shown in *Figure* A.11 looks complicated. However, if you advance step by step using computational graphs, obtaining derivatives (the procedure of backward propagation) will be much less troublesome. When you encounter a layer that looks complicated (such as the Batch Normalization layer), other than the Softmax-with-Loss layer described here, you can use this procedure. This will be easier to understand in practice rather than only looking at equations.

Index

About

All major keywords used in this book are captured alphabetically in this section. Each one is accompanied by the page number of where they appear.

Printed in the USA
CPSIA information can be obtained
at www.ICGtesting.com
CBHW081121260524
9116CB00018B/1373